This resource provided by:

S0-AHO-054

The Coming Home Network International

PO Box 8290
Zanesville, Ohio 43702
Phone: 740-450-1175
www.chnetwork.org

The Apostasy That Wasn't

The Extraordinary Story of the
Unbreakable Early Church

Rod Bennett

The Apostasy That Wasn't

The Extraordinary Story of the
Unbreakable Early Church

Catholic Answers Press

Published by Catholic Answers, Inc.
2020 Gillespie Way
El Cajon, California 92020
1-888-291-8000 orders
619-387-0042 fax
catholic.com

Printed in the United States of America

Cover design by Devin Schadt
Interior design by Sherry Russell

978-1-941663-49-3 hardcover
978-1-941663-50-9 paperback
978-1-941663-51-6 Kindle
978-1-941663-52-3 ePub

To Dorothy Carter Bennett
Of all wives, most patient

"Remove not the ancient landmark
which your fathers have set."
Proverbs 22:28

"You shall not make a schism. Rather, you shall make
peace among those that are contending."
The Didache, c. A.D. 70

I believe in God,
the Father almighty,
Creator of heaven and earth,
and in Jesus Christ, his only Son, our Lord,
who was conceived by the Holy Spirit,
born of the Virgin Mary,
suffered under Pontius Pilate,
was crucified, died and was buried;
he descended into hell;
on the third day he rose again from the dead;
he ascended into heaven,
and is seated at the right hand of God the Father almighty;
from there he will come to judge the living and the dead.
I believe in the Holy Spirit,
the holy catholic Church,
the communion of saints,
the forgiveness of sins,
the resurrection of the body,
and life everlasting. Amen.

The Apostles' Creed
Second century A.D. or earlier

Contents

Acknowledgments

The inspiration for this book came largely from the historical works of Hilaire Belloc; his lively approach to the task of explaining difficult historical material opened my eyes to many subjects that had always been obscure to me before. Other writers whose stylistic influence will probably be recognized deserve a "shout out" as well; Robert Riskin, Robert Hugh Benson, and Tom Wolfe. And the book is so full of quotes from Robert Payne, Guiseppe Ricciotti, G.K. Chesterton, and John Henry Newman that a separate acknowledgment here seems almost superfluous—but is gratefully offered anyway.

Personal friends and relatives were hugely helpful as well: people like Mike Aquilina, Franklin Jones, Jim Henry III, Dave Armstrong, and Mark Shea.

God bless all of these—and you, my readers, as well!

Introduction

In the green hills of western North Carolina, not far from the Tennessee line, lies a sunny Southern tourist attraction called Fields of the Wood. Advertising itself as the home of the world's largest Ten Commandments (spread across the face of a small mountain), the world's largest open Bible (made of concrete and twenty feet high), and an authentic walk-through replica of Christ's empty tomb at Jerusalem, this out-of-the-way corner of roadside America sounded, when I first discovered it in the 1980s, like just exactly my cup of tea. Ever since I was a kid I've had a real soft spot for these quirky little outcroppings of mom-and-pop piety and I seldom miss an opportunity to turn off the main highway into whatever wax museum, tourist cave, or historic shrine happens to present itself. I must say, however, that I got a good deal more than I bargained for on this particular trip. I expected to find travel brochures, snow globes, 3-D View-Master reels, foldout picture postcards with twelve different Tru-Color views—and I found them. But I found something else, too. I uncovered an enormous blind spot in my own faith; a kind of a cancer, really, of bad information that was threatening (though I hadn't realized it until then) to eat up all the rest of my beliefs as an Evangelical Christian. So right then and there I was forced to embark on a course of study I'd never bothered to look into before—a quest to make sense of my own religion. I hope you will enjoy tagging along as I try to retrace my steps.

Fields of the Wood, I learned, memorializes the place where, on June 13, 1903, the one true Church of God was restored to the earth after an absence of nearly 1,600 years. Early that morning, a self-taught former Quaker named Ambrose Jessup Tomlinson climbed alone to the top of one of the Blue Ridge Mountains determined to grab hold of God and not let go. Frustrated and confused by the multiplicity of competing sects swarming over the Southern mountains in those days, A.J. Tomlinson wanted to know where was simplicity, where was certitude, where, in short, was "the church of the living God, the pillar and bulwark of the truth" (1 Tim. 3:15). And according to the stone tablet that now marks the spot, Preacher Tomlinson "prayed and prevailed." He came down from the mountain, came down as Moses came down from Sinai, unshakably convinced that he had just been party to a sacred encounter of truly biblical proportions. Staggering back to the tiny congregation of mountaineers for whom he served as pastor, Tomlinson announced the revelation he had just received; to wit, "that this small group was in reality the Church of God of the Bible, for they had agreed together to accept the whole Bible rightly divided and to walk in all the light as it shined on their pathway . . . This was the event and the place where David's prophecy [Ps. 132:4–6] was fulfilled, 'I will not give sleep to mine eyes, or slumber to mine eyelids, until I find out a place for the Lord, an habitation for the mighty God of Jacob. Lo, we heard of it at Ephratah: we found it (the Church) in the fields of the wood.'"

My traveling companion on that visit was another theologically minded Evangelical and he and I spent quite an entertaining afternoon clambering over every inch of Fields of the Wood trying to piece the full story together. The entire twenty-acre site is thickly forested with granite monuments, biblical plaques, and the like, so checking them all against each other to develop some kind of systematic theology for Tomlinson's group became a bit like a scriptural scavenger hunt. What Reverend Tomlinson does seem unquestionably to have established is a minor Pentecostal denomination called the Church of God of Prophecy (Cleveland, Tennessee); it was what he claimed to have *reestablished* that we were having trouble getting our minds around. Were the friendly mountain folk we saw running the place really claiming to be the only true Christians on earth? Did they really believe that the Holy Spirit had totally withdrawn himself from humanity for sixteen centuries? It certainly seemed so: "Fields of the Wood is not just a religious retreat or a tourist attraction. It marks and beautifies the very spot where the Church of God emerged from the deep blackness of the Dark Ages to become once more the great beacon of truth to a world still groping in spiritual darkness.

The Church of God lay desolate and lost through the centuries; we found it again in the Fields of the Wood."

I hate to admit this but my friend and I responded at first with laughter. A concrete pillar solemnly declared, "THIS IS WHERE DAVID SAID THE CHURCH WOULD BE FOUND." An old airplane on display, out of which some tracts had been dropped back in the forties, was solemnly declared to be the fulfillment of Isaiah 60:8 ("Who are these that fly as a cloud, and as the doves to their windows?"). Yet as we continued to explore those hushed, wooded hillsides, all of the repeated assurances that we were walking on holy ground began to have their effect. A pensive mood came over us; then deeper, more edifying thoughts came slowly to mind. Why had our laughter and unbelief come so easily? What made us so sure A.J. Tomlinson *hadn't* restored the true faith to the world? Was it because he was nothing but an uneducated yokel? So were Peter, James, and John. Was it because his holy place was tacky and run-down? So are many of the shrines at Bethlehem and Jerusalem. True, my friend and I thought we could "rightly divide" the Bible better than A.J. Tomlinson— but then, of course, A.J. Tomlinson had felt the same way about people like us. All in all, it was a dappled, dozy, and strangely disquieting way to pass a summer's afternoon.

Central to Reverend Tomlinson's claim, of course, is this idea of the "deep blackness" and the "Dark Ages." "Acts 20:29" he claimed, "foretells the great falling away, or apostasy, which would plunge the early Church into darkness." Now, as it happens, I had heard about this Great Apostasy before—heard about it and always thought it smelled fishy. Once, as a volunteer with a nondenominational missions group, I had argued for a good two hours with a pair of my fellow missionaries, two modern-day Pentecostals who told pretty much the same story about the world before the Azusa Street revival of 1906. Just as in the Tomlinson version, the Holy Ghost had withdrawn himself completely and for the better part of the entire Church Age it had been as if Christ were never born at all. What about Jesus' promise in Matthew 16, I protested—that "the gates of hell would not prevail" against his Church? What about Matthew 5:14, where Christ tells us that a city set on a hill can never be hidden? I vividly recall being shocked that people with these kinds of opinions had been allowed into an Evangelical missionary work in the first place; their ideas sounded "cultic" to me, like something one might hear among the Mormons or Jehovah's Witnesses.

And indeed, the Great Apostasy is a foundational tenet of both the Watchtower Society and Mormonism. As a matter of fact, there are remarkable similarities between A.J. Tomlinson's mountaintop experience of 1903 and that of Latter-Day Saints founder Joseph Smith eighty years earlier. Both men had become perplexed by the rampant denominationalism of rural America; both climbed a hill to pray; both were allegedly told to join no existing religion but to found a new one of their own—a new one that would, in reality, constitute the true restoration of the old. So the more I heard about this Great Apostasy business the less I liked it. Seventh-day Adventists taught the concept, I'd been told, and it led them to their notion that Sunday worship is the Mark of the Beast prophesied in the Book of Revelation. Even so-called liberal Christianity had a version, wherein crafty politicos and conniving clergymen had conspired together to turn the "simple message of Jesus" into that dreadful monstrosity known as "organized religion." For all their manifold differences, each of these movements had that one striking dogma in common: That the original Church founded by Christ and his apostles went bust. Thank God it has been restored by Joseph Smith/Charles Russell/Ellen G. White/A.J. Tomlinson . . . you fill in the blank.

My reaction then, to Fields of the Wood and its Great Apostasy, might easily have gone no further than this simple instinct of suspicious dislike. Or I might have managed, I suppose, to just start laughing again—to dismiss the whole thing as simply too fringy or kooky to get exercised over. But then another disquieting thought crept into my head: "How different is all this from my own picture of Church history? Don't the Dark Ages figure pretty prominently in my own outlook? Don't

I assign a similar importance to the Protestant Reformation of the sixteenth century—with Martin Luther standing in for A.J. Tomlinson? Don't I have, when it comes right down to it, a 'Great Apostasy' theory of my own?"

It was a startling epiphany. In fact, it exposed for the first time a whole host of deep, embryonic misgivings I'd been half-consciously suppressing my whole life. Basically, they boiled down to this: *Why was the Church Age such a terrible letdown?* Why, when it came right down to it, had the heroic efforts of the New Testament saints ended up amounting to so very little? I mean, the Old Testament leads up to Christ's advent in just the same way that an exciting movie builds up to its climax. Miracle after miracle, prophecy after prophecy, the whole story of Israel builds inexorably toward that stupendous eucatastrophe at Bethlehem, the moment in which Israel is at last to be transfigured into something greater and more powerful and more real than anything she ever had been as a mere tribe or nation. Yet somehow, some way, the picture of Church history I'd been given all my life was totally different—a Grand Anticlimax. We might have wanted to finesse the phraseology a bit at my church but we too saw the triumphs of early Christianity as a brief temporary set of victories followed by near-total collapse. Just as surely as Preacher Tomlinson's, my Church history timeline had a 1,500-year gap; a period of time roughly equal, mind you, to *the entire history of Israel from Moses to John the Baptist.* As far as I ever heard, it was an age without heroes, without conquests, without miracles, an age in which help and salvation were not *less* difficult but *more* difficult to find than they had been under the synagogue. And here at Fields of the Wood I suddenly realized—with a shock—that this problem had been somewhere in the back of my mind, troubling me, since I was about ten or twelve years old.

It is true that up to this point I would have tried to differentiate my view by maintaining that the original Church had not actually become apostate but had merely been *obscured*, leaving a "remnant" of true believers hiding somewhere in secret, waiting to reemerge someday like the first crocuses of spring.

Yet now I saw clearly how little this notion had ever satisfied me. Whenever I'd pointed this problem out in the past, my religious teachers would invariably begin spinning what I, even at the time, regarded as airy conspiracy theories straight out of Oliver Stone. I was often told (without any evidence to back up the assertion) that the true Christians had been there all right, thinking and worshipping just as we do here at our church today, only the "powers that be" have doctored the records, so that no trace of their existence has been left behind. Or, occasionally, I was sent to shabby, disreputable sects like the Montanists and the Albigenses as examples of God's true remnant. These, oddly, always turned out to be weird gnostic splinter groups whose real doctrine (as far as we can reconstruct it) was as divergent from my own as any other brand of "dark ages" Christianity. How important, then, was my distinction between obscurity and apostasy if one was forced to go rooting around in history's rubbish bin looking for true Christianity? Just how obscure do things have to get before we can go ahead and declare an apostasy?

Another set of voices, on the other hand, more moderate in tone, took the opposite tack, directing me to examples of genuine Christianity lingering *within* the mainstream of Dark Ages religion. Ambrose, Augustine, Thomas à Kempis, even Francis of Assisi were sometimes cited as "crypto-Evangelicals"—genuine Spirit-filled Christians struggling to survive amidst the general wreck of the Church, and secretly on the outs somehow with the authorities of their day. Yet once again, even the most cursory examination of the facts made nonsense of the claim. Every one of these men, I quickly discovered, had readily and even enthusiastically accepted the entire package of doctrines that, to me, had always been the very hallmark of the collapse: baptismal regeneration, purgatory, confessions to a priest, and so forth. If a man could believe all these things and still qualify as an authentic Christian . . . well, then it became difficult to see how Francis Xavier, Aloysius Gonzaga, and Pope Innocent III weren't authentic Christians, too. This did solve the problem of A.J. Tomlinson, I suppose, but it didn't seem to leave much for Martin Luther to do, either. Which brought me neatly back around to square one, searching for the Great Apostasy once more.

No, my friends, Fields of the Wood had thrown me quite a curve. I realized it more and more in the days and weeks ahead. For the first time in my life I started asking questions such as these: Is such a picture of Church history even scriptural? Could such a radical breakdown ever happen to a Church "built upon the foundation of the apostles and prophets, Jesus Christ himself being the chief corner stone" (Eph. 2:20)? And just how much real history did the A.J. Tomlinsons of the world actually know? Trying to sort it all out seemed like an incredibly daunting prospect, even for a lifelong history buff like myself. Then again, I had noticed at least one fact that seemed clear enough; though everyone differed about which prophet had put things right again, there was a surprising amount of agreement about *when things first went off the rails.* "The final act of this tragedy" according to Tomlinson in a little tract popular at Fields of the Wood (and his opinion is fairly representative), "occurred in A.D. 325 at the Council of Nicaea when the Church became a mere instrument of the Roman state, and substituted a creed for the Word of God." We may all agree to disagree, it seems, when choosing our reformers, but when it comes to the villain of the piece—well, the verdict is in. Even Dan Brown, author of the blockbuster conspiracy thriller *The Da Vinci Code*, concurs entirely. The instigator of the Nicene coup, the man who undid what had been done by Christ himself, was one Flavius Valerius Constantinus, better known to history as Constantine the Great.

Here, at least, was a solid place to start. Constantine, after all, was a real man and his council was a real event; it ought to be possible to examine the facts of the matter and draw a real conclusion. And, indeed, my early investigations here were quite encouraging since most of my sources did, at least, agree on the basic outline of the tale. It seemed that when the emperor allowed himself to be converted in 313, he transformed the Christian Church from a simple body of pure, New Testament believers into the state religion of the Roman Empire. In doing this, he made Church membership socially advantageous and this brought in a vast flood of half-converted pagans who were admitted with minimal fuss by a mere external act of baptism. These pseudo-converts retained, naturally enough, more than a few souvenirs of their old beliefs and they mixed these into their new faith in a kind of syncretist hodgepodge. Where once Christians had met secretly in the catacombs, enormous gilded basilicas were now raised; in fact, preexisting pagan temples were often rededicated (with some slight remodeling) as ersatz Christian cathedrals. Ancient pagan festivals like Easter and Halloween were given an after-the-fact Christian reading, then incorporated into an elaborate calendar of holy days, with newly minted Christian saints shoehorned into slots that had once been reserved for Venus and Mercury.

Worst of all, perhaps, Christianity gained a clerical class. Where once there had been equality, democracy, and the priesthood of the believer, Constantine gave the Church an ecclesiastical hierarchy just like Mithraism, Zoroastrianism, and a host of other mystery cults. In order to solidify their hegemony, these state-appointed officials cooked up elaborate sacrificial rituals that only they could understand and locked the Bible away in languages only they could interpret. As for the Nicene Council itself—well, none of the emperor's accusers seemed quite sure what *that* had been all about. They only knew that Constantine had done it, and that the Church was never the same afterward.

This all *sounded* plausible—but did it really happen this way? Did politics and paganism so easily overcome, in the space of two or three short decades, a Church that had held fast through ten bloody persecutions, for nearly 300 years? Or had I missed a step somewhere—and a lot of other good Christians missed it with me? Already I saw glaring gaps in the apostasy scenario that seemed to suggest the latter. I noticed, for instance, that the charges brought against the emperor were so wildly discordant it seemed impossible to decide what I was and wasn't being asked to verify. A.J. Tomlinson, as we have seen, blamed Constantine for preferring his own creed to the Bible; Dan Brown says

Constantine invented the Christian Bible in the first place. The Jehovah's Witnesses damn Constantine's council for fabricating the divinity of Christ; the Mormons fault it for denying the divinity of Man. Seventh-day Adventists reproach Constantine for dropping too much of the Old Testament law; my own Baptist church blamed him for keeping too much of it. It was as if the same man were being criticized at the same time for being both too fat and too thin. To top it all off, I also learned that many Protestant denominations (including some I had always considered to be Bible-believing) happily *accept* the creed drawn up at Nicaea! Even the most Evangelical of Lutheran churches, for instance—with my own personal anti-Constantine, Martin Luther, at their head—still recite the Nicene Creed every single Sunday morning! So where on earth could I go from there? What hope for little old me to find the answers when most of my fellow Protesters couldn't even agree on the questions?

I hope you won't imagine that I was ready to look into any medieval alternatives just yet; in fact, I stayed stuck in a mental loop about all this for quite some time. I think most Evangelicals are stuck in such a loop; vaguely conscious of the riddle, perhaps, but no more attracted to the complexities of Catholicism, Eastern Orthodoxy, or any other form of pre-Reformation Christianity than they are to the wacky speculations of the Great Apostasy groups. And to tell you the truth, this is probably a healthy impulse, a sound instinct for conservatism that has done more good than harm. But I'd seen too much there at Fields of the Wood—had my nose rubbed in the problem, so to speak. And now it looked as if I, too, like A.J. Tomlinson before me, was going to have to grab hold of God . . . and hang on for the ride.

The big breakthrough, I suppose, came when I happened upon a dusty set of forgotten books languishing on the back shelf of a local Christian bookstore. Distributed years ago by a respected Protestant publisher, these formidable-looking tomes were called *The Fathers of the Church*, and they contained something I never knew existed—a vast selection of Christian documents from the period *between* Christ and Constantine. How these writings altered my understanding of first- and second-century Christianity is a story I have already told, in a book called *Four Witnesses: The Early Church in Her Own Words*. This current volume may be considered a follow-up to that story, though you need not have read the first book to understand the second.[1] But *The Fathers of the Church* also contained, to my amazement, a very full contemporary account of third- and fourth-century Christianity as well; thousands of pages, in fact, amounting to a complete history of the period in question. The rise of Constantine is there; his conversion, such as it was; his complicated relationship with the Church and what came of it. All of this is covered quite thoroughly in the writings of early Christian historians such as Eusebius, Theodoret, Sozomen, and Socrates Scholasticus.

I also learned that I could review, if I liked, the surviving books and letters of the principal actors in the drama—men such as Alexander of Alexandria, Eusebius of Caesarea, Basil the Great, and even the Emperor Constantine himself. In fact, the actual canons and decrees of the Nicene Council were available for evaluation! Here then, was an out I never expected. Here was the raw historical data. If the true Faith really was fumbled away during this era then these were the fools and knaves who did it. If there really was some kind of a cataclysm in 325—so bad it sent the Holy Ghost running for cover—then there ought to be traces of it preserved in these pages, like the evidence of an ancient asteroid impact preserved in the bedrock. Were these "Fathers of the Church," in fact, fools and knaves? And how would their doctrinal teachings compare (or perhaps contrast) with those of pre-Constantinian Christians? My big dusty set of books appeared to offer the answers. So I rolled up my sleeves, stuck a pencil behind my ear, and got to work.

What I learned astonished me. The minute I turned to these source materials (and away from old-fashioned denominational polemics), the fog began to clear. I found neither the apostasy I

---

[1] A brief compendium of this material is available in this volume as Appendix One: Christian Teaching Before Constantine.

had been led to expect nor its mere opposite; I found a *drama*—even a melodrama. I found combat, siege, disaster, despair, and relief. I found one of the darkest chapters in Christian history and one of the most glorious. Paganism really did make an unprecedented assault on the Church during the fourth century; not a slow, secret, insidious assault such as I had imagined, but direct open warfare! And Christianity met it with direct heroic resistance—the very opposite of the cringing, fawning retreat implied in the pop version. Those "doctored" records, supposedly swept clean, stored instead a blow-by-blow account of the magnificent conflict . . . and hardly anything else for a hundred years. False creeds *were* proposed—and mandated. And there *were* emperors who tortured to have them received. Important Church leaders turned traitor; but when they did, the faithful Christians of the fourth century made their mark on history as well. Cities burned, Caesars fell, bishops were tarred and feathered, and heads, as they say, rolled. Miracles took place and immortal champions arose. It was the epic of our race, we Christians—nothing less. And how I had ever done without it was the main question I had left when my researches were through.

So I'd like to tell you this extraordinary story. I think it will captivate you, as it did me, and strengthen your faith, as it did mine. Better yet, I'd like these Fathers (and Mothers!) of the Church themselves to do most of the telling—in their own words once again. These early brethren of ours were, after all, eyewitnesses to the enormous change that took place during their lifetimes and far better judges of its meaning than any latter-day interpreters could ever hope to be. This is, however, an extraordinarily complex story, one that does not yield easily to simplification (which is, come to think of it, perhaps the reason it isn't better known or why it has encouraged so many to give it up in frustration and simply treat the whole period as an inkblot test on which to project doubts and fears). One of the ways I've tried to make the tale more accessible is to employ, as I did in *Four Witnesses*, some of the techniques of the novelist—dramatized vignettes that might be inappropriate were I attempting to write a straightforward book of history. There are plenty of those on the market already, however, with no real need for anyone to produce another. What there *is* a need for is a good popularization of this important narrative, a "foot in the door," so to speak, for John Q. Christian sitting in the pews of our churches—and that is what I've aimed at here, even at the risk of oversimplification. To those who might be tempted to wonder if a mere storyteller like myself might deliberately distort the picture where a real scholar would not, I can only reply that if my efforts serve only to send more Christian believers back to the source materials (in a skeptical mood or not), then I will be content to have achieved that happy purpose, at least.

St. Francis de Sales—another commonly offered example of "crypto-Evangelicalism"—was a seventeenth-century bishop noted for the affection he earned among people on both sides while trying to ease cross-communion hatreds. He sometimes encouraged deeper thoughts about the Great Apostasy by refer-ring to the words of our common savior in John's Gospel: "Now is the judgment of this world: now shall the prince of this world be cast out. And I, if I be lifted up from the earth, will draw all men unto me" [John 12:31–32 KJV]. "Was he not lifted up on the cross?" Francis would ask, with questions that are still worth pondering as we begin our journey:

> Did he not suffer?—and how then having drawn to himself the Church, should he let it escape so utterly from him? How should he let go this prize which had cost him so dear? Had the prince of this world, the devil, been driven out with the stick of the cross for a time of three or four hundred years, to return and reign a thousand years? Would you make so abso-lutely vain the might of the cross? Are you ignorant that our Lord has purchased the Church with his own blood?—and who can take it from him? Think you that he is weaker than his adversary?
>
> Ah! I pray you, speak honorably of this captain. . . .[1]

~

A note on the term "Universal Christianity": This entire story takes place in the days of the *Undivided Church*: during the first millennium of Christianity, that is, in which all believers other than those who had chosen to join isolated cults or small splinter groups were "peaceably united in one faith." Such cults would have been recognized as such by practically all traditional Christian churches today—seriously defective, theologically speaking, not only by the standards of the historic liturgical communions but by those of Evangelical Christianity as well.

The Age of Constantine and of Athanasius predates the Great East/West Schism that produced our modern "Catholic" and "Orthodox" terminology by over 700 years. It predates the still later Western division into "Catholic" and "Protestant" churches by nearly 1,200 years. The titles we use when describing these later divisions today were originally held in common by the one, original Undivided Church:

That Church was *Catholic* because it was intended by its divine founder to be *universal*—found everywhere, united wherever it was found, meant for everyone, the new spiritual home of humanity.

This same Church was *Orthodox* because it was *"right-thinking"* in matters of the Faith—because it believed and proclaimed the unspoiled doctrine of its divine founder as he taught it to his apostles, and that was passed down by them to future generations.

The Undivided Church was *Bible-believing* and *evangelical* as well, because it cherished the Holy Scripture handed down by the apostles and took them seriously in the sense originally intended; and because it understood its whole mission to be that of spreading the Christian gospel—the *Evangelium*, in Latin—by word and by deed.

Catholic, Orthodox, Bible-believing—all of these are legitimate terms to describe the ancient Church that existed for so long before any of the current divisions within Christianity took place. Whether any of these titles became the exclusive, legitimate property of any one community after the subsequent splits is a topic outside the scope of this present volume. I have, in fact, tried scrupulously to avoid addressing any later developments at all.

Because these terms are, however, so generally associated in modern usage with one particular group or set of denominations it has seemed worthwhile to coin, for the purposes of this book, a neutral title, free—hopefully—of any later connotations. To that effect, I have chosen "Universal Church" to describe the Body of Christ during these early centuries and "Universal Christianity" as the Faith that Body held in common. Of course, the various historians and other experts quoted in these pages were not privy to this decision; I wish to suggest, for that reason, that when these authorities are found employing one or the other of the aforementioned terms in their comments, readers will choose to interpret them interchangeably in the sense described here, without worrying too deeply, in this context, about whether the expert quoted intended the later identification or not.

All this having been said, it must also be emphasized that Universal Christianity is not simply, like C.S. Lewis's famous "mere Christianity," a theoretical construct invented in retrospect to highlight a basic minimum of shared generalities; it is actually a verifiable historical reality. The Universal Church—the Bride of Christ, particularly as she lived her life in the three centuries prior to Constantine—had a very definite set of doctrines and practices that can be ascertained beyond any reasonable doubt by examining the many thousands of pages of writings left behind from that era; and not all of these teachings have been preserved intact by every modern church that agrees with her in the main. The story of how the emperor might or might not have changed what he found in place on the day he came to power could prove difficult to understand without at least some awareness of these facts.

One more caveat: though readers of *Four Witnesses* may be aware of my affiliation—an ordinary Catholic layman attending Mass at today's ordinary Catholic churches—I would like to stress once again that the issues dividing that type of church from other Christian bodies are no part of my purpose here. This book aims merely to demonstrate, as the title implies, that the widely believed "Great Apostasy" simply *wasn't*—that Athanasius did save Christianity and that the Universal Church survived intact into the second millennium, whatever else may have happened to it since then.

1

Redheaded Stepchild

Then the disciples of John came to him, saying, "Why do we and the Pharisees fast, but your disciples do not fast?" And Jesus said to them, "Can the wedding guests mourn, as long as the bridegroom is with them? The days will come, when the bridegroom is taken away from them, and then they will fast" (Matt. 9:14–15).

So piercing were the stars, so black the firmament overhead, the air so still and devoid of moisture that mother and child might have been standing on the surface of the moon. The great metropolis of Alexandria lay only a few miles to the north; but the sky was darker everywhere in those days and the atmosphere cleaner, so that the Milky Way spangled over their heads like a sack of multicolored jewels scattered across black velvet. At their feet spread the great Egyptian desert, a shadowy ocean of sand rolling southward into Africa. The woman, a pale, Gaulish redhead with dark rings of sorrow under her eyes, had otherwise the look of ease and city life about her. She was plainly out of her element here at the edge of the wilderness. Her child seemed even more incongruous: a scrawny, big-eyed boy, five, perhaps, six years old, with an ominous, unending cough; a dark, mixed-race runt with a head of kinky yet unmistakably Celtic red hair.[II] Most Roman women would have exposed this child at birth, or aborted him early on, at the first signs of a difficult pregnancy. This woman was different. She clung to her pathetic little offspring as if he were a bag of gold and even now she was taking terrible risks, breaking Caesar's law,

[II] Gregory of Nazianzus (c. 329–90), among others, preserves the fact that Athanasius had "auburn hair," although several other writers mention his very dark complexion. The hostile Emperor Julian, as a matter of fact, called Athanasius bluntly a "black dwarf."

on his behalf. Yet she was not alone. Other mothers were nearby, perhaps eight or twelve of them, with other children, all boys. They stood together in a group at the prearranged meeting place. They stood together with only the occasional whimper of grief, Christian mothers, patiently waiting for the gaunt, somber men who were coming to carry their sons away.

With the first sight of an approaching camel the sounds of prayer, too, came within hearing; low, dirge-like chants of lament in the Coptic language native to Egypt: *"In Rama was there a voice heard, lamentation, and weeping, and great mourning, Rachel weeping for her children, and would not be comforted, because they are not."* Presently, the riders themselves came into view, "the Children of Israel," as they had been derisively known by the city Christians, five tall, bearded men between eighteen and thirty, deep voiced, dressed in skins, courtly and old-fashioned in their speech. The woman had, like most people, laughed at them during happier times. Now they seemed like time travelers from the past, stepping out of the pages of early Church history on a mission to save the future. These were the watchful servants, she now knew, the wise virgins, the only ones whose lamps were still burning now that the day of Antichrist had arrived. The rest of us, she reflected bitterly, the whole of Christendom, she supposed, had been living in a fool's paradise this past half century and more.

As the brothers sidled up to the group and began to dismount, the woman looked down suddenly into the eyes of her son. This was it, she realized—the final moment. All around her, she sensed the other mothers coming to the same realization, felt them instinctively tighten their grip on the boys. What, she wondered, would become of these women once the children were safe? They would all wander back into the city, of course; the desert was death to city folk. But would the city be any safer in these Last Days? She had heard that just in the previous month all the Christian women of nearby Heliopolis had been rounded up and sold to brothels in the East, from the most dignified matron down to the last adolescent girl. She herself could hold up in such straits, she knew. She had come late to Christ, after a whole youth of sordid

adventures in just such places. But the rest of these girls were cradle Christians, born in suburban homes, raised on sunshine and
their daddy's doting. She caught her breath at the thought. They
needed her, then. They needed her to go ahead and be strong
on their behalf. Maybe she really had frittered away most of her
Christian life. No doubt she had, these last few years, fallen into
the trap of looking to God mainly for worldly success, in a world
that was now passed away. Never mind that. None of it mattered
anymore. Jesus, in his infinite mercy, had sent her a gift—one last
chance to make it up here at the end.

The mother gathered her child into her arms. She kissed him
roughly on the side of the face and then thrust him into the
hands of the closest brother.

"His name is Athanasius," she told him.

"We will take him to Antony," the quiet, cow-eyed man
answered.

At last, with all eyes fixed in her direction, the woman turned
decisively away from her baby. "The Lord is my shepherd," she
called out in her distinctive foreign brogue. "I shall not want.
He makes me lie down in green pastures: he leads me beside still
waters." The other mothers looked at her in wonder, in disbe-
lief—and then slowly, one by one, they found the courage to join
her. "He restores my soul. He leads me in paths of righteousness
for his name's sake. Even though I walk through the valley of
the shadow of death, I fear no evil; for thou art with me; thy rod
and thy staff, they comfort me." The brothers began to move
quickly among them, gathering up the children. There would
be no time for extended farewells tonight; Caesar's spies might
have followed this little exodus, might be watching even now.
"Thou preparest a table before me in the presence of my enemies;
thou anointest my head with oil, my cup overflows." In minutes,
the transfer was complete. The boys cried out for their mothers
from the arms of their new fathers; as the caravan remounted,
the men pronounced a final word of benediction. Then it was all
over. The Christian daughters of Alexandria finished their psalm
alone. "Surely goodness and mercy shall follow me all the days

of my life; and I shall dwell in the house of the Lord forever."

Most of us today will have noticed the biblical parallels in this story. The Holy Child of Bethlehem, for instance, was carried, three centuries before, into this very same desert to escape the wrath of another tyrannical potentate, King Herod the Great. As a matter of fact, little Athanasius's departure may actually have happened during the Christmas season, though at this point in history none of the actors in the drama would have known it, or much cared. The year was 304 and Christmas was, as yet, a very minor feast on the calendar, celebrated nowhere with any particular fervor and not at all in many Christian communities.[III] In this story, however, the tyrant is the Roman Emperor Diocletian, and his late campaign to finally extirpate "the Christian superstition" once and for all is known to historians as the Great Persecution, the final and fiercest of the ten general persecutions through which the early Church had been destined to pass. And in his own unique way, this new Holy Innocent is also "set for the fall and rising of many in Israel, and for a sign that is spoken against" (Luke 2:34). There are no angels or shepherds in this Christmas story; no one here knows any Christmas carols to sing. The only music is the cry of a lost, imperfect child receding slowly across the sands, swallowed finally by the vastness of the desert. Yet this pitiful runt, this redheaded stepchild, is fated, though no

---

[III] Not that holy days themselves were anything new at this time: one of the very oldest Christian documents in existence, *The Martyrdom of Polycarp*, records the keeping of a "saint's day" nearly 150 years earlier, complete with the exposition of his relics! Likewise, the memorial of the Resurrection has been observed with great solemnity since the very beginning; its connection with the lunar calendar is a legacy from Passover and the Church's Jewish roots. The English word *Easter* (which is, indeed, related to a preexisting Anglo-Saxon festival celebrating the rising light of day and Spring) is merely a local nickname, used only in English- and German-speaking parts of the world. Elsewhere in Christendom some derivative of the Hebrew word *Pesach* (Passover) is used, i.e., *Pascha* in Greek, *Pasqua* in Italian, *Pascua* in Spanish, *Paschen* in Dutch, and so forth; even in the Catholic portions of Germany the Resurrection feast is known as *Paisken,* not *Ostern.*

one knows it yet, to save Christianity—to save, in fact, the world. Had anyone thought to spare him his compromised quality of life, to put him "out of his misery" after the fashion of the pagans, that world never would have been saved. If it is to be saved again, from the new and frightening rebirth of paganism happening in our own time, we would do well to remember Athanasius. His is a Christmas story worth telling again, even in the twenty-first century, full of new life and hope.

The Ghetto Church

Because the Great Persecution does form such a natural watershed between the Age of Constantine and all that went before, modern believers have fallen into the habit of lumping everything prior to it in a big mental pot called "early Christianity." In that pot, we tend to imagine the Church of the third century acting and relating to Constantine's Roman Empire exactly as it did to Nero's more than 200 years earlier—something akin to passing a Quaker meetinghouse on a modern highway and imagining the people inside dressed like William Penn. Actually, the age of early Christianity covers quite a long span of time (longer, in fact, than the entire history of the United States), and many of the common misconceptions about it are rooted in nothing more than anachronism. Big-screen epics like *Constantine and the Cross*[IV] have sometimes reinforced these myths, portraying the period we are now investigating with costumes and imagery from a much earlier era. In these popular representations, Christians of the late 200s look just like their brethren from Bible days: a pure, persecuted band of New Testament believers huddling together in caves and catacombs, hunted down by a ruthless, uncompromising strain of pagan totalitarianism. In reality, this fanciful portrait falsifies the paganism of Constantine's day almost as much it does the Christianity.

[IV] In justice, 1962's *Constantine and the Cross*, directed by Lionello De Felice, is actually a pretty good movie; in spite of the anachronisms it ranks as one of the more intelligent religious spectacles of its era.

Prior to Diocletian's outbreak in 303, the paganism of Rome had not been tyrannical for decades and did very little persecuting. Precisely what the empire had become by then was a vast early experiment in multiculturalism. Over the previous years the Romans had been engaged in a titanic civilizing campaign that brought law and order to practically the entire known world. The making of that enormous omelet had, admittedly, required the breaking of a few eggs; but the goal was never conformity—no, just the reverse. The ultimate goal was the establishment of a stable, neutral matrix in which every citizen of whatever race and creed was free to buy and sell, to enter sexual partnerships, to propagate ideas, and to worship and believe exactly as they chose. Third-century Rome, in other words, was a libertarian's paradise.[v] It is true that every citizen swore an absolute oath of allegiance to the state; but this swearing came easily to most pagans since the state, in practice, exerted its authority over such a narrow range of human behaviors. "[O]ne reason for Roman military success," according to historian Henry M. Chadwick, "was believed to be the fact that, while other peoples worshipped only their own local deities, the Romans worshipped all deities without exclusiveness and had therefore been rewarded for their piety. . . . Even the apparently exclusive religion of Judaism had been welcomed into the loose amalgam of polytheism by identifying the God of the Jews with Dionysus or (since they reverenced Saturday) with Saturn."[2] So in a nutshell, the empire's characteristic attitude toward religion was indifference cloaked in the language of respect, and her official "polytheism" was really an effort to honor many religions rather than many gods. The only thing Rome ever actually required

---

[v] "Rome put no pressure on the manifold peoples of the Empire to conform, destroyed no cultural traditions, and suppressed no difference of language. Instead, she imposed the way of peace, and built up the institutional framework which all men took for granted as they went about their daily concerns." T. Robert S. Broughton, *Imperial Rome* (New York: Time/Life Books, 1965), 44.

in this area was an official nod to the city's all-inclusive pantheon, an act that was, in effect, the ceremonial acceptance of a doctrine very like our own separation of Church and state.[VI] To make any single religion, then, into the state religion of the empire was a concept utterly alien to pagan Rome. The empire had no state religion in those days and had no business to ever get one, as far as most of her citizens were concerned. The business of Rome was business.

So if the Christians weren't cowering under persecution during the 200s, just what were they doing? Oddly enough, they were a well-known segment of Roman society. They were in the minority, of course—perhaps 15 percent of the empire's fifty million inhabitants were Christian by 250—but they were everywhere and their numbers were steadily increasing.[VII] The catacombs had been left far behind by this time; Christians of the mid- to late-third century had no need to hide their faith and they did not hide it. The Church owned property during this period and built churches on it. "By 250," according to Chadwick, "there were about 100 episcopal sees[VIII] in Italy. . . . By the year 251 the resources of the church in Rome had grown so much that it was

---

[VI] Religion in Rome, according to Paul Johnson, was "valued as an aid to public decorum. . . . The state's compulsory but marginal civic creed . . . imposed no burden on conscience." Johnson, *History of Christianity* (New York: Macmillan Co., 1976), 6.

[VII] Pliny the Younger, writing from Italy about A.D. 112, complains that Christianity had already become so popular that the pagan Temples were nearly empty and it had become difficult to sell meat sacrificed to idols. "By Tertullian's time [eighty or ninety years later], the Christians were numerous enough to overthrow the Empire, had their intentions been hostile." Johnson, *History of Christianity*, 70.

[VIII] An episcopal see is the geographical district under the authority of an individual bishop. Sometimes called a diocese or bishopric, these administrative divisions of the Universal Church are akin to the counties in an American state. For questions regarding the role of the bishops themselves in early Christianity, please refer to Appendix One, Christian Beliefs Before Constantine.

supporting from its common purse not only the bishop, forty-six presbyters, seven deacons, seven subdeacons, forty-two acolytes, and fifty-two exorcists, readers, and doorkeepers, but also more than 1,500 widows and needy persons, all of whom were 'fed by the grace and kindness of the Lord.'"[3] Believers served in the army, often in positions of authority and respect; even important provincial governors were known to be Christian by this time. Sixty or eighty years earlier the obligation to offer sacrifice to the gods would have precluded such service, since refusal to do so was to declare oneself, in effect, a traitor to the Roman way of life. Yet by 270, Christians were so common and so integral to life in the empire that what had been an absolute requirement in Grandpa's day was now being silently excused by practically all the authorities. Even the Emperor Diocletian himself had shown great tolerance for the Faith. Lucius Lactantius, a poet and rhetorician in his court, tells us that Diocletian's own wife and daughter had been interested in learning Christianity prior to the outbreak. And why not? A large Christian basilica was located directly across the street from the emperor's house! Clearly then, Christians of the late 200s had every reason to think that the "Age of Martyrs" was ancient history. Indeed, the famous stories of Polycarp and Blandina, Justin and Agatha must have seemed as remote to them as the tales of Valley Forge and Nathan Hale seem to us. No wonder that Christian believers like Athanasius's mother, swallowed up so unexpectedly in Diocletian's fury, might have seen the hand of Antichrist at work and the advent of the End Times.

Not only was this "pure early Church" not persecuted in the decades before Constantine, it apparently wasn't very pure either. The great Christian thinker Origen (who lived right at the heart of the period in question) says flat out that the Church was "whoring" in the third century. And Eusebius Pamphilus, writing in 325, had this to say about the Church of his youth:

> As always happens when there is abundance of liberty, our lives became indolent and careless; we envied one another and did harm to our brethren; any wretched excuse

was sufficient to start a war of arms—as it were—with a
spearthrust of words; leaders poured ill fame on other
leaders; nation rose against nation; pretense and damned
hypocrisy seemed to reach the limits of their evil height. . . .
Like senseless people we did not trouble to make our God
propitious and benevolent toward us but like certain atheists
who consider that human affairs are neither guarded nor
watched over (by God) we piled wickedness on wickedness.
Those who were supposed to be our pastors disdained the
paths of divine piety and inflamed their hearts in contests
one with another, only adding thus to the quarrels and
threats, the rivalry, the envies and hates of the times. They
filled their time in striving for position in no different a
manner than from the princes of this world.[4]

The abuses were so bad that many local Church synods were
called to try and bring in some reform. One of these, the Council of Elvira, was held in Spain in 300 and its surviving records
give us a pretty harrowing list of crimes going on well before the
"deep blackness and the Dark Ages" set in. The catalog includes
the following: pastors loan-sharking the faithful; money-grub-
bing bishops living the high life out of church funds; presbyters
shacking up with female parishioners; deacons visiting and par-
ticipating in pagan worship; a clergy winking at and routinely partaking in gambling, divorce, and adultery. As for abuses
among the laity, the council lists routine fornication before marriage, rampant divorce and remarriage, and the abortion of children conceived in adultery. If anything, the pure early Church
seems to have been more pure (in its morals, at any rate) after
Constantine than it was before.

In real life—as opposed to popular mythology—the third
century was the age of the Ghetto Church. Like the Jews in
Europe prior to World War II, the Christians of the Roman
Empire, living in their own enclaves, close to their places of
worship, talking, dressing, thinking, believing differently than
their neighbors, were disliked precisely because of their ubiquity

and their growing influence.[IX] Christians really were doing well under the *Pax Romana*; too well, in fact, for their own spiritual good. Called by the Lord to be salt and light to the dying world, the third-century Church was getting along just fine as a middle-class, quasi-ethnic Roman minority, with no vision higher than what Evangelical philosopher Francis Schaeffer used to call "personal peace and affluence." So long as it was content to be nothing more than that—just one more "denomination" on the empire's crowded religious scene—the Church would achieve assimilation eventually, just as the synagogue had. Such, at any rate, seems to have been the best hope of many. This hope, however, was fragile. *Real* Romans tended to chafe at the spectacle and got more and more riled as the century wore on to see the old laws against Christianity being so routinely winked at. In response, Christians ended up compromising even more than they had already; learning to "play ball," as it were, to live and let live, to keep silent when they ought to have spoken, to render unto Caesar the things that were God's. Yes, the third-century Church had found a way to make peace with paganism—and it was proving deadly.

JESUS FREAKS

In the midst of this whoring one young man made a desperate grab at authenticity and wound up saving the whole bucket of milk. His name was Antony of Coma, the son of well-to-do Christian parents in Roman Egypt. Born about 251, Antony

---

[IX] The idea that Christians lacked all power or political sway prior to the rise of Constantine—and thus retained a New Testament-era innocence of its corrupting force—is one of the silliest aspects of the popular apostasy myth. The most easily accessible of all Church histories (that of Eusebius Pamphilus) records that Church leaders of the late 200s "were courted and honored with the greatest subserviency by all the rulers and governors" and that the splendid churches they had erected by this time were, if anything, a cause of jealousy to the emperors! (VIII:I).

was twenty years old, living the comfortable life of a rich young ruler, wholly unmolested by the Roman authorities, when both his mother and father passed away, leaving to him the care of his younger sister as well as all their worldly possessions. It was a crossroads in his life. Had he been a more typical member of the Ghetto Church, Antony would have picked up right where his father left off and carried on with business as usual. Antony, however, had always been a little odd—sensitive, troubled, disinterested in schooling or, really, success in any form. Most of all, he seems to have taken his childhood Bible lessons a bit too seriously; more seriously, at any rate, than anyone had ever really intended. One day, not long after coming into his fortune, he was walking to church, pondering the disparity between his own lifestyle and that of the early Christians. An ancient biography has preserved the scene for us:

> [H]e meditated as he walked how the apostles had left all and followed the savior; and how those in the Acts brought the price of what they had sold, and laid it at the apostles' feet, to be given away to the poor; and what and how great a hope was laid up for them in heaven. With this in his mind, he entered the church. And it befell then that the Gospel was being read; and he heard how the Lord had said to the rich man, "If thou wilt be perfect, go, sell all thou hast, and give to the poor; and come, follow me, and thou shalt have treasure in heaven" [Matt. 19:21]. Antony, therefore, as if the remembrance of the saints had come to him from God, and as if the lesson had been read on his account, went forth at once from the Lord's house, and gave away to those of his own village the possessions he had inherited from his ancestors (300 plough-lands, fertile and very fair), that they might give no trouble either to him or his sister. All his moveables he sold, and a considerable sum which he received for them he gave to the poor.

The next week Antony was back in church again, a poorer but wiser man—but God still had more to say:

Having kept back a little for his sister, when he went again into the Lord's house he heard the Lord saying in the Gospel, "Take no thought for the morrow" [Matt. 6:34], and, unable to endure any more delay, he went out and distributed that too to the needy. And having committed his sister to known and faithful virgins, and given her wherewith to be educated in a nunnery,[X] he himself thenceforth devoted himself . . . to training; taking heed to himself, and using himself severely.[XI]

Fasting and self-denial have been part of our Faith since Elijah lived beyond Jordan, where the ravens brought him his food and the brook brought him his drink. But in the Ghetto Church these practices had fallen into almost complete disuse—as badly, perhaps, as they have in our own sad time. Although not everyone, by any means, is called to excel in these pursuits, certainly there are still many demons besetting the Church (both literal and figurative), which "will not come out without much prayer and fasting" (Matt. 17:21). Seeing this truth, Antony made a momentous decision at his personal crossroads; he turned radical to save himself from nominalism. In the Gospels, the rich young ruler went away sorrowful, for he was very wealthy; Antony left the wealth behind and went away with joy.

[X] Women certainly were living together in Christian communes by this point and had been dedicating themselves to Christ alone with vows of virginity since apostolic days. Paul himself gives instruction to virgins "devoted to the Lord in both body and spirit" (1 Cor. 7:32–35 KJV) and two of the earliest post-apostolic writers, Tertullian and Justin, bear witness to the existence of this institution in writings which date from A.D. 170 or earlier. Athanasius says that such women were referred to as "the spouses of Christ" in his day and had been since even earlier times.

[XI] This ancient *Life of Antony* (the earliest known Christian biography, by the way) was composed by his disciple Athanasius, writing late in his own career. More will be said about its composition on later pages. This book was, incidentally, a major influence on the conversion of St. Augustine of Hippo. The translation here is by Rev. Charles Kingsley in his book *The Hermits* (New York: Macmillan & Co., 1913), 36.

At first, he lived in the town, sleeping in haystacks, going without, praying most of the time—yet working as a basket weaver so as not to suffer the apostle Paul's censure, "If anyone will not work, let him not eat" (2 Thess. 3:10). Most of the proceeds, however, he gave to the destitute. "And all in the village who loved good, seeing him thus, called him the friend of God; and some embraced him as a son, some as a brother." Later, Antony left the company of his fellow men and went fasting, like his Lord, into a desert place—the great blistering desert of the Upper Thebaid. He crossed the Nile, climbed the barren mountains on its east bank, and found an old, abandoned fort, where he established his residence. And there, in the words of the great patristic scholar Johannes Quasten, "the spread of worldliness was counteracted by a flight from the world."[5]

He slept on the ground, ate nothing but bread with salt, drank well water, stayed up all night, and lost himself in desperate intercession for the Church—a Church, as he believed, well-nigh on its deathbed. Antony knew from Scripture that "The prayer of a righteous man has great power in its effects" (James 5:16). He also knew, like Peter, that he was not a righteous man (see Luke 5:8) but a sinful man, from whom the Lord, by all rights, ought to depart. Antony needed purification. So he set out to buffet his body to bring it into submission (see 1 Cor. 9:27) and when it became exhausted, he would repeat that other saying of Paul, "When I am weak, then am I strong" (2 Cor. 12:10). And like Christ fasting in the wilderness, Antony was tormented by Satan. Many times, even in visible form, devils tried to turn him from his path, often resorting to physical blows.

Word of his vigil began to circulate back in the towns. Once, a group of curious young men came out to the fortress to speak with Antony and learn what he was up to. The hermit denied them admission, but he did allow the youths to toss some loaves of bread over the wall. The men—not more than teenagers, probably—refused to leave right away. They camped out at the base of the wall and spent the night. During the hours of darkness, they had an uncanny experience; they heard, as it were,

crowds inside clamoring, thundering, lamenting, crying—
"Depart from our ground. What dost thou even in the desert?
Thou canst not abide our onset." At first those without thought
that there were some men fighting with him, and that they
had got in by ladders; but when, peeping in through a crack,
they saw no one, then they took for granted that they were
demons, and being terrified, called themselves on Antony . . .
his acquaintances came up continually, expecting to find him
dead, and [instead] heard him singing, "Let the Lord arise, and
his enemies shall be scattered; and let them who hate him flee
before him. As wax melts from before the face of the fire, so
shall sinners perish from before the face of God" [Ps. 68:1–2].
And again, "All nations compassed me round about, and in the
name of the Lord I repelled them" [Ps. 118:10].[XII]

Antony never did come out of his fortress—not for twenty
long years. It had never been his intention to found any kind
of movement anyhow or to influence anyone but God. Yet the
young men stayed anyway, and stayed by the dozens. A steady
trickle of them came out of the cities from then on, warned

[XII] To those who tend to dismiss such stories when found in the lives of
the saints, John Henry Newman had this to say: "Supposing I found a
narrative, such as Antony's, [dating from] *the apostles' age*; it would be sufficiently agreeable to the narratives of Scripture to make me dismiss from
my mind all *antecedent* difficulties in believing it. On the other hand, did
the miracle of the swine [Matt 8:28–34] occur in the life of St. Antony, I
venture to maintain that men of this scientific day would not merely sus-
pend their judgment, or pronounce it improbable (which they might have
a right to do), but would at once, and peremptorily, pronounce it altogether incredible and false." Newman, *Historical Sketches* (London: Longmans, Green, 1917), 109–10. Eventually, the Protestantism of Newman's
day learned to recognize this double standard, and straightway began to
debunk the miracles of Scripture and hagiography alike. Thus so-called
"liberal Christianity" was born. Those of us hoping to save a lively, supernatural faith today would do well to ponder the consequences of that
nineteenth-century mistake.

somehow in their spirits to "flee from the wrath to come" (Matt. 3:7). They moved into nearby caves and other ruins, into empty sepulchers and the tombs of their ancient ancestors. They separated and lived alone, in imitation of Antony, and like Antony, they "used themselves severely" and begged God for revival in the churches. Occasionally, these would-be disciples joined to form a delegation, turning up at the wall of the old fort, begging their role model to come out and become their spiritual guide. To their astonishment, Antony did finally open the gate one day, that gate which had been shut a score of years. He stepped out into the open air, purified like Moses from the wilderness of Shur, and embraced them one by one. Antony was ready to embark on a new phase of his mission.

In Antony, the early Church was born again. Modeling himself on the Baptizer, he resurrected John's ancient order for a new age. The world needed to hear once more the voice of one crying in the wilderness, needed to see again a group of men living out "those commands of Christ which all the rest of the world explained away to nothing."[6] While the Ghetto Church ate, drank, and made merry, Antony's boys kept themselves alive on locusts and wild honey. While the city Christians normalized their own decayed state of affairs, speculating idly that miracles had ceased with the death of the last apostle, Antony's boys were filled with the Holy Spirit, who confirmed their mission with signs and wonders. Demons were cast out, lepers were cleansed, the lame made to walk, the blind made to see. Equally reminiscent of the Apostolic Age were the pristine gospel teachings of Antony and his disciples, resplendent with the unmistakable sound of primitive Christianity. Once, a young man asked Antony, "'What shall I do?' Quoth the old man, 'Trust not in thine own righteousness; regret not the thing which is past; bridle thy tongue and thy stomach.'" Another time, he related a heavenly vision to his students: "I saw all the snares of the enemy spread over the whole earth. And I sighed, and said, 'Who can pass through these?' And a voice came to me, saying, 'Humility alone can pass through, Antony, where the proud can in no wise go.'" Asked if his austerities sprang from a servile fear of God's judgment, Antony had this to say: "I do not now fear God, but love Him, for love drives out fear."[7]

All of Antony's teachings are like this: simple, direct, uncluttered by the technical jargon of the theologian. Though he was practically illiterate, he knew the Gospel of Luke by heart, having memorized it like a song. One time, according to the biography,

> two Greek philosophers came to him, thinking that they could tempt Antony. And he was in the outer mountain; and when he went out to them, understanding the men from their countenances, he said through an interpreter, "Why have you troubled yourselves so much, philosophers, to come to a foolish man?" And when they answered that he was not foolish, but rather very wise, he said, "If you have come to a fool, your labor is superfluous, but if ye think me to be wise, become as I am; for we ought to copy what is good, and if I had come to you, I should have copied you; but if you come to me, copy me, for I am a Christian."

Another academic once asked the hermit, "How art thou content, father, since thou has not the comfort of books?" Antony replied, "My book is the nature of created things. In it, when I choose, I can read the words of God."

Nature, as a matter of fact, was central in the lives of the desert monks. Dwelling in the mountains for decades at a time, they became mountain men, veritable walking almanacs of the rhythms of the stars and the ways of the winds. Of time for meditation there seemed an endless supply; time enough to start seeing, almost literally, God's "invisible nature, namely, his eternal power and deity" in the things that have been made.[8] Kingsley describes it well in *The Hermits*:

> The eastward view from Antony's old home must be one of the most glorious in the world, save for its want of verdure and of life. For Antony, as he looked across the blue waters of the Gulf of Akaba, across which, far above, the Israelites had passed in old times, could see the sacred goal of their pilgrimage, the red

granite peaks of Sinai, flaming against the blue sky with that
intensity of hue which is scarcely exaggerated, it is said, by the
bright scarlet color in which Sinai is always painted in mediaeval
illuminations. . . . Day by day the rocks remained the same. . . .
Silently [the sun] passed in full blaze almost above their heads
throughout the day; and silently he dipped behind the western
desert in a glory of crimson and orange, green and purple; and
without an interval of twilight, in a moment, all the land was
dark, and the stars leapt out, not twinkling as in our damper
climate here, but hanging like balls of white fire in that purple
southern night, through which one seems to look beyond the
stars into the infinite abyss, toward the throne of God himself.[9]

It was into this spectacular orphanage that the Christian women
of Alexandria consigned their sons. At the onset of the Great Persecution, Antony's desert became a safe haven for a few Christian
refugees, a chosen few and no more. The desert, obviously, could
support only a handful. An "underground railroad" carried them
in, seldom carried one out. For the most part, the boys became
monks themselves and joined Antony's long-haired band of Jesus
Freaks and goatherds. This, at any rate, seems to have been the
case with little Athanasius. He seems to have revived in the desert
air. He grew up under the discipleship of Antony and his brethren.[XIII] Closeted away on the backside of the wilderness, he was

---

[XIII] Though some skeptical authors have questioned this, the (admittedly
circumstantial) evidence for Athanasius's sojourn in the desert does seem
pretty strong—seems, in fact, to be the only way to reconcile the few discordant facts we do know about his youth. Born in Alexandria, where the
Great Persecution was especially fierce, Athanasius explicitly denies having
experienced it in any manner other than secondhand; but his experience of
Antony, on the other hand, seems very personal indeed: "I was his attendant
for a long time." "Athanasius was so early and so completely engulfed in
public affairs," according to the editors of *De Incarnation* (St. Vladimir edition), "that there seems no place for this companionship except in boyhood
. . . his parents may well have sent him to the safety of the desert during the

held for safekeeping against a day when the Church would need him desperately. Something else was kept safe there as well, stored away as the treasures of civilization were stored at Shangri-La in Hilton's famous novel *Lost Horizon*. This treasure was the gospel itself, the authentic Faith, rusting away from disuse in the world outside, threatened, in fact, with the prospect of slow, inexorable extinction. For an age was soon coming, and indeed, now was, in which the very existence of the Bible would be jeopardized by the nominalism of the Ghetto Church.

persecution." Most tellingly, when young Athanasius finally steps onto the world stage at the Council of Nicaea he is introduced as "one of the ascetics."

2

Bringing in the Sheaves

"It shall come to pass in the latter days that the mountain of the house of the Lord shall be established as the highest of the mountains, and shall be raised above the hills; and all the nations shall flow to it, and many peoples shall come, and say: "Come, let us go up to the mountain of the Lord, to the house of the God of Jacob; that he may teach us his ways and that we may walk in his paths" (Isa. 2:2–3).

The opening salvos were aimed at the officers of the Church. Early in the year 303, all Christian clergymen were ordered to report to their local authorities and sacrifice publicly to the gods. Having done so in the presence of competent witnesses, they would receive a sworn affidavit protecting them from any further disciplinary action. Eusebius records that many of them renounced Christ immediately, without the least hesitation. Then, in 304, the laity was commanded to follow suit: everyone, man, woman, and child, must sacrifice or die. Given the state of the Church revealed at Elvira, we should not be surprised to learn that whole parishes, whole districts of the Ghetto Church, apostatized *en masse*. As an example, we may inspect the records of a city called Lucernaria, in proconsular Africa. In July of that year the governor gathered the entire Christian population together and notified them that they were to sacrifice on the spot or undergo torture. "The Proconsul's announcement was like an earthquake. All the Christians gave in at once—including priests, deacons, and other clergy—and everybody offered the pagan sacrifice."[XIV] As the Great Persecution wore on, several

---

[XIV] Ricciotti, *Age of Martyrs,* 99. The distinct offices of the clergy—bishop, priest, and deacon—were already clearly delineated by the time of Ignatius (A.D. 107), a disciple of Peter himself.

such apostates actually began to write anti-Christian books, urging their former brothers and sisters to abandon the cruel and ridiculous religion that had brought them to such straits. Worst of all were the actions of the *traditores*—an old Latin name given to the nastiest Benedict Arnolds of the lot, those bishops and other clergy who handed the Scripture over to be burned. Since all Bibles were hand-copied in those days, there were far fewer copies in existence and thus a far greater danger that all known copies might be lost. Thank God, "the resulting destruction of the scriptures was not complete but it was very extensive—this is shown by the fact that none of the great uncial codices of Scripture which exist in modern times dates any farther back than the fourth century."[10] It is possible that some of the actual New Testament manuscripts penned by the apostles themselves were lost during this phase. This was a targeted attack, then, on the very bedrock of the Church, designed to eradicate the Faith of Christ root and branch.

Who started this bloody campaign of repression—and why? Most Roman citizens would have seen it as something out of the history books, something backward and archaic, like the outbursts of lynching that occurred in the segregationist South during the very same years NASA was learning to put men in space.[xv] And it was presided over by an emperor whose reputation was that of a patient, tolerant man; an emperor, if anything, a bit too soft on all these "illegals." How is it that Diocletian, a stable, patriotic gentleman with a rural background, a man whose greatest love in life was puttering around in the garden with his cabbages, happens to have presided over the worst of all Roman persecutions? Diocletian was even noted for his family values! Not long before the persecuting began, he introduced a

---

[xv] "[By 300] actions against Christians were increasingly unpopular. Whereas, in the first and second centuries, official hostility was a response to anti-Christian feeling among urban mobs, from 250 onward the state usually had to act alone, indeed against public criticism." Johnson, *History of Christianity*, 74.

controversial law aimed at strengthening the role of traditional marriage in the empire. So how do we account for his sudden, violent change of policy? What was going on there at the turn of the fourth century? Is there something hidden in the backstory, something in Rome's recent past that might create an understandable framework for this event?

There is indeed. A colossal revolution was in the air in those days, a sea change for Roman culture so tremendous that the emperors came to dread it in much the same way that Western leaders feared the spread of communism in the twentieth century. Simply put, the demographics of Rome were changing. Roman paganism—the whole political and philosophic basis of the empire, that is—was dying, slowly but surely, and *something else* was taking its place. The emperor knew it. The senate knew it. Everyone knew it. And all through the first three centuries A.D. the power of this force increased, like water building up behind a decrepit earthen dam.

Though the Romans often end up wearing the black hats in dramas about the early Church, the empire itself was not an evil institution. It was simply inadequate, running, for lack of God's revelation, on a tank half empty. Like the American nation today, it was noble enough as a secular enterprise, with high ideals and lofty dreams. It had been, in spite of its crimes, a grand experiment, making through the centuries a confused but rather gallant attempt to bring basic decency into a world of far worse things. G.K. Chesterton put it well: "It was the best thing the world had yet seen, all things considered and on any large scale, that ruled from the wall of the Grampians to the garden of the Euphrates. It was the best that conquered; it was the best that ruled; it was the best that began to decay. . . . the Roman Empire was recognized as the highest achievement of the human race; and also the broadest. [But] a dreadful secret seemed to be written as in obscure hieroglyphics across those mighty works of marble and stone, those colossal amphitheaters and aqueducts. *Man could do no more.*"[11] The Romans had, by 50 B.C., pacified the nations, watered the desert, and crisscrossed the continent with superhighways. After that they found themselves with no more worlds to conquer and nothing left to do but try and live on bread alone.

Any literal belief in the old gods had died long ago, certainly among the educated classes. The language of religion was retained, of course, just as modernist Christianity retains much of the terminology of the historic Faith, but Apollo and Venus and all the rest had long since been reinterpreted as allegories or metaphysical abstractions after the manner of Porphyry and Iamblichus. The explosion of grotesque immorality we associate with imperial Rome—open prostitution and perversion, the bloody gladiatorial combats, and so forth—is best understood as a response to this religious collapse: a mass of hopeless, worn-out cynics trying to shock themselves awake whether with pleasure or pain. Yet deep inside, they were hungering for something higher. What the Romans needed, and in the worst way, was a religion worthy of them—something they had always had to do without. This last fact ought never to be forgotten; it might help us temper our criticism of a people who are, after all, our own ancestors, culturally and often literally.

Fulton Sheen, that great evangelist of early television, chronicled this hunger in a memorable talk:

> More than 500 years before the Christian era lived the great dramatist Aeschylus, who wrote *Prometheus Bound*. Prometheus is pictured as bound to a rock because he had stolen fire from Olympus and given it to mankind. An eagle comes and devours his entrails—a symbol of modern man, whose heart is being devoured, not by an eagle, but by anxiety and fear, neuroses and psychoses. For these thousands of years mankind had been yearning for some kind of deliverance; that aspiration found its answer in the speech of Hermes to Prometheus, "Look not for any end, moreover, to this curse, until some God appears to accept upon his head, the pangs of thy own sins vicarious" . . .
>
> [Later] Suetonius, in his life of Augustus, continued the traditional aspiration: "Nature has been in labor to bring

forth a personage who would be king of the Romans." The Senate was disturbed by this general expectation and passed a law forbidding anyone to let a male child live *that year*. The order was not executed because many of the senator's wives were with child. But it did show how much the ancient air was filled with a hushed expectancy that some great king was coming to the world. Tacitus confirmed this in his *History*: "Mankind is generally persuaded that the ancient prophecies of the east will prevail, and it will not be long until Judea would bring forth one who would rule the universe."[12]

As the old containers for faith failed one by one, Roman civilization went shopping for new wineskins. Nothing really suitable was found. The mystery cults of the East became fashionable for a while, mostly with the wealthy, but they had no real life in them. Truth be told, their elaborate rites and invocations were not much more than playacting—the same sort of whistling in the dark heard among our own Wiccans and other urban neo-pagans. Elsewhere, earnest philosophers were making rudimentary attempts to create a new Roman monotheism from the ground up. *Sol Invictus*—the Unconquered Sun, upon which all life on earth does, in fact, depend—was being put forward as the closest thing available to a living, all-powerful deity. It was felt that such a god might provide a last, rational rallying point for all who wished to avoid outright atheism, somewhat like the watchmaker God offered up in the eighteenth century by Hobbes and Robespierre. This effort, too, was doomed to failure. Then, as now, this kind of religion was too transparently man-made to evoke any real feelings of duty or devotion. Men never have been able to satisfy their hearts for very long with a faith they know they themselves have concocted.

There was, however, one option in this race to replace polytheism that had a unique if problematic appeal all its own. Not just another fad, here was a system old and established, a going concern, and already active all over the empire. It had lofty standards of clean, wholesome morality. It had mysterious books of deeply stirring scripture, books already ancient even in that long-ago era. It came, as prophesied, from Judea, and like several of the mystery cults, preached repentance and practiced baptism—but it was not Christianity. No, the Romans had been coming into daily contact with people who practiced this religion for 200 years *before* Christ. Like Judaism it was strictly and impressively monotheistic, just as Socrates had deduced the true faith would be—but it was not Judaism (not in the ordinary sense of that term, anyway). Its adherents did not strain at gnats or tithe of mint and cummin; they hardly troubled themselves about kosher foods at all. They knew not a word of Hebrew, most of them, and had never been within a hundred miles of Jerusalem. Most tellingly, hardly any of them were circumcised, that curious, painful sign so repellent to all pagans yet so all-important to the Jews. Who were they, then? The answer is difficult to express without giving a false impression. What we really need is a new name to describe this strange, now-vanished faith tradition; none of the old ones really fits. Perhaps we may, for want of a better term, go ahead and call this vast body of believers what history will prove them to have been all along: the Proto-Christians.

The Jews called them God-fearers—or the more broadminded of them did, at any rate. These were Gentiles, Roman pagans, who had come into contact with Judaism outside Palestine, been attracted to it, and adopted it in varying degrees without actually becoming Jewish themselves. By the time of Christ, the empire was thick with them, from Cadiz to the Crimea. They read the Old Testament avidly (in the famous Greek translation called the Septuagint), learned to adore the one true God they found there, and tried to keep his Ten Commandments. These were the parts of the Hebrew faith that seemed meaningful to pagans and they took them up enthusiastically, in great numbers, without really asking anyone's permission. All the rest of it—the aspirations of political Israel, the ethnic component, and all the Levitical minutiae—made little impression and they left it pretty much alone.

Closely allied with the God-fearers (and, indeed, hardly distinguishable from them in practice) were the Hellenized Jews of the Dispersion, from whom they had learned the tenets of

Judaism in the first place. These were the descendants of those Jews Zerubbabel left behind in Persia at the close of the Babylonian Captivity. When, as Daniel prophesied, that Persian Empire was supplanted by the Greek and then the Roman empires, these long-lost cousins of Israel found themselves subjects of Caesar, scattered throughout the length and breadth of his vast domain. By the time of the apostles the numbers of these Hellenized Jews had grown into the millions. In fact, they eventually came to outnumber Holy Land Jews by a margin of at least four to one. But just as in the days of Ezra and Nehemiah, they prayed for the peace of Jerusalem and sent large sums of money for her support. The Jerusalem Jews accepted these offerings, to be sure, but grudgingly and with sniffs of superiority.

These Jews of the Dispersion, you see, were lousy Jews by Hebraic standards—almost as bad as the God-fearers. The Holy Land Jews considered them half pagan. They talked like pagans (in Greek or Latin), dressed like pagans, and in many ways thought like pagans. Most of them had Greek names. Most scandalous of all, they allowed these so-called God-fearers to hang around their synagogues—people who claimed to love Jehovah but could not see how vitally important it was to wash one's hands at the correct times or carefully count one's footsteps on the Sabbath day. God-fearers and Hellenists, Hellenists and God-fearers—it was all one and the same to the Pharisees, and the whole vast phenomenon was nothing but an embarrassment as far as they were concerned.[XVI]

Because they vanished completely within a few centuries, most of us have heard little about these God-fearers and Hellenized Jews. But make no mistake: they represented a huge and tremendously successful movement—more important to history, perhaps, than the smaller, ethnically focused remnant in Pales-

---

[XVI] Though the Hellenized were still ethnically Jewish in the eyes of more traditional Hebrews, their culture and practices so strongly resembled those of the Gentile God-fearers that the two groups gradually came to be considered one movement in practice.

tine. At the city of Rome itself there were a dozen large Hellenized synagogues by the year A.D. 100. Roman Egypt was particularly blessed: over a million Proto-Christians by the middle of the second century. Most of them were Roman citizens and influential in the affairs of their day. The famous historians Philo and Josephus were among the Proto-Christians, and Julius Caesar himself expressed a warm admiration for the movement. Philo, as a matter of fact, is one of the great witnesses to just how influential Proto-Christianity really was. He wrote during the lifetime of Christ and his whole outlook shows how much more missionary-minded were the Dispersed Jews and how little like their Pharisaic cousins as depicted in the Gospels.

"There is not a single Greek or barbarian city," Philo writes with pride, "not a single people, to which the custom of Sabbath observance has not spread, or in which the feast days, the kindling of the lights, and many of our prohibitions about food are not heeded."[13] What a contrast to the situation in Jerusalem at that time! There, the "Great Unwashed" were not welcome and were made to realize it. The Proto-Christians, on the other hand, loved their fellow Romans and wanted the best for them. Every day they prayed that God would fulfill his ancient promise to make them "a light to the Gentiles" and a "blessing to all the nations."

CRUMBS FROM THE MASTER'S TABLE

Was this, then, the new monotheistic faith Rome so badly needed—the one unifying world religion to go with their one unifying world civilization? In spite of its great potential, several thorny internal problems kept this from happening. The one making news in the first and second centuries was the constant recurrence of terrorism in Palestine, born of the ugly, radical politics of Jewish Zealotry. Most Jews, even in the Holy Land, had made their peace with Rome by this time and many of them had even come to appreciate the blessings of stability their arrangement with the empire included. Rome, after all, ruled Palestine very loosely and allowed the Jews a measure of autonomy unique among her vassals. Still, there was a party of far-right Jews who wanted so little to do with Rome and anything Roman that they carried out a violent, continual insurgency against imperial oversight, characterized by assassination and sabotage. By A.D. 70 this revolt had provoked a brutal military crackdown; and by 135, after yet another sanguine uprising, Caesar felt compelled to liquidate the Jewish nation entirely and sent even the Holy Land Jews into exile. All this turmoil left a bad taste in the mouths of most Romans and would have disinclined many of them from considering any religious option even remotely smacking of Judaism. Never mind that the Proto-Christians tried to distance themselves from Zealotry and Pharisaism—this, in fact, only made things worse. It served to highlight the fatal, internal paradox at the center of their movement, the philosophical dead end that acted as a permanent cap on its growth potential. Which paradox was that? Namely this: everyone knew that Diaspora Judaism wasn't the real McCoy. Even the Dispersed themselves half admitted it.

Judaism had all the earmarks of God's own truth. It had grandeur and clarity in all the places that paganism was most puerile and silly. It stood for chastity and the stable family life Rome was so starving for. It ought have fit the bill exactly. But Judaism was for the Jews. The Jews themselves (all the most authentic ones, anyway) had made that clear enough. No Roman could ever be truly Jewish in the eyes of Jerusalem, even if he did finally submit to all the rigors of the law. Not without learning a foreign tongue, totally repudiating his nation, turning his back on his family, his culture, his heritage—simply writing it all off as a dead loss. And even then his very face and features would be there to undermine any claim to have Abraham for his father. So the vast majority of the Proto-Christians stayed stuck in a mental loop. To know Jehovah was to love him; they had learned too much to ever go back. Yet they also knew that they could never be truly acceptable to him. The best they could hope for (and even this kept the movement's numbers in the millions!) was to eat of the children's crumbs as they fell from the Master's table.

All this explains why, when the Ruler of the Universe did finally arrive in Judea, he found more faith outside Israel than in.[14] In fact, the group most uniquely ready to receive his message was precisely this huge mass of God-fearers and Hellenized Jews. The Holy Land Jews were too narrow and hidebound, too invested in the existing system (or their distortion of it, anyway) to even feel the need for Messiah very strongly anymore. Actual pagans, on the other hand, needed too much remedial training to get up to speed; even the bare idea of one God or the simple morality of the Decalogue was a radical, advanced lesson in their eyes. But the God-fearers, the Hellenized Jews—these saw the meaning of Christ instantly, felt it in their very souls. Unlike the rest of the Gentiles, they were well schooled in Bible doctrine; indeed, whole generations of them had been, like Timothy, "acquainted with the sacred writings since childhood" (cf. 2 Tim. 3:15). But unlike most Hebrew students of Hebrew scripture, they also understood that Messiah, when he came, would be less interested in the worldly fortunes of a chosen race than in the spiritual salvation of a whole world.

Peter encountered a good example of these early on, "a man named Cornelius, a centurion of what was known as the Italian Cohort, a devout man who feared God with all his household, gave alms liberally to the people, and prayed constantly to God" (Acts 10:1–2). Like his Lord before him, Peter was astonished to see so much faith in a Roman. In that astonishment he spoke words that sent a shock wave rolling across the empire: "Truly I perceive that God shows no partiality, but in every nation anyone who fears him and does what is right is acceptable to him" (Acts 10:34–35). A few years later (c. A.D. 49), Peter presided over the apostolic Council of Jerusalem, which ruled once and for all that the rites and restrictions incumbent upon Jews had been for Jews only and were not binding on any Gentile converts. Then, when Paul, in his letter to the Galatians, told the listening world, "There is neither Jew nor Greek, there is neither slave nor free, there is neither male nor female; for you are all one in Christ Jesus" (Gal. 3:28)—well, it was off to the races.

God had "opened a door of faith to the Gentiles" (Acts 14:27).

The building force of which we spoke earlier, then, threatening to collapse the crumbling dike of Roman paganism, was this rising tide of Proto-Christianity and its steady metamorphosis into the real thing over the course of the first three centuries.

Many modern Christians still labor under the impression that Jesus failed in his appeal to the Jews; indeed, that the Old Testament itself was a failure—a failed covenant, a false start, an aborted mission that required, finally, a complete "reboot" from heaven. What this viewpoint misses are the profound differences between Hebraic and Hellenized Judaism. Yes, the scribes and the Pharisees drove Peter and Paul out of their synagogues and continued to do so until there was a permanent breach between the two faiths, but the much larger and more messianic body of Hellenized Jews welcomed the apostles with open arms.[XVII] We have every indication that they flocked into the churches in huge, startling numbers.[XVIII]

The Pharisees, of course, continued to claim that *they* were the true Jews, the true followers of Moses. The Christians responded exactly as they had been taught, denying this claim as Christ himself denied it: "If you believed Moses, you would believe me, for he wrote of me" (John 5:46). We can see this spiritual dynamic in

[XVII] Speaking to the unbelieving Jews at Rome, the apostle Paul prophesied that this would happen: "The Holy Spirit was right in saying to your fathers through Isaiah the prophet: 'Go to this people, and say, You shall indeed hear but never understand, and you shall see but never perceive. For this people's heart has grown dull, and their ears are heavy of hearing, and their eyes they have closed; lest they should perceive with their eyes, and hear with their ears, and understand with their heart, and turn for me to heal them.' Let it be known to you then that this salvation of God has been sent to the Gentiles; they will listen" (Acts 28:25–28). Other important prophecies of these events may be found in Deut. 28:12; Ps. 18:43; Isa. 2:2, 11:10, 49:22, 55:5; Jer. 16:19; Mic. 4:2; Zech. 2:11; and Matt. 21:33–46.

[XVIII] The cities, for instance, where Christian growth was most explosive in the second and third centuries—Antioch and Alexandria—also happen to have been the cities with the largest pre-Christian populations of dispersed Jews.

action in the writings of Irenaeus of Lyons, one of the earliest of the Fathers. Pastor of a large church in Gaul during the late second century, Irenaeus baptized many of the Proto-Christians himself and observed the phenomenon firsthand:

> [T]he scribes and the Pharisees . . . who from the times of the law had begun to despise God, did not receive his Word, that is, they did not believe in Christ. Of these Esaias says: "Your princes are rebellious, companions of thieves, loving gifts, following after rewards, not judging the fatherless, and negligent of the cause of the widows" [Isa. 1:23]. And Jeremias, in like manner: "They," he says, "who rule my people did not know me; they are senseless and imprudent children; they are wise to do evil, but to do well they have no knowledge [Jer. 4:22]. But as many as feared God, and were anxious about His law, these ran to Christ, and were all saved."[15]

Here, at last, is the key to understanding the causes of the Great Persecution that sent little Athanasius into the desert: one good dose of genuine Christianity destabilized the old prototype. Stuck in their mental loop, the Proto-Christians posed no threat to Rome at all; they were nothing but a loose association of enthusiasts cleaving to an interesting foreign religion. Freed from that paradox, however, those many millions began to look something like a Trojan horse, like a virus lying dormant, long neglected, waiting to infect the whole body. At first, the danger would not have been apparent; in fact, the Romans must originally have perceived Christianity only as a new, more robust variety of the Proto-Christianity with which they were already familiar. At this stage, Christians came into conflict with Rome almost by accident. Christ himself was crucified by the empire only because his religious foes managed to get him tagged as a disturber of the peace.

But by the turn of the second century the truth was becoming apparent: this new thing, this *katholike ekklesia* or Catholic Church, as they called it, was more than just a movement, it was a real society, "a true political organism," as Hilaire Belloc writes, and "the only subsidiary organism which had risen within the general body of the empire."[16] As we have seen, this Church owned property, had its own officers and laws. It was strong, unified, and filled with an energy and vitality not seen since the empire itself was a new and inspiring thing. In fact, if you squinted your eyes a bit, this *katholike ekklesia* almost looked like a little empire. It was, at any rate, something that might just conceivably be a rival to Rome someday.

So during the second and early third centuries the emperors persecuted to suppress. Christianity made people unpatriotic, made them intolerant and dogmatic, willing to criticize other people's gods and alternative lifestyles. They were only a fanatical minority, of course, but they were making sparks—and making them over the powder keg of a large, receptive body of Proto-Christians and other sympathizers. This, in fact, was what finally caused most of the attacks to cease by the latter half of the 200s: persecution just made martyrs of the Christians—literally. It made them look heroic in the eyes of their hoped-for audience and ended up furthering their recruiting goals rather than hindering them. So the decision was made to stop all active or systematic harassment of Christians in hopes that the trend would burn itself out given half a chance. And this strategy was effective for a time. It produced the Ghetto Church we saw earlier, and the bad example she set did slow the rate of conversions during the late third century. Even so, the floodwaters continued to build, and before long the empire was persecuting not by accident, not simply to suppress, but persecuting for its very life.[XIX]

[XIX] "The Christians had been constantly increasing, both among the soldiers and the civil officials. Magnificent churches were being erected in the large cities, and the time seemed not far distant when the new religion would gain the ascendancy over the old. Christianity had, therefore, to be rooted out, the Holy Scripture abolished, the churches destroyed, and the cemeteries confiscated. The Christians themselves were degraded to the condition of pariahs." "Valerius Maximianus Galerius" in *The Catholic Encyclopedia*, Vol. II (New York: Robert Appleton Co., 1907).

As it turns out, there were other forces at work besides individual conversion; those iron laws of demographics we mentioned had kicked in by this point. As a pagan culture, as a libertarian culture committed to allowing people to formulate their own ideas of good and evil, Rome was, par excellence, a culture of death. Abortion, contraception, infanticide, and all forms of sterile sexual perversion were not only rampant, they were the norm. And quite apart from their disastrous effect on the Roman spirit, these practices brutally stifled the birth rate among pagans. The sterility in their hearts became literal sterility and a massive baby bust began, bringing with it all the corrosive effects on a civilization that usually accompany population decline. Simply put, the pagans were aborting their future.

The Christians, however, lived differently. Theirs was a culture of life. From the beginning, Christians had held all these practices in abomination and despite numerous individual lapses avoided them as a society.[xx] Naturally, their population growth rate followed accordingly. Even the halfhearted adherence to Christian morality shown by the Ghetto Church was enough to skew the numbers heavily in their favor over time. So the authorities began to feel threatened going and coming: from

---

[xx] A few examples: "You shall not murder a child by abortion nor kill one that has born." *The Teaching of the Twelve Apostles* (*Didache* 2:2), c. 70 A.D. "For us, since murder has been forbidden, it is also not permitted to dissolve what is conceived in the womb while the blood is being formed into a human being. It is an anticipation of murder to keep one from being born; nor does it make a difference whether one takes the life of one already born, or disturbs one in the process of being born: even the one who is going to be a human being is one," Tertullian, *Apologeticum* 9:8, 197 A.D. "Marriage in itself merits esteem and the highest approval, for the Lord wished men to 'be fruitful and multiply.' He did not tell them, however, to act like libertines, nor did He intend them to surrender themselves to pleasure as though born only to indulge in sexual relations. . . .Why, even unreasoning beasts know enough not to mate at certain times. To indulge in intercourse without intending children is to outrage nature, whom we should take as our instructor." Clement of Alexandria, *Paedagogos* 2:10, 202 A.D.

the remaining body of Hellenized Jews waiting to fall into the Church like so many dominoes, and from the ongoing Christian population explosion that was threatening to wipe them away as a simple matter of mathematics.[XXI] And feeling threatened, the emperors became dangerous—even stable country gentlemen like Diocletian.

The fall of the Roman Empire (which had begun more than a hundred years earlier under the idealistic but ineffectual Marcus Aurelius) had already progressed a long way by 303. The barbarians were hammering steadily at the northern frontier and the alien, Oriental culture of the Persians was encroaching from the East. Diocletian took office at a time when Rome needed every man to come to the aid of his empire. Even so, it was not actually Diocletian who gave the order to begin persecuting. For greater ease in administration, Diocletian had partitioned his huge realm into two halves early in his reign, with himself as emperor of the East and an associate emperor, Maximian, ruling in the West. Each of these, in turn, had a kind of vice-emperor ruling with him; Constantius Chlorus assisted Maximian at the ancient capital of Rome, and a brutal, stupid man named Galerius acted as Diocletian's own subsidiary in the Eastern capital of Nicomedia. It was this Galerius, vain, ferocious, and jealous of worship, who pulled the trigger on the Great Persecution; yet Diocletian seconded the evil command, turning his back on a lifetime of mild, intelligent rule, ensuring that his own name would, rightly or wrongly, live forever in infamy as the author of the terrible work. He also set into motion, though he little knew it at the time, forces that would turn the next decade—303 to 313—into one of the most tumultuous periods of social upheaval in world history.

To compare this decade to our own turbulent 1960s would be only a dim parallel. By the end of it, all four of these emperors

---

[XXI] Much additional information on this fascinating subject can be found in *The Rise of Christianity* by University of Washington sociologist Rodney Stark (San Francisco: HarperSanFrancisco, 1997).

had been swept away; a devastating civil war had taken place, some of it fought in the very streets of Rome; and inconceivable new laws had been written, fundamentally altering the ancient constitution of the empire. Most significant in the long term: the Proto-Christians watched, fascinated, as the Ghetto Church passed through the hottest fury of God's refining fire.

QUITE AN EYEFUL

Standing in the quiet of Antony's desert and watching them come had been like watching woodland creatures come pouring out of a burning forest long before any actual sign of flame is visible—wave after wave, with only the faintest smell of smoke in the air. Little Athanasius had come in the first wave, just after the initial outbreak. Later, adults came, too—dazed, somber, nearly mute, but able finally, under the gentle hospitality of the desert hermits, to tell stories of what they had seen. Antony and his brethren gathered up those stories and, along with other eyewitnesses, patiently preserved them for us.

In Alexandria and Roman Egypt alone,

> thousands of men, women, and children, despising the present life for the sake of the teaching of our savior, endured various deaths. Some of them, after scrapings and rackings and severest scourgings, and numberless other kinds of tortures, terrible even to hear of, were committed to the flames; some were drowned in the sea; some offered their heads bravely to those who cut them off; some died under their tortures, and others perished with hunger. And yet others were crucified; some according to the method commonly employed for malefactors; others yet more cruelly, being nailed to the cross with their heads downward, and being kept alive until they perished on the cross with hunger. . . . Women were bound by one foot and raised aloft in the air by machines, and with their bodies altogether bare and uncovered, presented to all beholders this most shameful, cruel, and inhuman spectacle. Others being bound

to the branches and trunks of trees perished. For they drew the stoutest branches together with machines, and bound the limbs of the martyrs to them; and then, allowing the branches to assume their natural position, they tore asunder instantly the limbs of those for whom they contrived this.

All these things were done, not for a few days or a short time, but for a long series of years. Sometimes more than ten, at other times above twenty were put to death. Again not less than thirty, then about sixty, and yet again a hundred men with young children and women, were slain in one day, being condemned to various and diverse torments.[17]

Yes, the great tribulation of 303 went on for eight full years, all across the vast Roman Empire, with scarcely a lull. Our "red-headed stepchild" passed through childhood, through adolescence, entered his teenage years, and still the Christian refugees came stumbling in out of the wastes—likely the commonest and most characteristic memory of Athanasius's youth. They brought with them, among other things, the last testimony of Bishop Phileas of Thmuis who, before being beheaded himself, recorded with unmistakable pride the Spirit-inspired heroism he had seen exhibited by members of his own flock:

Having before them all these examples and models and noble tokens which are given us in the divine and sacred scriptures, the blessed martyrs who were with us did not hesitate, but directing the eye of the soul in sincerity toward the God over all, and having their mind set upon death for religion, they adhered firmly to their calling. For they understood that our Lord Jesus Christ had become man on our account, that he might cut off all sin and furnish us with the means of entrance into eternal life. For "he counted it not a prize to be on an equality with God, but emptied himself taking the form of a servant; and being found in fashion as a man, he humbled himself unto death, even the death of the cross" [Phil. 2:6–8]. Wherefore also being zealous for the greater gifts, the Christ-bearing martyrs endured all trials and all kinds of contrivances for torture; not once only, but some also a second time. . . .

And they endured this, not merely as long as the governor talked with them or was at leisure, but through almost the entire day. For when he passed on to others, he left officers under his authority to watch the first, and observe if any of them, overcome by the tortures, appeared to yield. . . . [When] they were ordered to choose whether they would be released from molestation by touching the polluted sacrifice, and would receive from them the accursed freedom, or refusing to sacrifice, should be condemned to death, they did not hesitate, but went to death cheerfully. For they knew what had been declared before by the Sacred scriptures. For it is said, "He that sacrifices to other gods shall be utterly destroyed" [Exod. 22:20] and, "You shall have no other gods before me" [Exod. 20:3].[18]

This cheerfulness the bishop writes of became one of the most commented-upon aspects of the Persecution. It was nothing actually new, of course; Christians had been facing death with a smile on their face and a hymn on their lips since the days of Nero, some 240 years earlier, but now the number of victims was far greater, the stakes of the combat far better understood— and the world was watching much more carefully.

That the spectacle really did begin to have an effect on even the pagans is a fact attested to by Athanasius himself. Before the coming of Christ, for instance, paganism had little to point to in the way of altruism or philanthropy as the modern West understands them; charity hospitals and other such institutions were virtually unknown in pagan Rome, with orphans and the sickly poor left to wander the streets just as in Mother Teresa's Calcutta. After all, the gods themselves were, often as not, petulant and capricious gluttons and adulterers in this system, rather than self-sacrificing saviors, so there was simply no organic place from which the root of charity might spring in the empire or, once sprung, find depth of earth. Yet here in the midst of the Great Persecution one suddenly finds (as recorded in one of

Athanasius's adult works) the fascinating tale of a pagan "Hiding Place"—with its strong prefigurings of the famous Evangelical heroine Corrie Ten Boom and the risks she and her family took sheltering wanted Jews from the wrath of the Nazis:

"I have heard from our fathers," he wrote, "and I believe their report to be a faithful one, that . . . Gentiles concealed our brethren the Christians,[XXII] who were sought after, and frequently suffered the loss of their own substance, and had trial of imprisonment, solely that they might not betray the fugitives. They protected those who fled to them for refuge, as they would have done their own persons, and were determined to run all risks on their behalf."[19]

All this the watching world saw. But what did the refugees see? What did those sadder-but-wiser Ghetto Christians find when they came looking at last for the half-legendary locust eaters, the wild-eyed prophets who had wandered off into the wastes (and to their deaths, as most supposed) way back in "the good old days"? Well, these refugees, it turns out, got quite an eyeful, too: "[By this time] the cells in the mountains were like tents filled with divine choirs, singing, discoursing, fasting, praying, rejoicing over the hope of the future, working that they might give alms thereof, and having love and concord with each other. And there was really to be seen, as it were, a land by itself, of piety and justice; for there was none there who did wrong, or suffered wrong: no blame from any talebearer: but a multitude of men training themselves, and in all of them a mind set on virtue."[20] The new arrivals found, in other words, a community of believers who didn't just admire, as their parents had, the sort of Christianity one found recorded in the scriptures, but who actually *imitated* it, as Sozomen records in his *Church History* of 439:

[XXII] Athanasius uses the word Gentile metaphorically here to mean any unconverted Roman; most of the Christian converts—now members of God's larger spiritual Israel—were as ethnically Gentile as their persecutors, as was Athanasius himself.

[Antony's monks] regard every man as wicked, who, though he abstain from evil, does not do good. For they do not demonstrate virtue by argument, but practice it, and count as nothing the glory current among men. They manfully subjugate the passions of the soul, yielding neither to the necessities of nature, nor succumbing to the weakness of the body. Having possessed the power of the divine mind, they always look away to the creator of the whole, night and day worshiping him, and appeasing him by prayers and supplications . . . They are not distressed when insulted, nor do they defend themselves when suffering from malice; nor do they lose heart when pressed by sickness or lack of necessaries but rather rejoice in such trials and endure them with patience and meekness . . . They regard the present life as a journey only, and are not therefore solicitous about acquiring wealth, nor do they provide for the present beyond urgent necessities. They admire the beauty and simplicity of nature, but their hope is placed in heaven and the blessedness of the future . . . They provided for their friends and strangers, imparted to those who were in want, according to their need, and comforted the afflicted.[21]

The refugees witnessed out-and-out miracles as well—another sign that Antony and his boys were still living, there in their desert time-capsule, the life of the early Church:

Many sufferers in body who were present did the Lord heal by [Antony's hand]; and others he purged from demons. . . . And concerning those who came to him, he often predicted some days, or even a month, beforehand, the cause why they were coming. . . . But we must not doubt whether so great wonders have been done by a man; for the savior's promise is, "If ye have faith as a grain of mustard-seed, ye shall say to this mountain, Pass over from hence, it shall pass over, and nothing shall be impossible to you" [Matt. 17:20]; and again, "Verily, verily, I say unto you, if ye shall ask my Father in my name, he shall give it you. Ask, and ye shall receive" [John 16:23]. And he himself it is who said to his disciples and to all who believe in him, "Heal the sick, cast out devils; freely ye have received, freely give" [Matt. 10:8]. And certainly Antony did not heal by his own authority, but by praying and calling on Christ; so that it was plain to all that it was not he who did it, but the Lord, who through Antony showed love to men, and healed the sufferers.[22]

Eventually, when Diocletian's monstrous folly had failed, when paganism had wrecked so hard and so publicly against the rock of Christianity that figments like Jupiter and Juno, Mars and Minerva could never again be taken seriously by European men, the refugees of the Upper Thebaid would come out of Antony's desert and return to the cities and towns of Roman Egypt, there to mix once more with their non-Christian neighbors . . . and compare notes.

Shortly before that glorious day, however, Antony himself went out—a tough, sinewy old man at sixty, long white beard stark against a skin as brown as cowhide. Feeling within himself, like Moses, that the time had come to leave the wilderness and stand tall before Pharaoh, to speak up himself for those called to make bricks without straw, Antony bid his brother monks farewell and turned his face again toward the city he had left so long ago behind.

"[W]hen the holy martyrs were brought [for sentencing] to Alexandria," records Athanasius in his *Life of Antony*, "Antony too followed, leaving his cell, and saying, 'Let us depart too, that we may wrestle if we be called, or see them wrestling.' And he [had previously] longed to be a martyr himself, but, not choosing to give himself up, he ministered to the confessors[XXIII] in the mines, and in the prisons."[23] When Antony finally was arrested himself, he made it his chief business to cheer and to strengthen the resolve of any wavering city Christians he found among the captives. "[H]e was very earnest in the judgment-hall to excite the readiness of those who were called upon to wrestle; and to

---

[XXIII] A confessor is a person who suffers any sort of pain or hardship for the Faith short of actual martyrdom.

receive and bring on their way, till they were perfected, those of
them who went to martyrdom."[24]

The surprising reaction of his judges to this ministry shows
the incredible power the fabled desert monks had already begun
to exercise over the public imagination. Simply put, Antony and
his brethren had become living symbols of the ancient, authentic Faith in its apostolic purity—symbols of it for both Christian and pagan alike. And since the judges in these cases prided
themselves on their ability to obtain recantations from waverers
(tallying them up, in fact, for bragging rights with their fellow
magistrates), the mere presence of one of the desert hermits in
the courtroom had come to spell disaster. And if, after all, Antony's mere presence could stiffen a hundred half-Christian spines,
what might happen if the obstinate old codger were actually
martyred—set up forever as a flag around which to rally?

> At last the judge, seeing the fearlessness and earnestness of
> him and those who were with him, [turned Antony out
> and] commanded that none of the monks should appear in
> the judgment-hall, or haunt at all in the city. So all the rest
> thought it good to hide themselves that day; but Antony cared
> so much for the order, that he all the rather washed his cloak,
> and stood next day upon a high place, and appeared to the
> General [charged with arresting Christians] in shining white.
> Therefore, when all the rest wondered, and the general saw
> him, and passed by with his array, he stood fearless, showing
> forth the readiness of us Christians. For he himself prayed to
> be a martyr, as I have said, and was like one grieved, because
> he had not borne his witness. But the Lord was preserving
> him for our benefit, and that of the rest, that he might be-
> come a teacher to many in the training which he had learnt
> from Scripture. For many, when they only saw his manner of
> life, were eager to emulate it.[25]

Who were "the rest" of whom Athanasius speaks? Who *can*
they be but the empire's many millions of Proto-Christians? The

final act had arrived at last, God's intended audience was watching in rapt fascination, and the persecutors of Rome could do nothing but confess their helpless impotence. They did this by willingly releasing, of all people, Antony of Coma and his desert monks— the one group of men whom everyone knew to be completely guilty, the most thoroughgoing Christians the judges had ever had in their custody. And when this happened . . . well, the dam could hold back its waters not a single moment longer.

3

Shooting for the Moon

"Then he said to them, 'Render therefore to Caesar the things that are Caesar's, and to God the things that are God's.' When they heard it, they marveled" (Matt. 22:21–22).

The gloom ahead was sundered suddenly by a star. Flashing, fiery, cutting the night with a silvery finger of light, this rotating orb was the brightest object in creation save the very sun and moon; yet it shone from a tower raised by the hand of man, a tower that scraped the sky, reaching like Babel of old almost to the throne of God. And when Eusebius saw it, still more than ten miles out, he knew, as any citizen of the year 319 would have known, that his destination was close at hand: Alexandria of the Egyptians, city of the future.[XXIV]

The ship's lookout saw it, too—*Pharos! The lighthouse of Pharos!*—and all over the chartered barque preparations began for the

---

[XXIV] This chapter speculates a bit about the activities and motivations of a real man, Eusebius of Nicomedia, destined to become a major figure in our story ahead. His "memories" about the historic events of the decade—about the Great Persecution, the fall of Galerius, and the rise of Constantine—are, as you will read them here, scrupulously fact-based and can be verified in any reputable work of Roman history.

Whether Eusebius, however, actually traveled to Alexandria at the outset of the Arian crisis, whether he dreamed of a new synthesis of science and religion, and what he personally was hoping for from the new emperor are matters open to conjecture. These devices have been created as a way to bring history to life; but the raw historical data is included as well, allowing readers to decide for themselves whether this imagined character study really is a plausible extrapolation from the bishop's actions as history records them.

conclusion of their voyage.[XXV] With a bracing salt spray in his nostrils, Eusebius of Nicomedia (not to be confused with his more famous contemporary, the Church historian Eusebius Pamphilus of Caesarea) remained at the rail, meditating on the enormity of his mission in Egypt; he had, after all, brought servants along to ready his baggage. This was by far the most important voyage of his career, perhaps the most important voyage any Christian clergyman had ever made. If this affair at Alexandria were handled badly it could alienate the emperor forever, might even bring the Persecution itself back with a vengeance. If, on the other hand, the crisis in that diocese were carefully managed and brought to a favorable conclusion, the benefits to the Church might be literally incalculable. Yet somehow no one but he seemed to recognize the moment for what it was! No one else knew, as he knew, what this particular crossroads called for.

Eusebius, as a matter of fact, could look back on his entire life as one long course of preparation for this defining moment. God knows, there had been any number of opportunities for things to have unfolded differently. His repugnance these last few months at the conduct of his more reactionary brethren in the episcopate had brought him to the point of schism again and again; yet he had always taken the high road, always chosen the path of peace. Even now, he was willing to undertake this crucial task entirely at his own expense and under his own recognizance. Perhaps there would be, someday, Christians ready to thank him, ready to bless their God that at least the bishop of Nicomedia had been awake when destiny called. But for now, Eusebius was content to labor behind the scenes, daring to take this new Christian emperor in hand when most other Christians were content to bask in the sunshine of his mere existence.

[XXV] The Pharos lighthouse, which stood at the entrance to Alexandria harbor, was listed by Herodotus as one of the Seven Wonders of the World. It stood 384 feet tall, equal to a forty-story building, and its fabled main beacon is said to have been powered by some mysterious elemental force. The tower was already more than 500 years old in Eusebius's day.

Who had ever dreamed of a Christian emperor, anyway? It was like expecting the devil to convert. Yet here it was: a naked, accomplished fact. What had been the odds? Every single historical event of the past fifteen years had to go exactly as it had gone for such a thing to occur. No one, for instance, would have predicted the sudden abdication (on May 1, 305) of Diocletian and Maximian. It was idealistic, well-meant, a noble gesture—and a complete calamity for everything they believed in. The naive act created a vacuum at the very center of power. Riot and revolution were the result, as even the most casual student of Roman history ought to have foreseen. Yet still the world was eons away from a Christian emperor. Constantius Chlorus had come to power in the West; and Constantius, it is true, had always been lenient toward Christianity. The brethren in his domains had every right to expect conditions to improve. But Christians in the West were such a small proportion of the overall population; no one, himself included, had seen anything world-shaking in the rise of a "Christian-loving" emperor way out there.[XXVI] Seen from the East—from Antioch, where Eusebius had been living at the time, enrolled in the underground seminary of Lucian—these remote developments offered little hope of relief, and the Great Persecution seemed fated to continue until every last Christian on earth had been sent to a martyr's reward.

What no one had counted on, not even the bishop of Nicomedia, was the spectacle of it all! No one had reckoned on the tremendous effect so many hundreds of martyrdoms would have on the population at large. For after the first terrible wave of apostasies, the Ghetto Church shook off its stupor. The casual, the merely hereditary, the

---

[XXVI] Contrary, once again, to the popular myth, neither Constantine himself, nor even his father Constantius Chlorus, was the first Roman emperor to be favorably inclined toward Christianity. Alexander Severus, who ruled in the early 200s, is supposed to have added a bust of Christ to his private chapel (along, it is true, with similar images of Abraham, Orpheus, and Apollonius of Tyana); and the *History of the Church* of Eusebius Pamphilus actually names Philip the Arab (who reigned from 244 to 249) as the first Christian emperor rather than Constantine!

hangers-on were stripped away, exposing a hard, jewel-like center that proved entirely immovable. Suddenly every pagan in the
empire knew at least one martyr personally. Suddenly the martyrs
were your barber, your fishmonger, your brother-in-law, your commanding officer.[XXVII] Conditions had changed in other ways as well.
The pagans were standing at a different place, Eusebius reflected,
watching from a new perspective. They had long envied us our internal network of hospitals and safe houses; we took care of our own,
no doubt about it, in an empire where no man was his brother's
keeper.[XXVIII] Yet there, near the end of the Persecution, they had
begun to envy us something else as well; something Romans had always admired above all things but which was becoming harder and
harder to find in the pagan world. That something was courage. We
Christians showed them courage—at a time when Galerius manifestly did not. It was the beginning of the end for imperial paganism.

Galerius had always been a fool and most people knew it, but it
was the whirling tempest of revolution that exposed him as a coward as well. When Constantius Chlorus died (in 306), his legions
in Britain proclaimed his rugged, soldierly son Constantine as his
successor. The natural heir, one might argue, was thus bypassed:
Maxentius, son of the original Western Augustus, Maximian. This
opened the door to a mad, years-long scramble to pick up the pieces
of the old tetrarchy and reassemble it into some new, streamlined
form. Yet for a while these two rival claimants, later to be the bitterest of enemies, made a temporary alliance—against Galerius. The
Eastern Augustus might have made a stand against this coup had he
been whole and in his right mind, but he was not. Like most of the
pagans, Galerius had contracted venereal disease at some point, and

[XXVII] No exact figure is possible at this late date, but all evidence indicates
that there were many thousands of executions during Galerius's reign.
Some of the more famous martyrs of this period are Crispina, Agnes,
Sebastian, Agatha, Lucy, and the Forty Martyrs of Sebaste.
[XXVIII] "Christians had picked up and "expanded the old charitable trusts of
the Jewish Diaspora. They ran a miniature welfare state in an empire which
for the most part lacked social services." Johnson, *History of Christianity*, 81.

his final outbreak came hard upon him just as his political fortunes were failing as well. To put it bluntly, he began literally to rot from the groin up, terrifying his physicians and anyone else unfortunate enough to have to enter his chambers.

Eusebius had heard, however, that one of Galerius's doctors during his last agony was secretly a Christian; and that this lone physician (who had doubtless seen his own circle of friends and family decimated by his patient's heartless policies) remained by the emperor's side, faithful to the end. Emboldened by the extremes of suffering Galerius was enduring, this brave Christian doctor spoke to him frankly at last, telling him that medicine could do no more because his torments were sent by God—the God of the Christians. His only hope of salvation, in this world or the next, was repentance and some attempt to atone for the horrible crimes that had been committed in his name. So (on April 30, 311) the proud Gaius Galerius Valerius, out of no consideration beyond simple fear of death, reversed his own settled policy overnight and issued an edict of toleration, legalizing Christianity and forbidding any further persecutions. He demanded only that Christians pray for the peace of the empire and for the health of her emperor, something everyone knew they were doing already and had been doing all along.

A few days later Galerius died, weeping and cursing, furious, it seems, that the Christian God had not responded to his munificent gesture with an immediate miraculous healing. All these things were made known to the pagan world at large and the effect was tremendous. Even now, eight years later, Eusebius recalled the aftermath with wonder. Pagans joined their Christian neighbors in the streets that week, in the joyous celebrations that erupted everywhere as every dungeon was emptied, every captive released, in a virtual Christian Exodus. "Great is the God of the Christians," some of them had cried, "great and true!" And suddenly the churches—most of which had been boarded up during the Persecution, or repurposed for pagan use—were filled to the rafters once again, not only with the surviving Christian population but with inquirers and seekers, with the God-fearers, the Hellenized Jews, and even many out-and-out pagans who had merely looked on with curiosity before. The steady inpouring of previous years became a veritable tsunami.[XXIX] Even so, Galerius's hasty edict had by no means settled the issue. There were still several pagan Caesars jockeying for position at that moment, including Constantine, and none of them had shown any inclination to become Christian themselves. The final distance to that incredible milestone—a Christian emperor!—was not crossed until October of the following year at the epic Battle of Milvian Bridge, the grand and startling climax of that "Christian Decade."

Up ahead, the Pharos beacon shone much brighter; Eusebius reckoned the remaining distance to Alexandria at not much more than a league and a half. And as he so reckoned, the sight of that shimmering sign in the heavens brought Constantine's famous "miracle" to mind. Every schoolboy knew the story by heart: after the death of Galerius, Maxentius and Constantine came into open conflict—a clash of titans, civil war between two ostensible "gods." Maxentius, who proved to be nothing more than a brutal tyrant, invaded Italy and installed himself at Rome, intent on becoming sole emperor of the West. Constantine marched to the aid of the city, with an army of 20,000 men, but was vastly outnumbered, and his thin supply lines to the north were in constant danger of severance. To succeed, Constantine would need nothing short of divine intervention. And that, according to his own sworn testimony, is exactly what he received.

It happened, he said, not long before the final battle. As he brooded over the long odds ahead, trying to decide "in which God he ought to put his trust," Constantine suddenly saw "a trophy in the shape of a dazzling cross in front of the sun" and with it the Latin words *In hoc signo vinces*—"With this sign thou shalt conquer." Afterward, many of his soldiers had been willing to vouch for the vision as well. Later, "while he slept there appeared to him Christ of God with the sign he had seen in the sky, who told him to make standards of that shape

<hr>

[XXIX] Some of the best modern scholarship estimates the rate of conversion as having reached a pace of almost 5 percent of the population per year.

to serve as a protection in his conflicts with the enemy."[XXX]

This had been good enough for Constantine. He rose and immediately designed an ornate cross formed from the first two letters of the Greek word for Christ—the famous "Chi-Rho" monogram which has, ever since, adorned so many Christian pulpits and Communion vessels. He then ordered this cross to be painted onto the shields and standards of his entire bewildered pagan army. The results, Eusebius reflected, certainly seemed to speak for themselves— or so they had to Rome's inhabitants, whatever their religious affiliation: Constantine's forces simply annihilated Maxentius's defenders, bottling them up against the main access point to the city, Milvian Bridge, routing all resistance, and leaving the usurper himself floating face-down in the Tiber below.[XXXI]

Had the alleged miracle actually happened? Did Constantine really see his crooked cross in the sky or hear the voice of Jesus as he slept? Eusebius himself had always been one of the doubters— though privately, of course. The story was just too pat, he believed, too perfectly in line with what Constantine happened to need at the moment. Not that Eusebius wished to be judgmental about the matter. In fact, the bishop now smiled at the thought, having always been, himself, an admirer of shrewdness and bold action in the service of a worthy cause. Certainly he would not begrudge the man a little white fib or two if told for the greater good, as this one so clearly would have been. Constantine, after all, loved Rome above all things. He was, by all accounts, the most sincerely patriotic man who had come to the purple in decades, if not centuries.

And when he did become emperor, the empire he found waiting for him was sick unto death with nothing but the old

---

[XXX] This and all the quotes in this paragraph are from the *Life of Constantine* (Book I) by Eusebius Pamphilus, who claims to have received the story—along with a solemn oath affirming its truth—from the lips of Constantine himself. Ricciotti, *Age of Martyrs*, 163.

[XXXI] "The impression which this victory made upon the pagan world was tremendous. The God of the Christians had proved His superiority over the gods of the Capitol." Fr. John Laux, MA, *Church History*, 76.

moribund paganism out of which to inspire any rebirth or recovery—that same tired tissue of superstitions for which even Galerius's racks and hot pokers had been unable to generate any further enthusiasm. So if Constantine wasn't going to be content, as so many of his predecessors had been, to simply lay the blame on the previous administration and ride the thing on into the ground, then he would have to actually *do* something. And the thing to do, surely, must have been all too obvious in such an increasingly Christian empire.[XXXII] Even for the majority still attached to the old religion it had become hard not to see Christianity as the most vital, healthy force left within it. Why not jump on the bandwagon, then? Why not arrest Rome's decline by taming this powerful new force so motivating to men—harnessing it to serve his beloved empire instead of competing with it?

Probably, guessed Eusebius, Constantine had been contemplating his audacious takeover plan for years and had dreamt up his "celestial sign" long before the dispute with Maxentius ever got started. Still, not even the emperor's bitterest enemies had ever called him a liar. Who knows? Perhaps an unusual cloud formation, some strange atmospheric anomaly, combined with the intense stress, the forced marches, the fatigue of the hard campaign, had allowed the future emperor to convince himself that he really had seen what he most needed to see, what Rome most needed him to see. Eusebius didn't know and, to be perfectly honest, didn't really care.

The bishop was, however, often queried about one aspect of the event toward which, as chief shepherd of the emperor's own

---

[XXXII] "The Christians themselves wondered at the speed and extent of the Church expansion before Constantine. It is hardly surprising that the Church felt itself to be riding on the crest of a wave, and faced the world with that confidence that is a marked feature of the early apologists." Chadwick, *The Early Church*, 66. "So long as nothing changed in the conditions that sustained the 40-percent-a-decade growth rate, Constantine's conversion would be better seen as a response to the massive exponential wave in progress, not as its cause." Rodney Stark; *The Rise of Christianity*, 10 (San Francisco: HarperSanFrancisco, 1997).

diocese, he could not decorously profess indifference: the question, namely, of whether the "converted" emperor had actually undergone any personal change of heart— that is, whether he had actually experienced conversion as the more sincere Christian understands it. Certainly Constantine was making many of the right noises: he had outlawed crucifixion as a form of capital punishment right away; he had ordered reparations to be paid to the surviving confessors and to the widows and orphans of the martyrs; and he had sponsored an important law, back in 316, outlawing the common practice of branding criminals on the cheek or forehead since, as the emperor himself wrote, "man is made in God's image." Constantine had shown favoritism, in other words, toward Christianity, much as his predecessor Marcus Aurelius, 150 years earlier, had shown favoritism toward the system of Xeno— Marcus's own best hope for Rome's philosophical future.

Still, the question remained for many; Constantine hadn't been baptized as yet, though the miracle that had supposedly stopped him in his tracks like Paul on the road to Damascus was now going on seven years in the past. And when pressed on the point, the new emperor became mysterious, evasive. He tended to emphasize his old pagan title of *Pontifex Maximus*—"chief bridge builder" of the Romans—and had, on at least one occasion, expressed his belief that while Christians had bishops to act as their spiritual guides, the remaining pagan population needed someone to shepherd them as well—a "bishop of those outside," as Constantine had put it. Once again, Eusebius smiled, reminded as he was of another of the emperor's traditional titles, that of *Pater Patriae*, father of his country. For that was just how Constantine was behaving: as yet another example of that well-known Christian type, the solicitous family father who insists that his children be taken to church each and every Sunday morning, but who always finds for himself somehow a good excuse to stay home.

And here was just the point at which Eusebius felt he could see further, more clearly than most of his brethren. Eusebius could understand a man like that, could still see the big picture. Constantine had decided, whatever his own personal beliefs might be (if any), that our Christian system was best for his empire—best for its peace, its prosperity, its happiness. And what Christian could argue with that? Who, indeed, could fail to be flattered by such a conclusion? Yet how was the Church repaying that compliment? With suspicion, with distrust, by poking and probing the emperor with indelicate questions about an inherently private matter. The theological busybodies had been at him already as well. When Constantine had proposed (very sensibly, in Eusebius's view) to head off any potential pagan/Christian rift in his realms by finding a bit of common ground for both groups via the old solar monotheism movement, most of the bishops had balked. Syncretism, they called it, and heathenish compromise. Yet the emperor had suggested nothing more radical than that the pagans be permitted to identify the Christian God with Sol and then to interpret his Son Jesus as an "emanation" of that God, just as Mithras or Apollo were considered emanations of the Sun God. And where was the harm in that? After all, did not both groups worship on the same day of the week—the day of the sun?[XXXIII] Hadn't the Old Testament writings prophesied a Messiah who would one day be called "the sun of justice" (Mal.

[XXXIII] Needless to say, Constantine had nothing whatever to do with the establishment of Sunday worship for Christians, which had already been in place for nearly three hundred years by his time. The early Christians referred to Sunday as "the eighth day"—a fresh start for all of Creation—commemorating alike the Resurrection of Christ and the coming of the Holy Spirit at Pentecost, both of which happened on a Sunday. The Acts of the Apostles and Paul's Second Epistle to the Corinthians both record the fact that the early Church met "on the Lord's Day," and Justin Martyr, writing just a few decades later, tells us explicitly that this term corresponds to the Roman Sunday, not with the Jewish Sabbath or any other day. So far, in fact, was the Church from deliberately patterning her practice on the Sun worship for which the Romans had named their first day, that she actually tried later to replace the old pagan names of the days of the week with simple numerical terms; she succeeded in the Greek-speaking East, but failed in the West, where paganism lingered much longer and where the terms still survive in all Western European languages except Portuguese.

4:2)?[xxxiv] And don't we Christians sometimes pray together *ad orientem*—while facing, that is, the rising sun?[xxxv]

As far as Eusebius was concerned, these coincidences between the two systems were, at the very least, a providentially provided "foot in the door" for the pagan population; and yet many of his fellow bishops seemed bound and determined to interpret Constantine's moves in this area in the worst possible light, exhibiting them as evidence of an "incomplete conversion." Had it not occurred to his zealous brethren that the emperor might come to resent all this spiritual psychoanalysis eventually and simply call off the whole experiment? Didn't they understand the terrible risk Constantine was

[xxxiv] Many of the early Fathers—such as Ignatius of Antioch, Clement of Alexandria, and Tertullian—had already noticed the fascinating coincidence between our Lord's Resurrection and the pagan day dedicated to the rising Sun and commented upon it in their writings, often linking it to Malachi 4:2.

[xxxv] The reason for this widespread practice (which survives even in many Evangelical churches in the form of the traditional Easter sunrise service) is rooted not in heathen Sun worship but in the promise of the angels at Christ's ascension: "This Jesus, who was taken up from you into heaven, will come in the same way as you saw him go into heaven" (Acts 1:11). Jesus rose from the grave at dawn and ascended from the Mount of Olives, which is east of Jerusalem; moreover, he himself compared his future return in glory to the lightning that "comes from the east" (Matt. 24:27). So prayer then, offered with outstretched hands while facing the rising sun, was a symbolic way of expressing the final petition of Scripture itself: *Maranatha!* "Come, Lord Jesus!" (Rev. 22:20). Writing in the mid-200s, Origen asserts that the practice actually originated with the apostles; and Clement of Alexandria, somewhat earlier, associates it with an old extrabiblical tradition about the martyrdom of Paul—to wit, that the apostle had turned and prayed facing eastward before laying his head upon the block. At any rate, whatever similarity the practice may share with solar monotheism long predates the Age of Constantine: the strongly messianic Essene sect of Jews (who probably gave us the Dead Sea Scrolls) seem to have practiced *ad orientem* prayer in their worship. Likewise, one can find the common misconception that Christians worship the sun in pagan writings dating from the early second century (a mistake that Tertullian explicitly attributes to the fact that "Christians pray towards the east").

still running over this daring Christian gambit of his? The Roman establishment, after all, remained overwhelmingly pagan, as was the entire army down to the lowest foot soldier—and emperors had been overthrown by their armies before. No, this was definitely not the time for the Church to start looking its fantastic gift horse in the mouth—not when the alternative had been men like Galerius! Had the other bishops so soon forgotten that devil in human form? God cared, perhaps, how personally gushy Constantine's feelings toward Jesus might or might not be; Eusebius would be content that he wasn't burning or disemboweling anyone at the moment.

Just then, the Pharos beacon upon which the bishop's attention had been fixed winked out suddenly. It took him a moment to realize why—but then he saw that dawn had broken and that the light had been deliberately extinguished as the night watch came to its end. And there, at last, across the shimmering harbor, was the huge circular dome of the Great Hall standing at the center of the fabled Alexandrian library! Any closer and Eusebius would be able to see the astronomers at work on the observatory terrace, scrutinizing, no doubt, the spectacular crescent moon dominating the purple pre-dawn sky. Now here was a place that captured the bishop's imagination like no other! This, after all, was where the whole thing began, was it not? Here it was, two centuries before the birth of Christ and under orders from Ptolemy II, that the seventy scholars had made the Septuagint, opening the Hebrew scriptures to pagans for the first time and to the Dispersed, fertilizing the world for Christianity, paving the way for Constantine.[XXXVI] It was here then, at the Alexandrian Library, that the new age had been born—or was being born, at any rate, with Eusebius himself acting as midwife.

[XXXVI] "[T]he Septuagint often ranked as an inspired version enjoying an authority that no other translation possessed. Only after the Christian appeals to it became embarrassing to the Jews were alternative, more literal translations favoured by the Greek synagogue . . . and some Rabbis, almost as hostile to liberal or hellenized Judaism as to Christianity, regretted that the Bible had ever been translated into Greek and denounced the making of the Septuagint as a sin like the worship of the golden calf." Chadwick; *The Early Church*, 12.

Oh, the wonders of that amazing library! Its lofty goal: nothing less than to acquire a copy of every book ever written and to keep, on site, fifty of the world's greatest minds at work at all times synthesizing the wisdom they contained. Yet more than just books, here were laboratories as well, lecture halls, and a large zoological park containing live specimens from every part of the earth. Here, physicians had advanced their art to previously undreamed of heights, attempting the most delicate brain surgeries in the best equipped operating theaters in the world.[XXXVII] Here, Euclid had invented geometry and Hero discovered hydraulics, using it to create an embryonic steam engine and a humanoid robot that, running on compressed air, sang and poured drinks![XXXVIII] Unlike many of his more backward-looking coreligionists, Eusebius kept himself well informed about such discoveries and prided himself on staying fully abreast of the new scientific spirit coming out of Roman Egypt. He thought of Eratosthenes, third librarian of Alexandria, who first calculated the circumference of the earth and who had suggested the startling (still unproved) idea that India could be reached by sailing westward from Spain.[XXXIX]

[XXXVII] Erasistratus of Ceos and Herophilus of Chalcedon (among other Alexandrian physicians) performed hernia operations, tracheotomies, lithotomies, and complex eye surgeries at the library in the third century B.C. Erasistratus, in fact, came very near to discovering the circulation of blood there, nearly two thousand years before William Harvey.

[XXXVIII] Hero of Alexandria(A.D. 10–70) is considered the greatest experimenter of antiquity. Though there is some question whether he actually built the robot described in his *Automata,* he certainly did complete his working *aeolipile* ("Hero's Engine") about A.D. 50.

[XXXIX] Despite the widespread misconception to the contrary, few educated people after about 300 B.C. have doubted that the Earth is spherical. As respected historian of science Stephen Jay Gould reports, "There never was a period of 'flat earth darkness' among scholars (regardless of how many uneducated people may have conceptualized our planet both then and now). Greek knowledge of sphericity never faded, and all major medieval scholars accepted the earth's roundness as an established fact of cosmology." *Dinosaur in a Haystack* (New York: Three Rivers Press, 1996), 42.

Eusebius thought of Aristarchus and his equally daring theory that the earth revolves around the sun rather than vice versa;[XL] and of Hipparchus, the first to accurately measure the solar year. Callimachus had labored at Alexandria, as had Archimedes, the world's greatest mathematician. The halls of this library were hallowed, then!—hallowed, as the bishop saw it, just as surely as the slopes of Mt. Sinai or the Holy Sepulchre so recently rediscovered by Helena.[XLI]

And who knew where this astounding march of progress might lead? If, that is, it were allowed to proceed (as it had not been allowed for more than half a century) in peace, uninterrupted by revolution, further threat of war, or other unrest. Why, any dream man might conceive seemed possible in such a world—a world united at last under one enlightened ruler, in the broadest principles of one sensible monotheistic religion.

Now the sacred memory of Archimedes, combined with the glittering vision of the moon overhead, sent the bishop's thoughts racing. Was it not Archimedes who had conceived of a

---

[XL] Aristarchus of Samos, rather than Copernicus, was first to put the sun at the center of our universe (and, incidentally, the planets in their correct order of distance around the sun) about 200 B.C. Though his heliocentric model was superseded for many centuries by the geocentrism of Ptolemy, it was never entirely forgotten and Aristarchus himself was never isolated or persecuted because of it.

[XLI] Constantine's mother, Helena, was converted to Christianity after his victory over Maxentius. "She became under his influence such a devout servant of God," writes Eusebius the historian, "that one might believe her to have been from her very childhood a disciple of the Redeemer of mankind." Under her title of Augusta—Constantine's Queen Mother—she built many beautiful churches in Rome and at Trier and then embarked finally on an expedition to the Holy Land, which she "explored with remarkable discernment," intending to recover whatever memorials of our Lord's life and Passion might still remain after nearly three centuries. Working with Macarius, bishop of Jerusalem (who likely had access to a large trove of local folklore on the subject), she discovered the site where the current Church of the Holy Sepulchre stands.

flying machine based on the great principle of buoyancy he discovered here at Alexandria? A ship of the ether, carried aloft by a gigantic canopy of heated air![XLII] And the great Aristotle—had not he, inspired by the sight of a crescent moon like this one, deduced that the moon must also be a sphere like the Earth? And if the moon were like the Earth—a whole new world with, as the astronomers tell us, vast *mare* or seas on its surface—was it unreasonable to suppose that there might be people alive there as well? Anaxagoras and Xenophanes had thought so, as had Pythagoras and Plutarch.[XLIII] And if so, if all these things are true . . . mightn't adventurous men of science someday drive, like Apollo of old, a chariot across these skies, based upon the principle of Archimedes's airship, and reach those men of the moon? Reach them in peace, for all mankind, in the name of the beneficent Constantine of Rome? Why, even his brethren in the episcopate might think such a project worthwhile, for would it not be the Church's duty to reach such men for Christ?—to preach, as

[XLII] Archimedes of Syracuse (c. 287–212 B.C.) discovered the principle of buoyancy upon which lighter-than-air aviation is based. Whether his researches progressed beyond the stage of small, experimental models is not known.

[XLIII] It was Plutarch (A.D. 46–120) who first conjectured that the dark areas visible on the face of the moon must be seas, though he was puzzled by the lack of atmospheric clouds such seas would naturally produce. "It is possible that some inhabitants exist on the Moon," he wrote, "and those who claim that these beings must need everything that is necessary to us, have never considered the variety that nature offers so that animals differ amongst themselves more than they differ from inanimate life." A few years later, the Greek poet Lucian wrote a speculative novel, *Facies in Orbe Lunare*, about a trip to the Moon, which is reached after a voyage of eight days and found to be inhabited by humans who ride on the backs of giant birds. "And if men," wrote Democritus (c. 460–370 B.C.), "then the men must have settled cities and cultivated fields as with us . . . and the soil grows all sorts of produce for them, the most useful of which they gather into their houses and use. . . . [These things] must have taken place not only where we live, but elsewhere also."

the biblical phrase goes, "the gospel to every creature?"[XLIV] And yet now, reflected Eusebius darkly, this wonderful dream was in danger—threatened by nothing more than a smelly desert relic from the bad old days, his narrow-minded fool of a bishop, and a precocious, barefoot boy!

The harbor dock was coming into view. Eusebius could already see the husky stevedores waiting to unload his luggage and the plush carriage-and-pair that stood ready to transport him directly to the episcopal manse. He felt his resolve stiffen as never before, his determination becoming fierce, unshakable. If the undreamed-of miracle was to be safeguarded, with all the marvelous possibilities it included, then someone needed to act—and act now. Eusebius must take charge of this crisis in the Alexandrian Church, must put out the fire that had been kindled here, and do it before the emperor has a chance to notice the turmoil. Didn't these wild-eyed fanatics see how important it was to send Constantine the right signals at this crucial

---

[XLIV] Our own Eusebius of Caesarea seems to have been the first writer to puzzle over the question of extraterrestrial evangelization. He maintains that Heraclitus (fifth century B.C.), as well as the Pythagoreans, taught that every star is a world and that a vast number of them must be inhabited—an opinion advanced in the Jewish Talmud as well, with which Eusebius was probably familiar. Sounding very modern indeed, Metrodorus of Chios (fourth century B.C.) wrote that "to consider the Earth as the only populated world in infinite space is as absurd as to assert that in an entire field of millet, only one grain will grow." Epicurus (third century B.C.) taught plainly "that in all worlds there are living creatures and plants and other things we see in this world." The cosmology of Democritus (fourth century B.C.) is perhaps most startling of all to modern readers: "There are innumerable worlds of different sizes. In some there is neither sun nor moon, in others they are larger than in ours and others have more than one. These worlds are at irregular distances, more in one direction and less in another, and some are flourishing, others declining. Here they come into being, there they die, and they are destroyed by collision with one another. Some of the worlds have no animal or vegetable life nor any water."

juncture? The Church, above all things, needed to show itself reasonable right now, to demonstrate to its new patron that it understood his dream for the future and the role it was expected to play. We Christians are a practical people! Patriotic and civic-minded. Willing to rise above our pointless theological scruples for the greater good. Ready to do our part. We are, as a matter of fact, a lot like Constantine himself, are we not?

Eusebius, at any rate, had now made it his life's goal to prove precisely that—to the rest of the Church and to the emperor himself. And Eusebius of Nicomedia, as anyone who knew Church politics could tell you, could be a very determined man.

4

Arius, Alexander, and Athanasius

"Do not think that I have come to bring peace on earth; I have not come to bring peace, but a sword. For I have come to set a man against his father, and a daughter against her mother, and a daughter-in-law against her mother-in-law; and a man's foes will be those of his own household" (Matt. 10:34–36).

Did Eusebius of Nicomedia—shepherd of souls at the empire's eastern capital early in the fourth century—did he really dream of a voyage to the moon? We have no way of knowing for sure, of course, though the scientific developments we pictured him contemplating are absolutely historical and would likely have captured the imaginations of most educated men during his era. For now, we should simply point out that Eusebius's "smelly old man" was our friend Antony of the Desert, that his "narrow-minded fool" of a bishop was a benign, white-headed gentleman named Alexander (who will be introduced more fully as we go), and that the barefoot boy was the frail and scrawny refugee Athanasius, who, having survived the Great Persecution, was now grown into an unusually devout and intelligent twenty-two-year-old. How these unlikely three came to constitute, in the eyes of an urbane cleric like Eusebius, such a desperate threat to world peace is a complex but fascinating story that might take a page or two to unravel.

Antony's oasis—that treasure chest of New Testament Christianity whose inhabitants had now leapfrogged safely over the age of the *traditores*—was cracked open at the close of the conflict and began to discharge its precious contents into the new world created by Constantine. Perhaps chief among these treasures was young Athanasius himself, physically unimpressive though he was with his short, delicate stature and thin strands of auburn hair pulled across an unusually large, brown forehead. Athanasius, it seems, had discerned a vocation to ordained ministry while growing up in the desert (the historian Sozomen writes of the "fitness for the priesthood" his brethren had sensed within him) and Antony honored this call by sending his charge back out to Alexandria to act as secretary and apprentice to the venerable bishop of that city, Alexander. We modern Christians might possibly be surprised at this; surprised, that is, that a "Lone Ranger" type such as Antony—who headed off, after all, under his own steam to try and find Jesus by himself in the wilderness—would so easily agree to do business with anyone so ordinary as the pastor of the vanilla-plain local church. Athanasius, however, didn't see it that way:

> [H]ow tolerant was [Antony's] temper, and how humble his spirit; for though he was so great, he both honored exceedingly the [laws] of the Church, and wished to put every ecclesiastic before himself in honor. For to the bishops and presbyters he was not ashamed to bow his head; and if a deacon ever came to him for the sake of profit, he discoursed with him on what was profitable, but in prayer he gave place to him, not being ashamed even himself to learn from him. For he often asked questions, and deigned to listen to all present, confessing that he was profited if any one said aught that was useful.[26]

It does not diminish these virtues of Antony's in any way to note the wonderful change that had come over the city churches by then and that made it possible for the great exile from nominalism to send one of his sons there so confidently. The Persecution, after all, had practically wiped out the trifling, peppercorn Christianity of the Ghetto era, a fact of which Alexander himself—a big city bishop who goes looking to the desert monks for his new priests and deacons—may be taken as proof.

So young Athanasius left the only home, the only family he could really remember, for the hustling, bustling metropolis; but not without the fondest possible memories of his time there and of the inspired leader who had made it all possible:

[Is there anyone] who met [Antony] grieving, and did not go away rejoicing? Who came mourning over his dead, and did not forthwith lay aside his grief? Who came wrathful, and was not converted to friendship? What poor man came wearied out, and when he saw and heard him did not despise wealth and comfort himself in his poverty? What monk who had grown remiss, was not strengthened by coming to him? What young man coming to the mountain and looking upon Antony, did not forthwith renounce pleasure and love temperance? Who came to him tempted by devils, and did not get rest? Who came troubled by doubts, and did not get peace of mind? . . . How many maidens, too, who had been already betrothed, and only saw Antony from afar, remained unmarried for Christ's sake! Some, too, came from foreign parts to him, and all, having gained some benefit, went back from him as from a father. . . . For to me, too, it is a great gain and benefit only to remember Antony; and I know that you, when you hear of him, after you have wondered at the man, will wish also to emulate his purpose.[27]

Besides his own self, Athanasius brought another treasure with him out of Antony's oasis. He brought a book, a book that he himself had written, and that is known today by the title *On the Incarnation*. Not much later, after he had been made a deacon by Bishop Alexander, this book was published—and almost instantly young Athanasius found himself at the center of an unexpected and ferocious Church controversy. Other than the quite considerable literacy he seems to have picked up somewhere (though Sozomen describes Athanasius as "self-taught," C.S. Lewis praised his book for the "classical simplicity" of its style), first-time readers nowadays would find little if anything to surprise them in Athanasius's short treatise. *On the Incarnation* is perhaps an unusually vivid but nevertheless perfectly ordinary expression of traditional Christian beliefs about the divinity of Christ; there isn't a single new or original idea in it, as anyone familiar with the writings of the apostles and Fathers of the first three Christian centuries must frankly admit.[XLV] It simply represents the Faith that Athanasius learned at the feet of Antony—and Antony was, happily, perhaps the least original of all our great Christian forefathers. Yet there is, it must be admitted, something bold, even daring in the book's phraseology, a new clarity of expression as compared to other contemporary works that does indeed tend to rub one's nose in the startling implications of the traditional doctrine.[XLVI] *On the Incarnation* might even be called impolite—a clean, hot wind of exultation on the great subject blowing in from the Upper Thebaid, where the absence of refined society had left young men like Athanasius woefully untrained in the fine art of parsing their words for those "slow to believe."

The book is addressed to a recent convert named Macarius, who had heard, as it seems, some puzzling objections to the deity of Christ from various perspectives and found himself at a loss to answer them all. In order to strengthen him and others like him against such attacks, Athanasius undertakes to provide Macarius with, "a rudimentary sketch and outline . . . of the faith of Christ and of his divine appearing to usward," claiming to have learned this outline from his own reading of Scripture but also from personal discipleship by "inspired teachers" who had

---

[XLV] Those who would represent the doctrine of the divinity of Christ as something new in the days of Constantine or even as the invention of the emperor himself only reveal their ignorance of the facts. Writing about A.D. 112 in a letter to Constantine's predecessor, Trajan, hostile witness Pliny the Younger testifies that the Christians he had observed "sang a hymn to Christ as God." (This passage happens, incidentally, to be the earliest surviving non-Christian account of Christian theology.) That there were those willing to deny of this truth during the early centuries is, of course, admitted; that they exemplified the remnant of some original, merely humanitarian understanding of Jesus and his mission flies in the face of all the evidence. For more information on this topic see Appendix One.

[XLVI] ". . . the correct intellectual image, from its hardness of outline, may startle and offend those who have all along been acting upon it." John Henry Newman, *Arians of the Fourth Century* (Notre Dame, IN: University of Notre Dame Press, 2001), 145.

actually gone on to "become martyrs for the deity of Christ"[28] (presumably during the Great Persecution). It was important, Athanasius believed, to show not only *that* Jesus had been "God with us," but also to show *why* "he came down from heaven." Commencing then, with the stories of Creation and the fall of man, our young deacon traces for his readers the cataclysmic circumstances that occasioned "so great a salvation."

DE INCARNATIONE

In the beginning, writes Athanasius, God

made man, and willed that he should abide in incorruption; but men, having despised and rejected the contemplation of God and devised and contrived evil for themselves . . . received the condemnation of death with which they had been threatened[29] . . . So then, men having thus become brutalized, and demoniacal deceit thus clouding every place, and hiding the knowledge of the true God, what was God to do? To keep still silence at so great a thing, and suffer men to be led astray by demons and not to know God? [And if so] what was the use of man having been originally made in God's image? For it had been better for him to have been made simply like a brute animal, than, once made rational, for him to live the life of the brutes . . . [Even] a merely human king does not let the lands he has colonized pass to others to serve them, nor go over to other men; but he warns them by letters, and often sends to them by friends, or, if need be, he comes in person, to put them to rebuke in the last resort by his presence, only that they may not serve others and his own work be spent for naught. Shall not God much more spare his own creatures, that they be not led astray from him and serve things of naught?[30]

"[T]o this end," Athanasius continues,

the loving and general savior of all, the Word of God, takes to himself a body, and as man walks among men and meets the senses of all men half-way[31] . . . [O]f his becoming incarnate we were the object, and for our salvation he dealt so lovingly as to appear and be born even in a human body.[32] . . . He took pity on our race, and had mercy on our infirmity, and condescended to our corruption . . . He takes unto Himself a body, and that of no different sort from ours. . . . [Though] from a spotless and stainless virgin, knowing not a man, a body clean and in very truth pure from intercourse of men. For being himself mighty, and artificer of everything, He prepares the body in the virgin as a temple unto himself, and makes it his very own as an instrument, in it manifested, and in it dwelling.[33]

But how did this Incarnation of the Word of God accomplish God's saving purpose? Why was it necessary?

[Because] the Word, perceiving that not otherwise could the corruption of men be undone save by death as a necessary condition, [also knew that] it was impossible for the Word to suffer death, being immortal and Son of the Father; to this end he takes to himself a body capable of death, that it, by partaking of the Word who is above all, might be worthy to die in the stead of all . . . For being over all, the Word of God naturally by offering His own temple and corporeal instrument for the life of all satisfied the debt by His death. And thus he, the incorruptible Son of God, being conjoined with all by a like nature, naturally clothed all with incorruption, by the promise of the Resurrection.[34]

Have we any proofs that all of this is, in fact, the true meaning of Christ's life and ministry? A great many, according to Athanasius:

He made himself visible . . . doing such works, and showing such signs, as made him known no longer as man, but as God the Word[35] . . . For his charging evil spirits, and their being driven forth, this deed is not of man, but of God. Or who that saw him healing the diseases to which the human race is subject, can still think him man and not God? For he cleansed lepers, made lame men to walk, opened the hearing of deaf men, made blind men to see again, and in a word drove away from men all diseases and infirmities: from which acts it was possible even for the most ordinary observer to see his Godhead . . . [H]e made even the creation break silence: in that even at his death . . . all creation was confessing that he that was made manifest and suffered in the body was not man merely, but the Son of God and savior of all. For the sun hid his face, and the earth quaked and the mountains were rent: all men were awed. Now these things showed that Christ on the Cross was God, while all creation was his slave, and was witnessing by its fear to its Master's presence. Thus, then, God the Word showed himself to men by his works.[36]

But . . . aren't there certain, shall we say, *logical* difficulties in such a mind-boggling conception? Who, for instance, was God while God was gone to Earth? And if God died on the cross, who raised him from the dead? "[H]e was not," answers Athanasius,

as might be imagined, circumscribed in the body, nor, while present in the body, was he absent elsewhere; nor, while he moved the body, was the universe left void of his working and Providence; but, thing most marvelous, Word as he was, so far from being contained by anything, he rather contained all things himself; and just as while present in the whole of Creation, he is at once distinct in being from the universe, and present in all things by his own power . . . He was, without inconsistency, quickening the universe as well, and was in every process of nature . . . And this was the wonderful thing that he was at once walking as man, and as the Word was quickening all things, and as the Son was dwelling with his Father . . . For not even by being in the universe does he share in its nature, but all things, on the contrary, are quickened and sustained by him.[37]

In addition to his repeated use of "the Word of God," Athanasius calls Jesus a great many other startling names in this small book: "the Power of God," "the Glory of God," "Image of the Father," "God the Word," "Maker and Lord," "Ruler and King of the Universe," and "God, and the true Son of God, his only-begotten Word." Every one of these titles, it must be repeated, can be found with variations in either the New Testament or the writings of one of pre-Constantinian Christianity's most respected leaders, men such as Justin Martyr, Ignatius, Irenaeus, and Cyprian of Carthage. These were mainstream authors representing the oldest and most apostolic churches on Earth. Even so, *On the Incarnation* does appear to have struck some hidden, sensitive nerve in a certain portion of its initial readers. Yes, everyone had heard these sorts of things before (impassioned Christian mystics had often been known to get rather carried away in their poetic praises of the savior; usually there was no harm in it), but this boy surely had gone too far. It almost looked as if Athanasius meant his immoderate panegyrics to be taken literally, as straight, sober theology! But that could not be, could it?

Consider another of the deacon's careless phrases, that passage wherein he calls Jesus "he who was from the beginning." This might even be taken as an attack on monotheism itself! After all, don't we all confess that Jesus is the *Son* of God? So if Jesus is God, how can he also be his own son? It makes no sense. Doesn't that very title of "Son" imply an origin in time, a moment in the past—however unimaginably distant, perhaps—when his Father could say (as he does in Psalm 2:7) "You are my Son, this day I have begotten you"? Whatever else could "Son" possibly mean? And besides, what son is as old as his own father?

It might be wise to pause a moment before going any further and try to block up one possible alley that seems likely to sidetrack us here. Doubtless for many readers, the word "Trinity" has already sprung to mind, offering a quick, "obvious" answer to difficulties such as these. Trouble is, this great theological term—so indispensable to historic Christianity for the last seventeen centuries—had not yet come into use in 319. However biblical the underlying idea might be, the word "Trinity" itself is not found in the Bible, nor are any of the famous formulas associated with it: "God in Three Persons," "the Triune God-head," and so forth. Scripture contains the *raw materials* for these terms, certainly, but not the formulations themselves, which would have been unfamiliar both to the young Athanasius and to his adversaries at this stage. It is true that a few of the Fathers had dallied with the Latin word *Trinitas* already—Tertullian, for example, and Hippolytus—but not even these early conjecturers had used it in exactly the later sense. To introduce "the Trin-ity" then, would be an anachronism at this point in our story; and to have offered it at the time *On the Incarnation* was written would have been like offering the phrase "general relativity" to nineteenth-century astronomers such as Herschel or Lowell in answer to their difficulties concerning the motion of the outer planets. Not only would the term itself be unfamiliar, but even the long thought-processes by which that correct answer would, in the future, be reached might require a good deal of time and effort to make clear.

But if, as we have said, the deity of Christ really was no nov-elty in 319 and if it is true that faithful Christians have believed it since the beginning, then there must have been *some* way of cop-ing, during those first three centuries, with the difficulties raised by the idea of the Incarnation. "If for instance," as John Henry Newman once put it, "Scripture bids us adore God, and adore his Son, our reason at once asks, whether it does not follow that there are two Gods; and a system of doctrine becomes unavoid-able."[38] So what was this system? How—on a day-to-day basis and minus our developed doctrine of the Trinity—did the early Church deal with these great puzzles and paradoxes?

The Faith Once Delivered

The answer lies in the character of a man like Antony, in a trait he shared with the apostles themselves and with all the best ele-ments of the pre-Constantinian Church. Antony was humble. He didn't create his own Christianity out of his own genius and vast knowledge of Hebrew and Greek (of which he had none); he simply accepted the original version, uncut and unedited. He accepted it ready-made, as an inheritance, to be cherished as "the faith which was once for all delivered to the saints" (Jude 1:3). Antony accepted the admonition of the apostle Paul in such matters: "[S]tand firm and hold to the traditions which you were taught by us, either by word of mouth or by letter" (2 Thess. 2:15). Now, Paul's letters (and those of the other apostolic writers) had been recognized as Scripture by Antony's time; and Antony, as we have already seen, took Scripture very seriously indeed. Scripture, nevertheless, did not seem to address these paradoxes directly. One could prove each of the individual truths from the Bible, yes, but resolving all of the seeming contradictions between them was not, apparently, a task that the inspired writers had chosen to undertake. Very well—word of mouth, then. Were there, in the early Church, old, unwritten customs regarding the handling of such delicate questions—questions that, unless approached with the greatest possible reverence, could even become blasphemous or presumptuous? History—as recorded in the lives of Antony and others during his era—shows that there were.

What was that tradition? It might well be described simply as *stubbornness*: a tradition of stolid, donkey-like stubbornness born out of humility and the fear of God. There was a *list*, that's all—an unwritten list of four rock-solid facts of our Faith, handed down by the saints gone before us. And the list—well, the list was the list:

1. That the Father is God;
2. That Jesus, his Son, is also God;
3. That Father and Son are not, however, mere names but real personalities who can relate not only to us *but to one another;*
4. Yet there is only one God.

This was the tradition—the Christian way. The piffling fact that one got to the end of the list and found logic sort of standing around looking foolish, like the guy who winds up the loser at a game of musical chairs, was not seen as particularly germane. Not to the issue, that is, of whether to go on believing in the ancient and apostolic list. Who knew? Given more time, the mystery might become plainer, might resolve itself altogether, in fact, with enough prayer, study, and meditation on our part. But until then, we Christians worship the Father, we worship his Son as well . . . and we let the chips fall where they may.

This is not to say that the early Christians did not value logic or reason; in fact, the great doctors and apologists of the third century did some of the finest brainwork our species has ever produced—writers like Athenagoras, Clement of Alexandria, and Dionysius of Rome. But Dionysius . . . well, Dionysius, as a matter of fact, happens to have demonstrated that donkey-like stubbornness we spoke of as well as anyone: "We must neither distribute into three divinities the awful and divine Unity, nor diminish the dignity and transcendent majesty of our Lord by the name of creature, but we must believe in God the Father Almighty, and in Christ Jesus his Son, and in the Holy Spirit; and believe that the Word is united with the God of the universe. For he says, 'I and the Father are One; and, I am in the Father, and the Father in Me' (cf. John 10:30, 14:10)."[39] Only by planting one's feet in this way, the early Church believed, and avoiding the very human itch to compromise one or the other of the points for the sake of "consistency"—only thus could the original Faith be kept safe from human tinkering, whole and unadulterated.

There was a man, however, who seems to have been so scandalized by Athanasius's enthusiastic little book that he chose to challenge its teaching openly, from the pulpit. This man was Arius, "a presbyter of the church at Alexandria in Egypt," one of Athanasius's superiors, and according to Sozomen, "a zealous thinker about doctrine . . . [whom Bishop Alexander held] in high repute, since he was a most expert logician." About this time, Arius nevertheless "fell into absurd discourses, so that he had the audacity to preach in the church what no one before him had ever suggested; namely, that the Son of God was made

out of that which had no prior existence, that there was a period of time in which he existed not."[40] Word of this novel line
of preaching got back to the bishop quickly, and Alexander, as
might be imagined, immediately felt that some remedial catechesis might be in order at the church of Alexandria. Acting
then, "in the fearless exercise of his functions for the instruction
and government of the Church, [Alexander] attempted one day,
in the presence of the presbytery and the rest of his clergy, to
explain, with perhaps too philosophical minuteness, that great
theological mystery—*the* Unity *of the Holy Trinity*."[41] (The historian Socrates is able to use the term "Trinity" here since he
records the event in hindsight, more than 150 years later.)

Arius was not impressed. "[I]magining that the bishop was
subtly teaching the same view of this subject as Sabellius the Libyan, [Arius] from love of controversy took the opposite opinion
to that of the Libyan, and as he thought vigorously responded
to what was said by the bishop. 'If,' said he, 'the Father begot
the Son, he that was begotten had a beginning of existence: and
from this it is evident, that there was a time when the Son was
not. It therefore necessarily follows, that he had his substance
from nothing.'"[42]

Sabellius the Libyan was a discredited Ghetto-era teacher
who, in attempting to make "the list" line up properly at his
church, had taught a doctrine known today as modalism. Arius
was trying (as he believed) to save strict monotheism by making the Son into a created thing, leaving his Father alone as "the
great I AM"—the one single self-existent Person; Sabellius had
taken the opposite tack, trying to preserve strict numerical one-
ness in God by denying that the Son has any real existence at all,
making him into a kind of mask the Father sometimes wears,
just one *mode* of representing himself (and thus the name "modalism"). Christian writer Lint Hatcher offered a memorable
shorthand for this approach recently when he dubbed modalism the "God's Three Hats" heresy, which pictures the Father
somewhat like the small-town mayor of lore who for budgetary
reasons keeps (along with the high hat of his most dignified of-

fice) the hat of a police captain and a fire chief on hand as well, should the need arise.[XLVII]

The trouble with this crude attempt at simplification is, of course, that it compromises the third item on our non-negotiable list: namely, that Father and Son are not just stage names for God, assayed on our behalf, but represent genuine, eternal realities. The Bible shows us the Father in a relationship with his Son—loving him, sending him out, and pleased with his work; and shows, likewise, the Son in a relationship with his Father— talking with him, obeying him, mediating between him and man. In the system of Sabellius, however, Christ was simply "the Incarnation *of* the Father"—the Father acting *as if* he were a Son, though the reality is quite otherwise. Yet "[even] on the very face of Scripture," as notes Newman once again, "the Christ who is there set before us, (whatever might be the mystery of His nature,) is certainly delineated as one absolute and real Person, complete in himself . . . this being the case, his Person could not be the same with that of the Father, who sent him, by any process of reasoning, which would not also prove any two individual men to have one literal personality." This, nevertheless, is what Arius accused his bishop of when he charged Alexander with subtly reviving the heresy of Sabellius the Libyan.

Was there any truth in Arius's accusation? Did the bishop of Alexandria—an elderly survivor of the recent persecution, "gentle and quiet" according to one of the Fathers, who kept every fast day assiduously and who never read from the Gospels without standing—did old Alexander really imbibe secretly of heretical opinions himself, though of the opposite sort of those of Arius?

The truth of the matter is more straightforward. Alexander had been installed in his position because of his saintly character, not because he was anyone's idea of a profound theologian.

[XLVII] Sadly, one has started hearing echoes of Sabellius again in the churches, any time the preacher proposes to explain that God really is just one person, but that he reveals himself in three ways, namely, Father, Son, and Holy Spirit.

Arius, on the other hand, was an extremely clever man who, by this time, had spent most of his life splitting hairs with his theological friends for fun.[XLVIII] Tall and thin, with a quick wit and a winning manner, he came out of the same Antiochian seminary as Eusebius of Nicomedia, a school whose graduates had, some of them, been in trouble before this for speculating a bit too close to the edge.[XLIX] So Alexander, it would seem, in undertaking to correct a pugnacious, professional debater like Arius, had simply gotten in over his head and wound up making a hash of the job. Historian Paul Johnson offers what is likely the best explanation for the bishop's "perhaps too philosophical minuteness": "A right-thinking theologian, anxious to remain orthodox, tended to smash his ship on Charybdis while trying to avoid Scylla."[L]

Arius, at any rate, declined to accept his bishop's fatherly correction and continued to insist that "there was a time when the Son was not." "Those who heard these doctrines advanced, blamed Alexander for not opposing the innovations at variance with doctrine. But this bishop deemed it more advisable to leave each party to the free discussion of doubtful topics, so that by persuasion rather than by force, they might cease from contention; hence he sat down as a judge with some of his clergy, and led both sides into a discussion. But it happened on

---

[XLVIII] According to Newman, Arius possessed an "almost satirical spirit" and his followers were "men destitute of religious seriousness and earnestness [who] engaged in . . . theological discussions, not with any definite ecclesiastical object, but as a mere trial of skill, or as a literary recreation . . . impatient of ignorance." *Arians of the Fourth Century*, 28, 32, 33.

[XLIX] The founder of this school, one Lucian of Samosata, was condemned by the bishop of Antioch for suggesting that the Son, though infinitely greater than the rest of Creation, is himself, nonetheless, a created being—a key tenet of the later Arianism.

[L] Scylla and Charybdis were mythical sea monsters described by Homer, guarding either side of a narrow sea channel; avoiding the one inevitably meant passing too close to the other.

this occasion, as is generally the case in a strife of words, that each party claimed the victory. Arius defended his assertions, but the others contended that the Son is consubstantial and co-eternal with the Father."[43] "Innovation" is the key word in this passage—a wonderful quality in the fields of science or industry, no doubt, but deadly when applied to a religion supposedly received intact from Christ and his apostles. Old Alexander may not have been the sharpest tack in the fourth-century Church's box, but he knew very well that Arius's ideas had a strange, unaccustomed sound. Logic or no logic, this was simply *not what Christians say*—not in three long centuries of praying, preaching, studying, and believing.[LI]

Probably, as the weary bishop must have hoped, it was all just some terrible misunderstanding; mere words were getting in the way and Arius actually had some perfectly orthodox point he was trying to make. So lengthy, vexing private interviews were conducted; and the two leaders prayed together repeatedly, asking God for light and harmony. Yet the more patiently Alexander behaved toward him, the more strident Arius and his emerging group of sympathizers became. Surely they didn't

---

[LI] Odd as it may seem to us, several important writers do insist that the Church had never deeply pondered Arius's blind alley before this. Sozomen asserts, for instance, that "religion was in a flourishing condition at this period, yet the churches were [suddenly] disturbed by sore contentions; for under the pretext of piety and of seeking the more perfect discovery of God, certain questions were agitated, which had not, till then, been examined. Arius was the originator of these disputations." *Ecclesiastical History*, I:15. Origen, it is true, had warned against the root idea some sixty years earlier: "The Word, being the Image of the Invisible God, must Himself be invisible. Nay, I will maintain further, that as being the Image He is eternal, as the God whose Image He is. For when was that God, whom St. John calls the Light, destitute of the Radiance of His incommunicable glory, so that a man may dare to ascribe a beginning of existence to the Son? . . . Let a man, who dares to say that the Son is not from eternity, consider well, that this is all one with saying, Divine Wisdom had a beginning, or Reason, or Life." Quoted in Newman, *Arians of the Fourth Century,* 97.

mean to intimate that God the Father has not always been a Father, but became such one fine day—like any other Dad pacing outside a maternity suite? But yes, Alexander was assured, that was exactly what they did mean to say. Surely they were not suggesting that he of whom John's Gospel says, "all things were made" and without whom "was not anything made that was made" (John 1:3)—surely Arius and company didn't mean to suggest that this Creator, this Word of God himself, was also *one of the things that was made?* Alas, that was, in fact, just precisely what they were suggesting. So finally, as Sozomen tells us, "the council was convened a second time, and the same points contested, but they came to no agreement among themselves. During the debate, Alexander seemed to incline first to one party and then to the other; finally, however, he declared himself in favor of those who affirmed that the Son was consubstantial and co-eternal with the Father, and he commanded Arius to receive this doctrine, and to reject his former opinions. Arius, however, would not be persuaded to compliance, and many of the bishops and clergy considered his statement of doctrine to be correct."[44]

Many of the bishops and clergy! How this last horrible fact must have stunned the gentle old shepherd. Incredibly, impossibly, a group of men whom their pastor had always considered sound as granite—a clergy with Galerius's scars still on their backs, who had labored side by side with Alexander and who had sat patiently for years as he preached exactly the opposite message—suddenly these same men were now ready to embrace a teaching the likes of which believers had scarcely imagined before. It was almost as if they had heard, over the last few days, some strange siren song in this man Arius's talk, something that captured them, charmed them, and then clicked for them, finally, some terrible switch inside. Facing then the crisis destined to consume his remaining years, Alexander (who was likely seventy-five or older at this time) must have groaned within and perhaps recalled the words of the blessed Polycarp, spoken in a similar situation: "O good God, to what times you have spared me, that I should endure such things!"[45]

POLITICS AND RELIGION

How did these dissidents at Alexandria justify themselves? Probably they hemmed and hawed a bit, knowing full well how out of step with tradition they sounded, but some semblance of an excuse likely emerged along the following lines. The Bible, they must have argued, is ambiguous on the topic in question. In addition to the aforementioned Psalm 2:7 ("today I have begotten you"), one could produce many other verses that might seem problematic to the more traditional view.[LII] And hadn't several of the early Church Fathers also used language that could appear favorable to Arius's interpretation? The innovators promised to investigate that line of attack fully.[LIII] Chiefly, they seem to have accused Alexander of narrowness, of an excessive rigidity about such things unbecoming in a leader of free Christian men. Many felt, possibly, that more room had been left in the past for different emphases, different schools of thought about the true nature of the savior, and that their viewpoint on the subject had been shortchanged of late. Very probably, the dissidents criticized their bishop for spending too much time with narrow-minded

[LII] Among these are: John 14:28; Prov. 8:22; 1 Cor. 8:5–6, 11:3; Col. 1:15; Mark 13:32.

[LIII] While arguing against Trypho the Jew, for instance, Justin had boldly referred to Christ as "another God"—and perhaps made things worse rather than better by quickly adding, "I mean in number, not in will." Elsewhere, however, he wrote that "the Word fulfills the Father's will," which would seem to imply two wills after all. Likewise, Clement of Alexandria asserts that "the Word is the Thought or Reflection of God," which could lend credence to the idea that the Son is a created "copy" of his Father. Many other examples might be cited, illustrating, once again, the same difficulty Alexander experienced—that of denying that the Son is a created being without seeming to imply that he is no Son at all (but merely one of the Father's attributes); or of emphasizing his personal distinctness without slipping into ditheism. What these defective phrases actually reflect is the primitive state of the Church's theological language during those early decades, rather than any actual heretical strain in the true thought of the Fathers.

rustics like Antony and his irritating protégé, Athanasius. The desert monks were colorful and inspiring, no doubt, but they had undergone little if any formal theological training and were notoriously naive about such things.

Perhaps ironically then, it seems to have been the "naive" rustic Athanasius—watching, as a mere deacon, from the sidelines—who began to recognize what it was that had really "thrown the switch" for his Church's emerging Arian minority.[LIV] While Alexander—guileless soul that he was, God love him—was busy taking Arius's theology far more seriously than it really deserved, Athanasius began to notice some recognizable patterns in the behavior of his bishop's dissenting clergy: "[Having failed to reclaim Arius,] Alexander, therefore, ejected him and the clergy who concurred with him in sentiment from the church. Those of the parish of Alexandria, who had embraced his opinions, were the presbyters Aithalas, Achillas, Carpones, Sarmates, and Arius, and the deacons Euzoïus, Macarius,[LV] Julius, Menas, and Helladius. Many of the people, likewise, sided with them: some, because they imagined their doctrines to be of God; others, as frequently happens in similar cases, because they believed them to have been ill-treated and unjustly excommunicated."[46]

Almost immediately, Arius and his partisans took their complaint to the streets, where they "excited many to a consideration of the question; and thus from a little spark a large fire was kindled: for the evil which began in the Church at Alexandria, ran throughout all Egypt, Libya, and the upper Thebes, and at length diffused itself over the rest of the provinces and cities. Many others also adopted the opinion of Arius; but Eusebius in particular was a zealous defender of it: not he of Caesarea, but the one who had before been bishop of the church at Berytus,

---

[LIV] "It is manifestly the opinion of Athanasius, that he [Arius] was but the pupil or tool of deeper men, probably Eusebius of Nicomedia." Newman, *Arians of the Fourth Century*, 39.

[LV] Is this the same Macarius to whom *On the Incarnation* was written?—a very sad thought, if true.

and was then somehow in possession of the bishopric of Nicomedia in Bithynia."[47]

To any churchman less innocent of politics than dear old Alexander, the sudden entrance of Eusebius of Nicomedia into the situation would have made everything clear. Eusebius—who had indeed started his ecclesiastical career as bishop of the church at Berytus, a lowly imperial backwater—had, by this time, finagled his way into the much more important episcopal chair at the eastern capital, even though the move was contrary to established Church law at the time. He seems to have managed this by means of a friendship with Constantia, the emperor's half-sister, and done it more or less openly with an eye toward influencing her kinsman's policies. Eusebius, in other words, was a well-known wire-puller and go-getter from way back, who had been dabbling in the art of mixing politics with religion before now, while Arius himself appears to have been an honest crank who thought his way into his theological corner in complete sincerity. Once turned out, however, from his place at Alexandria, Arius had taken refuge at Caesarea in Palestine, and his friends there, knowing he would need powerful allies in the fight ahead, suggested he write to his old schoolmate at Nicomedia. This is how Eusebius of Nicomedia first got involved in the Arian business, as it came to be known—and how Athanasius (along with other shrewd observers) knew there was a good deal more going on than a mere quarrel over conflicting sets of Bible verses.

Of Eusebius's interest in the affair (suggested in the harbor vignette above) there can be little doubt in light of his subsequent behavior.[LVI] The situation at Alexandria had a dangerous side—it had the potential to go, as they say, "all the way to the

---

[LVI] "[Eusebius] transformed what might have remained an Egyptian dispute into an ecumenical controversy. He was more an ecclesiastical politician than a theologian, experienced in worldly affairs and ambitious, ready for any intrigue." Quasten, *Patristics,* 191. Theodoret says frankly that Eusebius and his partisans were "slaves to ambition and vainglory."

top." It had, simply put, the capacity to exasperate the emperor. Constantine, after all, had chosen Christianity for its ability to unify, as a great new source of stability and permanence for his beloved Rome. What he hadn't yet noticed was that the Word of Christ has other potentialities as well; the power to bring "not peace but a sword" (Matt. 10:34), and to pierce hearts with its passion for truth "to the division of soul and spirit, of joints and marrow, and discerning the thoughts and intentions of the heart" (Heb. 4:12). It was precisely this aspect of Constantine's new religion that was beginning to show itself in the Church at Alexandria; and by choosing to intervene there the bishop of Nicomedia had been attempting to shield the emperor from it, hoping to safeguard the gains that his perhaps naive revolution had already wrought. Alas, the cat got out of the bag pretty quickly, and once it did there would have been nothing left for Eusebius and his ilk to do but to go all out for Arianism (as the new system was beginning to be called[LVII]): "There was a time when the Son was not."

Why? Because Constantine, to his credit, had chosen from the start to support the Christian Church as he found it; the existing society, that is, whose leaders—perfectly united up until now "in the same mind and the same judgment" (1 Cor. 1:10)— he had found already in charge. What this meant was that if the whole body of those leaders was ever called upon to adjudicate this Alexandrian matter for the entire Universal Church, then whichever of the two beliefs came out on top would be able to present itself simply as "Christianity," and thus to count upon the emperor's continued support. There was, mind you, no question yet of the emperor himself defining heresy or enforcing orthodoxy. That had always been the role of the bishops, and Constantine—who had never shown the slightest interest in metaphysics of any kind, pagan or Christian—would have been the among the last men to volunteer for such a task. True, Eu-

[LVII] Arianism should not, needless to say, be confused with Aryanism, the much-later white supremacy theory associated with Adolf Hitler.

sebius of Nicomedia appears to have been equally indifferent to truth in the abstract, but he certainly was not indifferent about which version of Christianity would be an easier "sell" where the public was concerned. Or which version of it would be more helpful to Constantine.

Arianism, after all, would—if adopted Church-wide—prove uniquely useful in getting "Christianity" accepted by a wide variety of otherwise hesitant Roman citizens. A Jesus who is not actually God but only a sort of Xerox copy of him, as Arius's group had begun to teach,[LVIII] would make things easier on any unconverted Jews out there or wavering philosophical mono-theists such as the Zoroastrians or Neo-Platonists; whereas a Je-sus who is, nevertheless, *a* god (like Perseus or Heracles, the ille-gitimate, half-human sons of Zeus) would be much more easily acceptable to pagans of whatever stripe. And wider acceptance of Jesus—whoever he might be—meant increased strength and permanence for Constantine's precarious regime and a greater sense of security for persecution-weary Christians.

Before long, Alexander himself began to realize the truth. In writing to warn the other churches about the mounting Arian calamity, our gentle, grandfatherly bishop cuts pretty quickly to the chase:

> Know . . . that there have recently arisen in our diocese law-less and anti-Christian men, teaching apostasy such as one may

---

[LVIII] "The fundamental tenet of Arianism was, that the Son of God was a creature, not born of the Father, but, in the scientific language of the times, made 'out of nothing' . . . [The Arians] maintained accordingly that the incarnate Logos was not the true Wisdom and Word of God, which was one with Him, but a created semblance of it . . . [They were] willing to ascribe to the Son all that is commonly attributed to Almighty God, His name, authority, and power; all but the incommunicable nature or being (*usia*), that is, all but that which alone could give Him a right to these prerogatives of divinity in a real and literal sense." Newman, *Arians of the Fourth Century,* 202, 204, 205.

justly consider and denominate the forerunner of Antichrist. I wished indeed to consign this disorder to silence, that if possible the evil might be confined to the apostates alone, and not go forth into other districts and contaminate the ears of some of the simple. But since Eusebius, now in Nicomedia, thinks that the affairs of the Church are under his control because, forsooth, he deserted his charge at Berytus and assumed authority over the Church at Nicomedia with impunity, and has put himself at the head of these apostates, daring even to send commendatory letters in all directions concerning them, if by any means he might inveigle some of the ignorant into this most impious and anti-Christian heresy, I felt imperatively called on to be silent no longer . . . [I write] that you might understand both who the apostates are, and also the contemptible character of their heresy, and pay no attention to anything that Eusebius should write to you . . . [Though] he affects to write in their behalf . . . the fact itself plainly shows that he does this for the promotion of his own purposes."

The complex biblical arguments included in this letter show signs of having been turned over to Athanasius, still the bishop's very junior secretary. But Alexander's own voice returns at the end, with some dire premonitions about what lies ahead for the Church:

Many heresies have arisen before these . . . exceeding all bounds in daring . . . but these persons, by attempting in all their discourses to subvert the divinity of the Word, as having made a nearer approach to Antichrist,[48] have comparatively lessened the odium of former ones. . . . We are indeed grieved on account of the perdition of these persons, and especially so because, after having been previously instructed in the doctrines of the Church, they have now apostatized from them. Nevertheless we are not greatly surprised at this, for Hymenæus and Philetus fell in like manner [2 Tim. 2:17–18]; and before them Judas, who had been a follower of the savior, but afterwards deserted him and became his betrayer. Nor were we without forewarning respecting these very persons: for the Lord himself said: "Take heed that no man deceive you: for many shall come in my name, saying, I am Christ: and shall many deceive many" [Matt. 24:4]; and "the time is at hand; Go ye not therefore after them" [Luke 21:8]. And Paul, having learned these things from the savior, wrote, "That in the latter times some should apostatize from the faith, giving heed to deceiving spirits, and doctrines of devils," [1 Tim 4:1] who pervert the truth.[49]

The Emperor Constantine was away on the battlefield at this time, engaged in a mopping-up operation left over from his war to unify the tetrarchy.[LIX] He had left behind him, as he believed, a solid, sensible, and flourishing religion for the populace to admire, which, when it came to purifying and uniting his ailing empire, had shown every sign of having been just what the doctor ordered. What would he find upon his return? Contrary to popular belief, Constantine had not "made Christianity the state religion of Rome," nor would he do so during his lifetime;[LX] he had simply bestowed his blessing upon it so that it might become a beacon to his pagan countrymen, a model of concord and harmony that might inspire them to overcome their petty squabbles and to reject the narrowly focused identity politics of their own tribe or section. How was that working out for the emperor, now that the Church herself was showing signs of party spirit and internal revolt?

And Constantine had wanted to revive the powerful old appeal to "God and Country" from which the empire had benefited in the past, but which had lost its influence as faith in the old gods withered. Yet religion as societal glue works best if

[LIX] The last of Diocletian's tetrarchs, Licinius, was defeated by Constantine at the battle of Adrianople, July 3, 324.

[LX] Catholic Christianity (as opposed to Arianism) was first "established," in the later sense, only by a joint declaration of Theodosius and Gratian in February of 380—more than forty years after Constantine's death.

clear, exclusive definitions—such as Alexander seemed determined to insist upon—are strongly discouraged. Constantine,
in other words, had welcomed a jealous God into the pantheon
when he pitched his lot with the Father of Christ, little realizing
what this would do to Rome's finely tuned balance of separation
between church and state.

But Eusebius knew; and now young Athanasius, by pondering what business a powerful, cynical bishop of Asia Minor
might possibly have meddling in the affairs of a foreign church
700 miles away, was beginning to glimpse the future as well.

5

Credo

"For it has seemed good to the Holy Spirit and to us to lay upon you no greater burden than these necessary things" (Acts 15:28).

The following remarkable missive—which author Robert Payne has called "one of the most astonishing letters ever written by an emperor to priests"[50]—was received by Alexander in Egypt, and by Arius in Caesarea of Palestine, early in the year 324:

> I call God to witness . . . that I had a twofold reason for undertaking this duty which I have now performed [the unifying of the empire, that is, and promoting the Christian religion]. My design then was, first, to bring the [various beliefs] formed by all nations [about God] to a condition . . . of settled uniformity; and secondly, to restore to health the system of the world, then suffering under the malignant power of [an angry tyrant]. . . . For I was aware that, if I should succeed in establishing, according to my hopes, a common harmony of sentiment among all the servants of God, the general course of affairs would also experience a change correspondent to the pious desires of them all.
>
> Since the power of divine light and the law of sacred worship [originated in the East], I naturally believed that you would be the first to promote the salvation of other nations . . . But, O glorious providence of God! How deep a wound did not my ears only, but my very heart receive when it was reported that divisions existed among yourselves more grievous still than those [I had sought to correct]! . . . [Y]ou, through whose aid I had hoped to procure a remedy for the errors of others, are in a state which needs healing even more than theirs. . . .
>
> I understand, then, that the origin of the present controversy is this. [It began when] you, Alexander, demanded of

the priests what opinion they [each] maintained respecting a certain passage in [Scripture], or rather, I should say, that you asked them something connected with an unprofitable question, then you, Arius, inconsiderately insisted on what ought never to have been [speculated about] at all, or if conceived, should have been buried in profound silence. Hence it was that a dissension arose between you, fellowship was withdrawn, and the holy people, rent into diverse parties, no longer preserved the unity of the one body. . . .

It was wrong in the first instance to propose such questions as these, and or to reply to them when propounded. For those points of discussion [are not commanded] by the authority of [any] law, but rather suggested by the contentious spirit which is fostered by misused leisure, even though they may be intended merely as an intellectual exercise, ought certainly to be confined to the region of our own thoughts, and not hastily produced in the popular assemblies, nor unadvisedly entrusted to the general ear. For how very few are there able either accurately to comprehend, or adequately to explain subjects so sublime and abstruse to comprehend in their nature? . . .

Let therefore both the [careless] question and the [ill-considered] answer receive your mutual forgiveness. For the cause of your difference has not been any of the leading doctrines or precepts of the divine law, nor has any new heresy respecting the worship of God arisen among you. You are really of one and the same judgment; and so it is fitting for you to join in communion and fellowship. For as long as you continue to contend about these small and very insignificant questions, it is not fitting that so large a portion of God's people should be under the direction of your judgment, since you are thus divided between yourselves. I believe it indeed to be not merely unbecoming, but positively evil, that such should be the case. . . . [Even pagan] philosophers, though they all adhere to one system, are yet frequently at issue on certain points, and differ, perhaps, in their degree of knowledge: yet they are recalled to harmony of sentiment by the uniting power of their common doctrines.

If this be true, is it not far more reasonable that you, who are the ministers of the Supreme God, should be of one mind respecting the profession of the same religion? . . . [S]ee whether it be right that, on the ground of some trifling and foolish verbal difference between ourselves, brethren should assume towards each other the attitude of enemies, and the Synod be rent by profane disunion, because of you who wrangle together on points so trivial and altogether unessential? This is vulgar, and rather characteristic of childish ignorance, than consistent with the wisdom of priests and men of sense.

Let us withdraw ourselves with a good will from these temptations of the devil. . . . I say [this] without in any way desiring to force you to entire unity of judgment in regard to this truly idle question, whatever its real nature may be. . . . [W]e are not all of us like-minded on every subject, nor is there such a thing as one universal disposition and judgment. As far, then, as regards divine providence, let there be one faith, and one understanding among you, one united judgment [concerning] God. But as to your subtle disputations on questions of little or no significance, though you may be unable to harmonize in sentiment, such differences should be confined to your own private minds and thoughts.

And now, let the preciousness of common affection, let faith in the truth, let the honor due to God and to the observance of his law remain immovably among you. Resume, then, your mutual feelings of friendship, love, and regard: restore to the people their [customary] embracings; and do ye yourselves, having purified your souls, as it were, and once more acknowledge one another. . . . Restore me then my quiet days, and untroubled nights, that the joy of undimmed light, the delight of a tranquil life, may henceforth be my portion. Else must I needs mourn, with constant tears, nor shall I be able to pass the residue of my days in peace.[51]

The Romans had always liked to pretend that their emperors were the personification of the Roman spirit or "genius," but in Constantine this flattering fiction almost came true. Like Rome itself, he had an almost abstract itch to find problems and fix them, to cut through the verbiage and put things right, to step into the middle of a row and restore order. This is not, however, to idealize the emperor; Constantine also had, in the words of that wise old French proverb, "the faults of his virtues." The flip side of his passion for stability and order was impatience; he never could stand to listen to a protracted debate, much less a quarrel, and quickly became irritated when presented with too much detail. At heart, Constantine was a soldier—but he didn't enjoy war for its own sake. He enjoyed it because it settled things, brought complex disputes to a definite end, and forced tricky, querulous people to sit down and shut up. It was, ultimately, this strong personal passion for law and order, peace and quiet, and stable business conditions, that occasioned the emperor's astonishing letter—also his uncharacteristic decision to intervene in Christian affairs, though he himself was still an unbaptized (and largely uncatechized, as it seems!) heathen.

Clearly, Constantine could not make heads or tails of the Arian kerfuffle—and was simply dismayed by it all; "very deeply grieved" according to Socrates, "regarding the matter as a personal misfortune."[52] The Christians now enjoyed a peace undreamed of by their fathers and what was the best thing they could think of to do with it?—to immediately gin up some kind of pointless war of words, as if they'd gotten used to strife over the years and were now getting bored without it. What kind of people had he gotten himself mixed up with, anyhow? People with too much time on their hands, obviously! So "Constantine was thereby greatly troubled; for just at this period, when religion was beginning to be more generally propagated, many were deterred by the difference in doctrines from embracing Christianity."[53] Though his Greek was bad, and every one of the documents in question (including the New Testament) was available exclusively in Greek, though it ought to have been clear to him that his understanding of the Faith was embryonic at best, Constantine had nevertheless leapt confidently to the assumption that he could tell the difference between an important and a trivial matter in Christian theology . . . and then, without missing a beat, go on to instruct two longtime clergymen in the matter!

"It is an ungrateful task," Newman reminds us, "to discuss the private opinions and motives of an emperor who was the first to profess himself the Protector of the Church, and to relieve it from the abject and suffering condition in which it had lain for three centuries." Nonetheless, Constantine's conduct

> still has somewhat of a warning in it, which must not be neglected. . . . Concord is so eminently the perfection of the Christian temper, conduct, and discipline, and it had been so wonderfully exemplified in the previous history of the Church, that it was almost unavoidable in a heathen soldier and statesman to regard it as the sole precept of the gospel . . . [Those] who receive scarcely more of [Christ's] teaching than the instinct of civilization recognizes (and Constantine must, on the whole, be classed among such), view the religious dissensions of the Church as simply evil, and (as they would fain prove) contrary to his own precepts; whereas in fact they are but the history of truth in its first stage of trial, when it aims at being "pure," before it is "peaceable";[54] and are reprehensible only so far as baser passions mix themselves with that true loyalty towards God, which desires his glory in the first place, and only in the second place, the tranquillity and good order of society.[55]

The emperor had sent his petulant epistle by means of a very distinguished courier: Hosius, bishop of Cordova, a personal friend of Constantine's and generally conceded to be his religious adviser. No one knows quite how this special relationship came about, but as Hosius was, by this time, one of the few remaining Western churchmen with any claim to worldwide importance, Constantine (a Westerner himself, living almost full time now in the Greek-speaking East) may have felt a kinship solely on the basis of their shared Latin tongue. Hosius carried the emperor's letter to Alexandria, was apparently able to arrange a few uncomfortable meetings there, but had, in the end, been forced to return with unhappy news. Neither Arius nor Alexander had been willing to yield to his appeals, and the tumult that had begun in the church of Alexandria was now running wild throughout all of Egypt, Libya, Palestine, and Asia Minor, with no obvious end in sight. "One saw not only the prelates of the churches engaged in disputing, but the people also divided, some siding with one party, and some with the other. To so disgraceful an extent was this affair carried, that Christianity became a subject of popular ridicule, even in the very theatres."[56]

Arius's phrase *"there was a time when the Son was not"* (which has a sing-song quality in the original Greek and can be chanted, almost like a nursery rhyme) was now heard in the streets as a rallying cry for his faction. Arius himself, in fact, "even went from house to house, endeavoring to make men the slaves of his error . . . These were, indeed, scenes fit for the tragic stage, over which tears might have been shed."[57]

And here, the world may owe a very great debt indeed to Hosius; for the Spaniard appears to have intervened at this critical juncture with a little fast diplomacy of his own—though no actual record of it survives. Constantine might easily have become angry at this point, perhaps made good on some of those not-so-veiled threats we saw in the letter: as, for example, when he wondered aloud to the disputants whether it might not be "positively evil" to allow them to retain the charge of their churches any longer. In an effort to prevent any such unfortunate outbursts, Hosius may have undertaken some remedial catechesis of his own. He may have begun tactfully, for instance, by sympathizing with Constantine's confusing new status. As Maximus Augustus, emperor of Rome, Constantine was, after all, absolute lord over these quarreling Roman citizens (who also happened to be Christian clergy); but as a Christian layman (which the emperor, as a catechumen, already was, even prior to baptism[LXI]) he was subject

---

[LXI] Partially due to the need for secrecy during the years of persecution and to the threat of infiltrators, the early Church put inquirers through a lengthy term of probation prior to baptism (normally two years). These catechumens (as they were called) were, nevertheless, considered part of the Church already and were said to have received a "baptism of blood" if martyred before the normal process could be complete.

to the bishops, as Scripture commands: "Obey your leaders and submit to them; for they are keeping watch over your souls, as men who will have to give account" (Heb. 13:17). Hosius may well have quoted the saintly Ignatius of Antioch here as well, that successor of Peter as bishop of Antioch who had spelled out the role of the clergy so well for the early Church: "See that you all follow the bishop, even as Jesus Christ does the Father, and the presbytery as you would the apostles; and reverence the deacons, as being the institution of God. Let no man do anything connected with the Church without the bishop."[58]

So was this new, previously unclassified animal—a Christian emperor—fish or fowl? Was he Caesar or was he someone's subordinate? Hosius wouldn't have blamed Constantine if he didn't know, for even the early Church Fathers hadn't known for sure: Melito of Sardis had wondered whether the emperor might someday become a Christian, but Justin and Tertullian seem to have decided it was impossible.[LXII] Constantine, as a matter of fact, may have meddled, initially, at Alexandria *because* he didn't know, simply from force of habit, since his age-old job description as *Pontifex Maximus* had always included his acting as a kind of "pagan pope" to the empire's myriad polytheistic cults. The emperor was simply *in charge of religion* in Rome—yet how? Now that the religion was also in charge of him? Hosius may also have convinced Constantine that he himself—Caesar's adviser and a reasonable man—also believed that the doctrinal issues involved were not trivial; that "the difference between Christ the Mediator and Christ the God is a very real one," as Payne puts it, "and a matter of importance to all Christians, not only theologians."[59] The emperor, at any rate, did not go ballistic.

Instead, he allowed Hosius to suggest an alternative. Hosius had seen Church trouble before this—had, in fact, been one of the

---

[LXII] So dramatic had the wave of conversions become by his day that Tertullian thought even "the Cæsars too would have believed on Christ, if either the Cæsars had not been necessary for the world, or if Christians could have been Cæsars." *The Apology*, 21.

bishops present at the Council of Elvira, that aforementioned African synod that worked to reform a morally compromised Ghetto diocese some twenty-five years earlier. So what if another synod were to be gathered?—a Grand Synod of *all* the world's bishops this time, an ecumenical council,[LXIII] something that had never even been possible while Christianity was illegal; or not, at any rate, since the apostles themselves had called the first one at Jerusalem in A.D. 49, to settle the matter of the Judaizers (Acts 15).

Constantine certainly had the resources to make such an event happen. Nor would the idea be new to him; the emperor had, about ten years earlier, been summoned to Arles, to lend his sanction to a smaller, local council gathered to address the matter of the Donatists—a hard, puritanical minority who had rebelled when they felt the Church was being too soft on repentant *traditores*. Would it not, at a general council of the whole Church, become readily apparent to the emperor which teaching about the savior really was traditional and which the innovation?—for Hosius had little doubt that Arius and his party would appear at any such council as a tiny, dissonant minority. The suggestion, at any rate, was broached, and Constantine assented. "When it was found that the event did not answer the expectations of the emperor, but that on the contrary, the contention was too great for reconciliation, so that he who had been sent to make peace returned without having accomplished his mission, Constantine convened a synod at Nicaea, in Bithynia, and wrote to the most eminent men of the churches in every country, directing them to be there on an appointed day."[60]

THE DELEGATES ASSEMBLE

We should pause a moment to notice that Constantine did not "order" the Council of Nicaea to be held; not, at least, in the

---

[LXIII] Derived from the Greek (oikoumene, meaning "the inhabited earth"), "ecumenical" means "worldwide"—which, in the fourth century, would have been synonymous with the Roman Empire.

sense that a subservient Christian clergy assembled there purely at his beck and call. After all, the emperors had been doing quite a lot of ordering over the past 300 years, a great deal of which the Church—and these very bishops, in fact—had flat-out refused, "in spite of dungeon, fire, and sword." No, the bishops responded to Constantine's call because they remembered the biblical admonitions of the apostle Paul: "Let every person be subject to the governing authorities. For there is no authority except from God, and those that exist have been instituted by God. Therefore he who resists the authorities resists what God has appointed, and those who resist will incur judgment" (Rom. 13:1–2). Though the time does surely come—as it had so recently—to "obey God rather than men" (Acts 5:29), this call from Constantine was not that time, for the bishops saw the wisdom in Hosius's suggestion as well as the emperor had. Constantine, after all, had given no instructions about *how* the Arian matter was to be settled, simply that it must be settled, one way or the other—and that was something that practically everyone agreed on.

Nicaea was a good choice of venue. It was only about twenty-five miles from the imperial residence at Nicomedia, on the Asiatic side of the straits of Bosphorus, in what is today Turkey. Well connected by excellent roads to nearly all of the provinces, easily accessible by water, Nicaea would have allowed the emperor to assemble the largest number of bishops possible without delaying the council and prolonging the crisis. Constantine also "pledged his word that the bishops and their officials should be furnished with asses, mules, and horses for their journey at the public expense. When all those who were capable of enduring the fatigue of the journey had arrived at Nicaea, he went there himself, with both the wish of seeing the multitude of bishops, and the yearning desire of maintaining unanimity among them. He at once arranged that all their wants should be liberally supplied. Three hundred and eighteen bishops were assembled. The bishop of Rome, on account of his very advanced age, was absent, but he sent two presbyters to the council, with authority

to agree to what was done."[LXIV] The date set for the opening
convocation was—according to most historians—May 20, 325.

[LXIV] Theodoret, *Ecclesiastical History*, I:6. Without entering the debate over
papal supremacy at all, we can, at the very least, conclude from this passage
that obtaining the pope's assent to the Nicene decision was considered a matter of great importance. First of all, Arianism had not reached the West at this
point and was of no immediate concern there; the heresy gripping Eastern
Christendom was little more than a topic of hazy news dispatches for most
Westerners. "How hazy is shown by the declaration of Hilary of Poitiers that
he had been a bishop for many years before he had even heard of the Nicene
Creed" (Chadwick). Yet the pope's physical absence at the council requires
a special explanation in this account and his legates travel a thousand miles
or more to be there, no doubt at great expense. Secondly, we may note that
when the time comes to sign the declaration of Faith drawn up at the conclusion of the council, the first names on the list are not those of the great Eastern
patriarchs, Alexander of Alexandria, or Macarius of Jerusalem, or Eustathius
of Antioch. No, the "John Hancock" of Nicaea was the Western bishop Hosius of Cordova, close associate of Pope Sylvester of Rome, who affixed his
signature and wrote: "I so believe as was written above." Next come the
signatures of no bishops at all, but "Victor and Vincent, Roman priests, for
the venerable man, our holy pope and bishop, Sylvester, [who] have signed,
believing as written above." Again, it is not necessary to our purposes here to
insist on a fully developed Catholic doctrine of Roman jurisdiction, a subject
that is outside the range of this book. Yet as early as A.D. 180, Irenaeus of
Lyons had written of "the greatest and most ancient Church known to all,
founded and organized at Rome by the two most glorious Apostles, Peter and
Paul" and prescribed comparison with her traditions as an unfailing barom-
eter of theological soundness. "With this Church," he continues, "because
of its superior origin, all Churches must agree, that is, all the faithful in the
whole world; and it is in her that the faithful everywhere have maintained
the Apostolic tradition." This special role for the Church at Rome was accepted—in theory, at least, and no doubt grudgingly at times—in both the
Eastern and Western halves of Christendom throughout the entirety of the
first Christian millennium and fully accounts for the prominence of these
Roman presbyters at the council. Hilaire Belloc sums the matter up with
admirable restraint when he writes "but for their adherence the decrees of the
Council would not have held."

The bishops, as they began to arrive with their accompanying retinues of servants and minor clergy, must have offered quite a spectacle to observers on the sidelines; every color and race of the Old World, a veritable parade of nations flowing into Nicaea. According to Eusebius Pamphilus (who was himself a delegate and an eyewitness), there were "Cilicians, Phœnicians, Arabs and Palestinians, and in addition to these, Egyptians, Thebans, Libyans, and those who came from Mesopotamia. At this synod a Persian bishop was also present, neither was the Scythian absent from this assemblage [both from outside the borders of the empire]. Pontus also and Galatia, Pamphylia, Cappadocia, Asia and Phrygia, supplied those who were most distinguished among them. Besides, there met there Thracians and Macedonians, Achaians and Epirots, and even those who dwelt still further away than these, and the most celebrated of the Spaniards himself [Hosius] took his seat among the rest."[61] Other famous members of the council included Eustathius, bishop of Antioch, and successor there to both Ignatius and to Peter; Macarius of Jerusalem, successor in that ancient bishopric to the apostle James; and also, according to some traditional accounts, Bishop Nicholas of Myra, destined to morph somehow, in the world's imagination, into Old Saint Nick, Santa Claus himself.

The list is heavily weighted toward Eastern bishops—understandable given travel conditions in those days—but this imbalance was not considered a problem since the crisis, up till now, remained largely an Eastern affair. "Many other excellent and good men from different nations were congregated together, of whom some were celebrated for their learning, their eloquence, and their knowledge of the sacred books, and other disciplines; some for the virtuous tenor of their life, and others for the combination of all these qualifications. . . . There were, likewise, [laymen] present who were skilled in dialectics, and ready to assist in the discussions."[62]

And along with this distinguished group, of course, came the disputants themselves: Arius, the man of the hour, currently living as a celebrity expatriate at Caesarea; Alexander of

Alexandria, his former bishop, now said to be entering his dotage by unfriendly watchers; and Eusebius of Nicomedia, the actual mastermind behind it all, as many of the bishops now realized. Arius likely made a very pleasing public entrance. He was tall and thin, just on the wrong side of sixty as the council convened, with dark, shoulder-length hair and dark, serious eyes that gave people the impression he'd done a good deal more thinking than they had. Nevertheless, he wasn't really stern-faced or dour; Arius often smiled as he explained his ideas and used a warm, compelling voice, with an interesting accent. He'd always tended, in fact, to unconsciously gather up little knots of female admirers who followed him around like groupies; the fact that he had, in spite of this, never been creditably accused of immorality only added to his mystique. Bishop Alexander, though probably not actually senile, really was very frail, and likely sad, by this point; white-headed, with kindly, watery eyes, he would count mostly upon his staff to present the case for orthodoxy. Eusebius of Nicomedia, quiet, well dressed, and crafty as Richelieu, preferred to hang back, to remain out of the spotlight and let the focus stay fixed on Arius.

While the delegates waited for everyone to arrive, they gathered in impromptu preliminary sessions that, perhaps unwisely, were open to the public. Sozomen sets the scene:

> As might have been expected . . . many different questions started out of the investigation: some of the bishops spoke against the introduction of novelties contrary to the faith which had been delivered to them from the beginning. And those especially who had adhered to simplicity of doctrine argued that the faith of God ought to be received without curious inquiries; others, however, contended that ancient opinions ought not to be followed without examination. . . .
>
> While these disputations were being carried on, certain of the pagan philosophers became desirous of taking part in them; some, because they wished for information as to the doctrine that was inculcated; and others, because, feel-

ing incensed against the Christians on account of the recent suppression of the pagan religion,[LXV] they wished to convert the inquiry about doctrine into a strife about words, so as to introduce dissensions among them, and to make them appear as holding contradictory opinions.

It is related that one of these philosophers, priding himself on his acknowledged superiority of eloquence, began to ridicule the priests, and thereby roused the indignation of a simple old man, highly esteemed as a confessor, who, although unskilled in logical refinements and wordiness, undertook to oppose him.

The less serious of those who knew the confessor, raised a laugh at his expense for engaging in such an undertaking; but the more thoughtful felt anxious lest, in opposing so eloquent a man, he should only render himself ridiculous; yet [the confessor's] influence was so great, and his reputation so high among them, that they could not forbid his engaging in the debate; and he accordingly delivered himself in the following terms:

"In the name of Jesus Christ, O philosopher, hearken to me. There is one God, the maker of heaven and earth, and of all things visible and invisible. He made all things by the power of the Word, and established them by the holiness of His Spirit. The Word, whom we call the Son of God, seeing that man was sunk in error and living like the beasts pitied him, and vouchsafed to be born of woman, to hold intercourse with men, and to die for them. And He will come

---

[LXV] These philosophers must have grown quite accustomed to their state-sponsored privileges, for Constantine himself did very little suppression of paganism and what he did do was of a very mild nature. He prohibited temple prostitution and animal sacrifice during their ceremonies (practices that seem to have been on their way out already), and he cut off state funding for the maintenance of their shrines, while simultaneously exempting Christian facilities (as well as the clergy themselves) from all taxation. Other than this, Constantine's sword remained in its sheath—though the same, admittedly, cannot be said of some of his later successors.

again to judge each of us as to the deeds of this present life. We believe these things to be true with all simplicity. Do not, therefore, expend your labor in vain by striving to disprove facts which can only be understood by faith or by scrutinizing the manner in which these things did or did not come to pass. Answer me, do you believe?"

The philosopher, astonished at what had occurred, replied, I believe; and . . . thanked the old man for having overcome him in argument." Confronted afterwards by his nonplussed brother philosophers, the Church's newest member—a bit dazed himself, perhaps—swore "that he had been impelled to embrace Christianity by a certain inexplicable impulse" and then "began to teach the same doctrines to others."[63]

THE EMPEROR'S KISS

"When they were all assembled, the emperor ordered a great hall to be prepared for their accommodation in the palace, in which a sufficient number of benches and seats were placed."[64] Each of the bishops "took his place with becoming modesty, and silently awaited the arrival of the emperor. The court officers entered one after another, though only such as professed faith in Christ." Hosius and Eustathius, representing the West and the East respectively, appear to have acted as co-presidents, taking seats near the head of the hall. "And now, all rising at the signal which indicated the emperor's entrance, at last he himself proceeded through the midst of the assembly . . . he surpassed all present in height of stature and beauty of form, as well as in majestic dignity of mien, and invincible strength and vigor."[65] Eusebius Pamphilus, always ready to magnify Constantine in his obsequious writings, makes much of the golden throne that had been provided for his use. Theodoret, on the other hand, records that the emperor asked for a "low stool" instead, and "did not seat himself [on it] until he had asked the permission of the bishops. Then all the sacred assembly sat down around him."[66]

This opening session was called to order by the Eastern pre-sider, Eustathius, who welcomed the emperor and asked him to address the gathering. Constantine rose and made the speech in his native Latin, with an accompanying translation into Greek, likely provided by Hosius. "It was once my chief desire, dearest friends, to enjoy the spectacle of your united presence; and now that this desire is fulfilled, I feel myself bound to render thanks to God the universal King, because, in addition to all his other benefits, he has granted me a blessing higher than all the rest, in permitting me to see you not only all assembled together, but all united in a common harmony of sentiment. I pray therefore that no malignant adversary may henceforth interfere to mar our happy state."[67]

Continuing in a tone that, unhappily, remained a little too reminiscent of his high-handed letter to Arius and Alexander, the emperor exhorted the bishops to unity

and recalled to their remembrance the cruelty of the late ty-rants, and reminded them of the honorable peace which God had, in his reign and by his means, accorded them. He pointed out how dreadful it was, aye, very dreadful, that at the very time when their enemies were destroyed, and when no one dared to oppose them, they should fall upon one another, and make their amused adversaries laugh, especially as they were debating about holy things, concerning which they had the written teaching of the Holy Spirit. For the gospels (contin-ued he), the writings, and the oracles of the ancient prophets, clearly teach us what we ought to believe concerning the di-vine nature. Let, then, all contentious disputation be discarded; and let us seek in the divinely-inspired word the solution of the questions at issue. These and similar exhortations he, like an affectionate son, addressed to the bishops as to fathers, laboring to bring about their unanimity in the doctrines.[68]

In the preserved records, however, Constantine's manner changes dramatically almost immediately after this oration; after

he would have been personally introduced, that is, to all of the gathered delegates one by one. If the emperor still labored, up to this point, under his impression that the whole dispute was merely a tiff between theoreticians, fostered by misused leisure, then he may not have been expecting to meet at Nicaea the kind of men with whom he was actually presented:

> Many individuals, like the holy apostle, bore in their bodies the marks of the Lord Jesus Christ . . .[69] Paul, bishop of Neo-Caesarea, a fortress situated on the banks of the Euphrates, had suffered from the frantic rage of Licinius [one of Constantine's persecuting co-emperors]. He had been deprived of the use of both hands by the application of a red-hot iron, by which the nerves which give motion to the muscles had been contracted and rendered dead. Some had had the right eye dug out, others had lost the right arm. Among these was Paphnutius of Egypt.

These delegates, many of them, had to be carried in on litters. Constantine also met simple, holy souls like Spyridion of Cyprus, who had continued his daily routine as a sheepherder even after being elected bishop of a major diocese; and James, a hermit of Mygdonia, who, the emperor was told, had raised a man from the dead with the very hands Constantine was now holding! "In short," as Theodoret concludes, "the council looked like an assembled army of martyrs." Caesar, not surprisingly, was moved, even shaken. "Observing that some among them had had the right eye torn out, and learning that this mutilation had been undergone for the sake of religion, he placed his lips upon the wounds, believing that he would extract a blessing from the kiss."[70] The world, surely, has witnessed few scenes so momentous: the successor of Nero, of Caligula, of Commodus and Diocletian, kneeling on the floor of his own palace, kissing the ugly face of Roman persecution. Later, when the actual debates got started, the emperor sat quietly on his low stool and "listened to all with patient attention, deliberately and impartially considering whatever was advanced."[71] He gave, after this, no more lectures.

Among these similar witnesses, too, came some of Antony's boys—the Jesus Freaks out of their desert time capsule. What these men believed about the matter at hand would be of the utmost interest to the assembly; and the records show that the Thebaid monks were received at Nicaea with the same kind of honor and deference shown to the confessors, having suffered, in their own way, a similar sacrifice for the health of the Church. Of this group—and looked upon by them as an old friend who had made good—young Athanasius was most prominent. Just shy of thirty, still too young to vote at the council, he was Alexander's archdeacon now, brought to Nicaea to argue the Incarnation when his bishop no longer could.

To Eusebius of Nicomedia this was simply additional proof of Alexander's decrepitude. These monks were embarrassing, especially standing here in Constantine's elegant hall; they were hairy and uncouth, illiterate and archaic, always seeing Jesus and performing faith cures. And Athanasius, too, though cleaned up a bit these days and a touch less ignorant, was unsightly as well; still the strange, mongrel runt who probably should have been drowned. Few could have imagined at the time—not even the farsighted Eusebius of Nicomedia—that little Athanasius would soon be the most famous Christian in the world, leading the entire orthodox cause long after Alexander and Hosius, Arius and Eustathius, Constantine, and even Eusebius himself had gone down to dust or to dungeon.

CREATING AND BEGETTING

Now the formal sessions began. Unfortunately, the actual word-for-word debates, if they were recorded at all, have not survived. We can, nevertheless, reconstruct the gist of what was said from various letters and other recollections written afterwards, often by the disputants themselves. We know, for instance, that Arius was allowed to speak first, and that "his first attack on the

Catholic doctrine was conducted with an openness which, considering the general duplicity of his party, is the most honorable trait in his character."[72]

"[Alexander] has driven us out of the city as atheists, because we do not concur in what he publicly preaches, namely, God always, the Son always; as the Father so the Son; the Son co-exists unbegotten with God; He is everlasting; neither by thought nor by any interval does God precede the Son; always God, always Son; he is unbegotten of the unbegotten; the Son is of God himself." Notice how Arius begs the question here; "the Son" is not contrasted, as in Scripture, with "the Father" but with "God"; and it is simply taken for granted that the biblical word "begotten" is nothing but a synonym for "created."

"But we say and believe, and have taught, and do teach, that the Son is not unbegotten, nor in any way part of the unbegotten; and that he does not derive his subsistence from any matter; but that by his own will and counsel he has subsisted before time, and before ages, as perfect God, only begotten and unchangeable, and [yet] before he was begotten, or created, or purposed, or established, he was not. For he was not unbegotten." Observe here that Arius is only too willing to call the Son "perfect God" and to say he existed before time, so long as he is allowed to deny him the single most essential divine attribute: that of being actually eternal and uncreated. "We are persecuted, because we say that the Son has a beginning, but that God is without beginning. This is the cause of our persecution, and likewise, because we say that he is of the non-existent [created, in other words, out of nothing]. And this we say, because he is neither part of God, nor of any essential being. For this are we persecuted; the rest you know."[73]

It is possible that Arius's well-known *Thalia* was brought forward at this time. Many of the bishops had been scandalized to learn that Arius, in trying to win popular support for his notions in Egypt, had set some of his theology to music for popular use—and that the irreverent tune he picked out for this purpose seems to have been some kind of an old drinking song (the word *Thalia* means a "song for merrymaking"). "God made the Son . . . and adopted him to be

his Son . . . the Father is foreign in substance to the Son . . . [but]
by God's will the Son became wisdom, power, the spirit, the truth,
the word, the glory, and the image of God . . . [And the Son] from
the time that he was made, being a mighty God . . . has hymned
the praises of his superior; that he cannot investigate his Father's
nature, it being plain that the originated cannot comprehend the
unoriginate; nay, that he does not know his own."[74] All of these
things proceed quite logically from Arius's original idea. In fact,
they had only one real defect: that neither Alexander—much less
Antony!—nor any other orthodox Christian had ever heard anything like them before.

Sensing, perhaps, from the coolness of his reception, that Arius
had expressed himself rather too plainly, Eusebius of Nicomedia
apparently asked for the floor. Anticipating their reaction—anticipating, that is, that the orthodox bishops would charge Arius
with introducing novelties and innovations—Eusebius brought
forward a list of his own; novelties committed, as he insisted, by
his opponents:

> We have never heard that there are two unbegotten beings,
> nor that one has been divided into two, nor have we learned
> or believed that it has ever undergone any change of a corpo-
> real nature. . . . We believe that the mode of his beginning
> not only cannot be expressed by words but even in thought,
> and is incomprehensible not only to man, but also to all be-
> ings superior to man. These opinions we advance not as hav-
> ing derived them from our own imagination, but as having
> deduced them from Scripture, whence we learn that the Son
> was created, established, and begotten in the same substance
> and in the same immutable and inexpressible nature as the
> maker; and so the Lord says, "God created me in the begin-
> ning of his way; I was set up from everlasting; before the hills
> was I brought forth" [Prov. 8:22–23].[75]

None of this seems to have gone over at all well. The bishops
were only too aware of the various problem passages for their

side of the dispute, just as much as Eusebius was aware of his; and the danger of the whole thing being reduced to an absurd tit-for-tat of proof-texting was something they had hoped everyone wished to avoid. Similarly, Eusebius's insistence on his having deduced Arianism from the perusal of Scripture alone (and the implication that his opponents must now confine themselves to terms found in that source as well) boded ill for the days ahead. No Christian had ever been able to do that when grappling with these questions, nor has any since. As we noted earlier, the word "Trinity"—even if some chance Tertullianist had picked it up and brought it to the council—is not found in the Bible, any more than commonly used Christian terms like *premillennial*, *substitutionary*, or *accepting Christ* are found there.[LXVI] Arius's ideas were foreign to the *meaning* of Scripture, not necessarily to the letter of it—not as filtered, that is, through the mind of some private individual hankering to resolve paradoxes.

What was needed was a Scripture-based *summary* of all the biblical data that avoided unfamiliar breaks with the Christian past; as opposed to wild, speculative "answers" to the mysteries of Scripture that just happen to be hard to disprove with a verse or two. Athanasius himself, at any rate, records that even though "the terms [the Arians] used were replete with irreligion . . . the assembled bishops who were 300 more or less, mildly and charitably [allowed them to go on, but] required of them to explain and defend themselves on religious grounds."[76]

As was fitting, Bishop Alexander was the first to rise in opposition. With little strength remaining for eloquence, he appears to have gone straight to the heart of the matter: the faulty usage of the word "begotten" his adversaries were insisting upon. Far from implying an origin in time (since time itself, not being part of God, must be one of the things he created—not something to which he himself is subject) the divinely chosen metaphor of

---

[LXVI] "Christian vocabulary is full of words that have come into use as the Christian mind has gone to work on what it finds in Scripture." Thomas Howard, *Evangelical Is Not Enough,* 105.

"begetting" actually points toward something else entirely. C.S. Lewis summarized it memorably:

> To beget is to become the father of: to create is to make. And the difference is this. When you beget, you beget something of the same kind as yourself. A man begets human babies, a beaver begets little beavers. . . . But when you make, you make something of a different kind than yourself . . . a beaver builds a dam, a man makes a wireless set. . . . Now that is the first thing to get clear. What God begets is God; just as what man begets is man. What God creates is not God; just as what man makes is not man.[77]

This, according to Alexander, is what Scripture actually means by calling Christ God's "only begotten Son" [John 3:16]—the very word itself denies that the Son is a created being. To this traditional Christian truth, Eusebius replied with another grab bag of Bible verses:

> If [as Alexander teaches] the fact of his being called the begotten gives any ground for the belief that, having come into being of the Father's substance, he also has from the Father likeness of nature, we reply that it is not of him alone that the scriptures have spoken as begotten, but that they also thus speak of those who are entirely dissimilar to him by nature. For of men it is said, "I have begotten and brought up sons, and they have rebelled against me" [Isa. 1:2]; and in another place, "You have forsaken God who begot you" [Deut. 32:18]; and again it is said, "Who begot the drops of dew?" [Job 38:28]. This expression does not imply that the dew partakes of the nature of God, but simply that all things were formed according to His will. There is, indeed, nothing which is of his substance, yet everything which exists has been called into being by his will. He is God; and all things were made in his likeness, and in the future likeness of his Word, being created of his free will. All things were made by his means by God. All things are of God.[78]

Alexander's patience may well have deserted him here, for the records tell us that he called upon his brilliant young disciple to take over once his own energy had gone. Athanasius, in any event, seems to have been well in charge once the debate entered the back-and-forth questioning phase.[LXVII] There must have been a bit of a hush in the hall when this odd little fellow stepped to the podium; quite apart from his curious appearance, Athanasius was underage, a complete unknown to many, and coming to the plate for his first big league at bat. His most essential quality, however, would not yet have been visible: Athanasius was stubborn. Where the ancient Faith was concerned, he was obstinate, intransigent, and stubborn as a donkey. And it was here at Nicaea that his soon-to-be legendary tenacity first took center stage.

He had already supplied his Bible verses, for all the good it had done anyone. They'd been included in his portion of Alexander's original letter. And for hearts ready to rest peacefully in the Faith once delivered, they are, indeed, decisive:

> Who that hears John saying, "In the beginning was the Word," [John 1:1] does not condemn those that say, "There was a period when the Word was not"? Or who, hearing in the Gospel . . . that "all things were made by him," [John 1:3] will not abhor those that pronounce the Son [himself] to be one of the things made? . . . Or how is he unlike the Father's essence, who is "his perfect image" [Col. 1:15], and "the brightness of his glory" [Heb. 1:3] and [who] says: "He that has seen me, has seen the Father?" [John 14:9] . . . One need not wonder indeed at their blasphemous assertion that the Son does not perfectly know the Father; for having once determined to fight against Christ, they reject even the words of the Lord himself, when he says, "As the Father knows me, even so know I the Father" [John 10:15].

[LXVII] Newman says Athanasius "conducted the controversy at Nicaea" and for him, according to scholar P.J. Harrold, "Arius conceived a particular hatred, which he seems to have transmitted to his children in heresy."

Athanasius may have given scriptural proofs one more try at the council but, to be honest, one doubts it. "We, by stating these things," as he recounts elsewhere, "and [by] unfolding the divine scriptures, have often confuted them: but again as chameleons they were changed, striving to apply to themselves that which is written, 'When the ungodly has reached the depths of iniquity, he becomes contemptuous' [Prov. 18:3]." To the Arians, Bible arguments alone were simply more grist for the mill.

Boldly then, Athanasius called the bishop's bluff instead. Were Eusebius's fellow partisans really ready to stick by him on this?— on his brazen assertion, that is, that Christ is begotten of God only in the same way as the morning dew? Created things, after all, are mutable and alterable by nature, quite unlike God "with whom is no variableness, neither shadow of turning" [James 1:17 KJV]. Such a "Son" then—not "the true and natural Logos" but totally unlike God in all the most essential ways—would be "foreign and external to God's substance . . . made [only] for our sakes." This being the case, "Someone asked them" (and here Athanasius is almost certainly referring modestly to himself) "if the Word of God could change, as the devil changed? They scrupled not to answer, 'Certainly, He can.'"[79]

Now, "stripping off all reverence," the Arians impudently avowed "that God, foreknowing and foreseeing [the Son's] obedience, chose him out of all creatures; chose him, I say, not as possessing aught by nature and prerogative above the others (since, as they say, there is no Son of God by nature), nor bearing any peculiar relation towards God; but, as being, as well as others, of an alterable nature, and preserved from falling by the pursuit and exercise of virtuous conduct; so that, if Paul or Peter had made such strenuous progress, they would have gained a sonship equal to his."[80] All of this from that seemingly simple phrase, *"there was a time when the Son was not"*!

Christian apologist and dramatist Dorothy Sayers, in her 1951 play *The Emperor Constantine*, imagines a direct cross-examination of Arius by Athanasius at this point:

ATHANASIUS
. . . And when he said to his disciples, "I and my Father are one"?

ARIUS
He meant that they were like-minded, in that he did the will of
the Father. For in him the image was uniquely perfect, not being
distorted by a fallible human soul.

*[ATHANASIUS is so astonished that he can hardly believe his ears.
But he leaps on this indiscretion like a cat on a rat]*

ATHANASIUS
You say that Christ had no human soul?

ARIUS
In Christ, the Logos took the place of the human soul.

ATHANASIUS
Then he was not true man, for man's nature consists in a fleshly
body and a rational soul. There are heretics who deny Christ's God-
head and others who deny his manhood—it was left for Arius to
deny both at once. . . . Tell me, how did this compound of half-man
and demi-god do the will of the Father? Freely, or of necessity?

ARIUS *(hesitating—he sees the trap but cannot avoid it)*
Freely.

ATHANASIUS
That which is created free to stand is created free to fall. Was
the Son, then, made fallible by nature, needing God's grace to
keep him from sin? If so, the second Adam is no more than the
first. Christ is but man—or at most an angel—and to worship
him is idolatry.

ARIUS *(sullenly)*
I did not say that.

ATHANASIUS

I am glad to hear it. But if he was created infallible, then he was not free, but did the Father's will of necessity, as the brutes do, and brute matter.

ARIUS

I say that he was made of like will with the Father, and therefore he cannot err.

ATHANASIUS

You mean that his nature is its own necessity?

ARIUS

Yes.

ATHANASIUS

Then he is God, for only God is his own necessity . . . Beloved Fathers, in whom will you believe? In the Christ of Arius, who is neither true man to bear our sorrows nor true God to forgive us our sins? Or in him who, being in the form of God, clung not to his equality with God, but was made in the likeness of man and became obedient unto death for our sakes?[81] Reasoning is but words—God's act is the living truth. I call upon the confessors to say for whom they suffered.

AMPHION[LXVIII]

For Christ our God.

PAUL[LXIX]

For Christ our God.

PAPHNUTIUS

For Christ who is over all, God blessed forever.

[LXVIII] Bishop of Epiphania.
[LXIX] Bishop of Neocaesarea.

ATHANASIUS
So speaks Paul the Apostle. So speak those who shed their blood
for Christ. But what says Arius?[82]

THE NICENE CREED

Lest we get too very lost in the thicket of Trinitarian controversy, it might be wise to pause a moment and restate the bottom
line: Arianism was nothing more or less than a clever attempt
to *save paganism*, to allow men to go on worshipping a creature
rather than the Creator, as they had since time immemorial. Perhaps Arius personally was troubled by an inability to reconcile
the divinity of Christ with his idea of monotheism, but for Eusebius and the rest, Arianism was nothing but "a bold endeavor
to reformulate Christian doctrine in a way more palatable to the
educated public of A.D. 320."[83] The Arians *took advantage,* in
short, of the paradoxes presented by the Incarnation, and they
did it in order to wage a program essentially political in nature.

It ought to be strongly emphasized, too, that there was no
humanitarian party present at Nicaea; no group of clergy advo-
cating, that is, a merely human Christ, a prophet or wise man
only. No, the Arians were thoroughgoing supernaturalists who
did not deny the Virgin Birth, the Resurrection, any of Christ's
miracles, nor his claims to divinity. The *Da Vinci* scenario, in
other words, which pictures the Council of Nicaea as the final
showdown between what became Roman orthodoxy and an
earlier, "purer" Christianity that followed an enlightened but
simply human sage, has no basis in fact at all.

The actual lines of demarcation at Nicaea were pretty clear
from the start. Of the 300-plus bishops present, the number of
out-and-out Arians is variously stated at thirteen, seventeen, or,
at the very outside, twenty-two. Though not many, the names
on this list include some remarkable ones: Maris, bishop of Chalcedon, site of a future council even larger than Nicaea; Meno-
phantus of Ephesus, successor there to Christ's own apostle John;
and even Theognis of Nicaea, the local bishop who was hosting

the council! All of these claimed to find Arius's arguments compelling and worth standing up for in front of the whole Church.

Lingering in the penumbra of this group was a larger minority of sympathizers, not actually committed to Arianism but willing to admit that the whole mysterious topic—the divine Sonship, that is—could stand a little talking over. Others of this group sympathized, instead, because—like the old man who converted the philosopher—they felt peace could have been maintained by *refusing* to talk the matter out, hoping that a house divided against itself might manage to stand after all, permanently half orthodox and half Arian. And some seem to have given the dissidents aid and comfort simply because the whole affair had been an ugly, embarrassing scene, because they were temperamentally disinclined to the taking of a strong hand in ecclesiastical matters, and because Arius's feelings appear to have been hurt.

Then there was a large, waffling middle: completely orthodox in their instincts, but still looking for that magic Bible verse, the one that would allow everyone to start miraculously getting along again. And the principal orthodox champions at the council were (along with Alexander and Athanasius, of course) Hosius of Cordova, Macarius of Jerusalem, Cæcilian of Carthage, Marcellus of Ancyra, and Eustathius of Antioch, heading up the strong bulk of Trinitarian traditionalists.

It was Athanasius's stratagem against the Nicomedian Eusebius that brought things to a head. Cornering him over Christ and the morning dew had caused the master maneuverer to stumble—as badly as Arius. "When they began to inquire into the nature of the faith," reports Eustathius, "the formulary of Eusebius was brought forward [a full summary of his position], which contained undisguised evidence of his blasphemy. The reading of it before all occasioned great grief to the audience, on account of its departure from the faith, while it inflicted irremediable shame on the writer."[84] The outcry was so great, in fact—even from those who had been among the waverers—that the paper containing the formulary had to be torn to pieces in front of them to restore order in the hall.

Eusebius Pamphilus now stepped in, casting himself as the head of the "peace party" at Nicaea. Hosius seems to have suggested earlier that some kind of doctrinal statement might be drawn up as a way to settle the issue. Eusebius picked this up and offered the Creed of Palestine he had grown up with at home, a teaching aid given to children and new believers.[LXX] Although it certainly would have brought peace—being very similar to the ancient "Apostle's Creed" used and accepted everywhere (and believed by many to have been composed by the Twelve themselves on the day of Pentecost[LXXI])—the bishop of Caesarea's suggestion had one major defect: his Palestinian creed would have left the entire matter exactly where it had been at the start of the Council. Though it called Christ "the Word of God . . . the only begotten Son . . . through whom all things were made" the Creed of Palestine contained exactly nothing that the Arians had not shown themselves perfectly capable of digesting. When they heard it, in fact, they saw a quick way out of the embarrassing box Arius and the Nicomedian had just built. "[They] were noticed making signs to one another to show that these declarations were equally applicable to us. For it is said, that we [humans, also] are 'the image and glory of God' [1 Cor. 11:7] . . . [and] the declaration that Christ is 'the true God' does not

---

[LXX] The Latin word *credo* ("I believe . . .") was usually the first word in such statements and has given rise to our English word "creed."

[LXXI] Ambrose and Rufinus, writing about A.D. 400, both credit the apostles with the composition of this earliest Christian creed, implying that the work was done in the Upper Room on the day of Pentecost. The Old Roman Creed—cited by Tertullian about A.D. 204 as something "received by tradition from Christ and the Apostles"—is practically identical minus a few small additions and may represent the Apostle's Creed in its original form. Augustine, Hilary of Poitiers, and Cyril of Jerusalem (fifth century) all record that candidates for baptism learned it by heart and they seem to connect it with Romans 6:17, wherein Paul gives thanks that "you who were once slaves of sin have become obedient from the heart to the standard of teaching to which you were committed." It was, at any rate, already venerable at the Council of Nicaea, whose final creed is an obvious elaboration upon it.

distress us, for, having come into being, He is true . . . Drawn aside by their own vile doctrine, [they] then began to say one to another, Let us agree, for we are also of God. . . ."[85]

"But the bishops saw through their evil design and impious artifice," according to Athanasius, "and gave a clearer elucidation of the words 'of God,' and wrote, that the Son is of the substance of God; in order that while the creatures, which do not in any way derive their existence of or from themselves, are said to be of God, the Son alone is said to be of the substance of the Father; this being peculiar to the only-begotten Son, the true Word of the Father. This is the reason why the bishops wrote, that He is of the substance of the Father."[86] This also the reason why the Council of Nicaea added to its Creed a word not found in Scripture; because the Arians forced them to it. That word was not "Trinity"—though that Latin term, of course, is what the biblical data ultimately signifies—but *homoousios,* a Greek word meaning "of the same substance." The eternal Son, begotten before all ages, is "of the same substance" as his Father.

Eusebius of Nicomedia hated this word above all others. He had announced, in fact, at the start of the council that he could in no wise accept *homoousios*—which is exactly why the council chose it here. It was deliberately picked as a way to force the Arians to deny their central tenets. The word, unfortunately, did have a bit of a checkered past, so Eusebius's compunctions about it had surface plausibility. What Athanasius and the others meant by *homoousios* was fairly simple; they used it to indicate that the Son is not foreign to his Father's nature as a created being would be—as the beaver is to his dam, and so forth. The Son is *one in being* with his Father. Alas, a previous revolutionary of the Ghetto era—one Paulus of Samosata—had once used the word in another, unnecessarily literal way. Paulus used *homoousios* to mean "made of the same stuff"—as if a part of God had broken off at Bethlehem and begun walking around on earth, while a correspondingly diminished Father, minus 25 percent or so of himself, watched approvingly from heaven. This use of *homoousios* had, indeed, already been condemned, several decades earlier, leaving Eusebius—with his trial lawyer's mentality—a perfect excuse for objecting to it here.

Some of the other objectors, however, had more honorable misgivings. The famous eighteenth-century historian Edward Gibbon, a noted deist and anti-Christian skeptic, asserts that the Council of Nicaea was sharply split over the divinity of Christ, and that the council fathers took a long time to decide the issue. In reality, the delay (which was only about four days, all told) was created solely by the large body of bishops who, despite their perfectly orthodox views, scrupled to use a word not found in the Bible. Nicaea really was, after all, a sort of "coming of age" for the Church—and like many adolescents, she hesitated to leave childhood behind. The Church really did have an old tradition of letting mysterious matters remain reverently mysterious—as evidenced by Antony's "illogical" list. It did discourage mere sophistry about the things of God, theological speculation as a parlor game for the pious on a dull winter's evening. And in the early decades, it did let Scripture work silently on the heart and the affections and not so much on the head. But when the Arians broke this peace, "insulting its silence, provoking it to argue, unsettling and seducing its members, and in consequence requiring its authoritative judgment on the point in dispute," the Church was, as Newman puts it, "obliged to change her course of acting . . . and unwillingly to take part in the theological discussions of the day, as a man crushes venomous creatures of necessity, powerful to do it, but loathing the employment. . . . The only alternative was an unmanly non-interference, and an arbitrary or treacherous prohibition of the discussion."[87]

Even so, approval for a new creed was, when it finally came, strictly limited; the new test would be imposed on the clergy only, on those acting as teachers of the Church and not on laypeople. This reflected the bishop's hope that those who continued in the simplicity of the early centuries—neither asking Arius's questions nor promoting his answers—might go on in that simplicity forever, in which the Bible is a "light and a lamp" rather than a sourcebook for theology.[LXXII]

The completed Nicene Creed,[LXXIII] a later recension of which is still used today in most of the world's Christian churches, was presented to the council on June 19, 325:

> We believe in one God, the Father almighty, maker of all things visible and invisible:—and in one Lord Jesus Christ, the Son of God, the only-begotten of the Father, that is of the substance of the Father; God of God and Light of light; true God of true God; begotten, not made, consubstantial [*homoousian*] with the Father: by whom all things were made, both which are in heaven and on earth: who for the sake of us men, and on account of our salvation, descended, became incarnate, and was made man; suffered, arose again the third day, and ascended into the heavens, and will come again to judge the living and the dead. [We] also [believe] in the Holy Spirit. But the holy Catholic and apostolic Church anathematizes those who say there was a time when he was not, and he was not before he was begotten and he was made from that which did not exist, and those who assert that he is of other substance or essence than the Father, or that he was created, or is susceptible of change.[88]

Dogmas Like Sausages

Homoousios, according to the bishops, expresses the true "signification of the [Bible] passages which have been quoted"—and

---

[LXXII] All the same, it is interesting to note that the old confessor himself—even while warning the delegates against "logical refinements" during the preliminary talks—had resorted to the use of an informal creed during his own outburst, perhaps composed by himself on the spot.

[LXXIII] This is the creed that was "substituted for the word of God" according to Rev. Tomlinson's Church of God of Prophecy; and yet every phrase of it is in full agreement with that church's own online doctrinal statement—which, incidentally, currently runs to twenty pages and includes sections on tobacco use and lodge membership!

they went on to note that "their murmuring, that the phrases are unscriptural, is exposed as vain by themselves, for they have uttered their impieties in unscriptural terms: (for such are 'of nothing' and 'there was a time when he was not'), while yet they find fault because they were condemned by unscriptural terms pious in meaning." The orthodox bishops, on the contrary, "not having invented their phrases for themselves, but having testimony from their Fathers, wrote as they did."[89] Here is express acknowledgment of Antony's ancient list, carried forward by him (and others, of course) out of the desert of early Christianity: *homoousios* is in accordance with "the testimony of their fathers." "Hear, O Israel: the Lord our God is one!" (Deut. 6:4)—and yet the Father and the Son are both true God, but the Son is not the Father and the Father is not the Son. The Nicene champions "did not find their expressions for themselves." They had not, in other words, taken it upon themselves to decide which doctrine was *true*, but merely which doctrine was *apostolic*—for Truth in the traditional scheme is not discovered but passed down, having been revealed by Christ to his apostles, and delivered intact by them to the Universal Church.

It is a very striking fact, actually, that the Council of Nicaea finished its work without making any attempt to explain the mystery that Arius had been trying to remove! How can there be a Three that is really One? Silence. To whom was the Son praying when he sweat blood in Gethsemane—to himself? No explanation. Those who have claimed that the Nicene Council substituted the Greek syllogisms of Plato and Plotinus for the simple gospel of Christ are just displaying their own ignorance of the subject, for Nicaea left the paradoxes of the divine Sonship as paradoxical as they found them. Forced to settle a dispute not of their own making, the bishops still left the word "Trinity" unused. They ruled out Arius's false answer but did not offer an explanation of their own. Despite every human urge to the contrary, they let the itch go entirely unscratched.

Constantine approached the matter in a very similar way. He "did not formulate the final creed, nor did he sign off on it—

being, again, an unbaptized nonbishop."[90] What the emperor was actually looking for was *the mind of the existing Church*, or, to put it more cynically, he was looking to determine which was the majority opinion. Eusebius Pamphilus suggests that it was Constantine himself who urged the bishops to go ahead with *homoousios*—but if this is true (none of the other ancient historians agree) it was surely not because he had any strong Christological opinions of his own, but because he quickly grasped that it would slam the door on a troublesome minority and thus get the whole commotion over with quickly. And, in fact, the *homoousios* did accomplish just that: "Finally all the priests agreed with one another and conceded that the Son is consubstantial with the Father. At the commencement of the conference there were but seventeen who praised the opinion of Arius, but eventually the majority of these yielded assent to the general view. To this judgment the emperor likewise deferred, for he regarded the unanimity of the conference to be a divine approbation."[91]

In a later postmortem on the council, Constantine makes the thought processes behind this deferral very clear indeed: "That which has commended itself to the judgment of 300 bishops cannot be other than the doctrine of God; seeing that the Holy Spirit dwelling in the minds of so many dignified persons has effectually enlightened them respecting the divine will . . . [Such a unanimously received doctrine] can only be *the* Faith."[92]

Of that original seventeen (or so), Eusebius and four others rejected the Nicene Creed. "'For,' said they, 'since that is consubstantial which is from another either by partition, derivation or germination' . . . they declared themselves unable to assent to this creed."[93] Here, the dissenters were insisting—at Eusebius of Nicomedia's recommendation, no doubt—on Paulus's narrow, materialistic definition for *homoousios,* even though the orthodox majority repeatedly condemned that usage and affirmed under oath that the false meaning Paulus had once put upon it was not their meaning. Eventually, however, as the final moments drew near, all but two of this remaining five gave way as well; a circumstance that Eustathius, the Eastern president, later explained pretty bluntly:

The Ariomaniacs, fearing lest they should be ejected from the
Church by so numerous a council of bishops, sprang forward
to anathematize and condemn the doctrines condemned . . .
[thus retaining] possession of their episcopal seats through the
most shameful deception, although they ought rather to have
been degraded. . . . So these men concealed their unsoundness through fear of the majority, and gave their assent to the
decisions of the council, thus drawing upon themselves the
condemnation of the prophet, for the God of all cries unto
them, "This people honor me with their lips, but in their
hearts they are far from me" [Isa. 29:13]. Theonas and Secundus, however, did not like to take this course, and were
excommunicated by common consent as men who esteemed
the Arian blasphemy above evangelical doctrine.[94]

Yes, Theonas and Secundus held out, but even Eusebius of
Nicomedia knuckled under—for the time being.

There is an old saying to the effect that "Religious dogmas are
like sausages; if you want to continue to enjoy them, you shouldn't
go and watch them being made." Matthew Tindal, for instance
(another famous English deist), said that if all the insults and libels
the delegates flung at each other had been preserved, few would
have any respect at all for the Grand Ecumenical Council of Nicaea.
And yet are the facts about it really so disedifying? Dan Brown's
Da Vinci Code claims that Christ's enthronement as the Son of God
was established there by "a relatively close vote." But in the end,
the Council of Nicaea excommunicated only Arius and his two
remaining adherents—about 1 percent of the delegates present. Everyone else willingly signed the Nicene Creed, the vast majority
having been willing to do so since day one. The emperor waited docilely in the wings, having not even a vote to himself. The
creed once signed (especially in its original form) added little to
the venerable old Apostle's Creed beyond the word consubstantial
(*homoousios*) and a few of its implications—the bare minimum of
what was necessary to address the Arian innovation. And far from
"substituting a creed for the Word of God," Constantine actually

ordered, around the time of the council, fifty new (and very expensive) Bibles to be made to replace some of the many that had been destroyed during the persecutions.LXXIV It may be, in fact, that the oldest intact Bible in the world today—the Codex Vaticanus—is one of these very fifty.

There is, however, one aspect of what happened at Nicaea that really was something new—and something rather portentous, as it turns out. The orthodox bishops merely *excommunicated* Arius and company; pronounced them cut off, that is, from communion with the Universal Church until such time as they became willing to repent and to submit to the authority of its traditions. The Arians were *turned out*, in other words, which is all that the Christian Church had ever done to heretics as of yet, and, in a sense, all that it ever would do to them in the future. It was Constantine, at this point, acting on his own initiative, who added something more.

The emperor had waited patiently to find out who was actually causing all the trouble, and while he waited he was perfectly willing to speak politely to everyone and to hear both sides of the story. But "when the decision was once announced, his tone altered, and what had been a recommendation of caution, at once became an injunction to conform. Opposition to the sentence of the Church was considered [by the emperor] as disobedience to the civil authority."[95] Constantine, in other words, had his own separate agenda at Nicaea and that agenda was, first and last, always and everywhere, *peace and domestic tranquility.* That peace he had already identified with an orderly and united Christian Church, and now that the

---

LXXIV Another of Dan Brown's absurdities is his claim that the Council of Nicaea created the Bible as we know it and then suppressed any early Christian book that did not meet the emperor's approval. In reality, Nicaea had nothing to do with the establishment of the biblical canon at all and the only books suppressed by Constantine were those written by Arius. The famous Muratorian Fragment—containing what appears to be the list of Christian scriptures employed at the Church of Rome around A.D. 170—shows that a New Testament canon identical to our own was already in use a full 150 years before Nicaea.

disturbers of the peace had been located, it was time for them to get with the program or suffer the consequences. So, the emperor

> punished Arius with exile, and dispatched edicts to the bish-
> ops and people of every country, denouncing him and his ad-
> herents as ungodly, and commanding that their books should
> be destroyed, in order that no remembrance of him or of
> the doctrine which he had broached might remain. Whoever
> should be found secreting his writings and who should not
> burn them immediately on the accusation, should undergo
> the penalty of death, and suffer capital punishment. [LXXV]
>
> The emperor wrote letters to every city against Arius
> and those who had received his doctrines, and commanded
> Eusebius and Theognis to quit the cities whereof they were
> bishops;[LXXVI] he addressed himself in particular to the church
> of Nicomedia, urging it to adhere to the faith which had been
> set forth by the council, to elect orthodox bishops, to obey
> them, and to let the past fall into oblivion; and he threatened
> with punishment those who should venture to speak well of
> the exiled bishops, or to adopt their sentiments.[96]

Sound theology was the clergy's business and Constantine was quite happy to leave that job to the professionals; but good

---

[LXXV] However threateningly worded, Constantine's decree here was, in fact, largely ceremonial. No executions were performed under this statute and—as we will see in the pages ahead—Arius's books were certainly not eradicated (though it is true that, like many more benign religious writings from the same period, no complete copy has survived). Suffice it to say for now, that many thousands of words from the Arian champions are preserved today as lengthy quotations in the writings of their orthodox opponents—proof, surely, that the decree cannot be taken quite at face value, since we know that Athanasius and company, at least, were allowed to retain copies for their research.

[LXXVI] Note that Eusebius was turned out of Nicomedia not for heresy but for refusing to approve the banishment of Arius—his lone holdout at the council.

order in the Roman Empire was his—and he meant to have it. And here, of course, is "Constantine's Sword"—the use of this-worldly punishments to address religious maladies—that has been so much objected to. This is also the limited sense in which the ancient churches can reasonably claim to be innocent of the charges of persecution or the burning of heretics so often hung around their necks: ever since Constantine, Church leaders have been called upon to *identify* offenders against religious order but have stepped aside to "let the law take its course" when it came to the punishment phase (which, in coarser times than ours, was often dreadful indeed). The broader charge—that Constantine's action offended the principle of separation of church and state—is based, once again, mainly upon anachronism. As historian Peter J. Leithart points out, "no one in the fourth century would have thought that a political regime could function without religious sanction, and it is naive to think that Constantine's conversion would have instantly turned him into James Madison."[97]

Still, this was definitely a watershed moment. Should the Church have objected to the civil punishments inflicted on Arius, Eusebius, and the rest? Or would that, too, have been an instance of Christians interfering with politics? Was this perhaps the time to rebel against the new Christian emperor—to take a stand against the dangerous precedent involved, even at the risk of reestablishing Arianism? Or worse—of possibly driving Constantine back to paganism? Perhaps it was . . . but it would have taken an extraordinarily farsighted churchman to think so. The issue, at any rate, was not raised at Nicaea.

For the moment, the bishops simply turned from the condemnation of Arius to a long list of other business at hand: secondary matters such as regularizing the dates for the annual Easter celebration and so forth. Despite a good deal of fog and fuddlement deliberately thrown up by Constantine-bashers in the years since, none of these other items was of any great long-term import. The council did not, for instance, establish Sunday worship for the first time (but merely ruled that the central Sunday prayers during communal worship should be said standing, rather than kneeling or sitting). Nor did Nicaea establish the celibacy of the clergy, the already-ancient mandate that men who have been ordained to the priesthood must not afterward take a wife;[LXXVII] the council simply passed a rule that clergymen must not have any woman living in their homes besides their own female relatives (probably this was a practical guard against the temptations presented by woman housekeepers, cooks, and so forth, living in the parsonage). The complete list of these (mostly obsolete) secondary rulings—twenty of them in all— still survives and can easily be accessed by the curious.

The First Ecumenical Council of Nicaea formally closed on July 25, 325 with a going-away party:

> At the very time that these decrees were passed by the council, the twentieth anniversary of the reign of Constantine was celebrated; for it was a Roman custom to have a feast on the

---

[LXXVII] Following the example of the apostle Paul, as well as his admonitions in 1 Corinthians 7—"It is well for a man not to touch a woman. . . . The unmarried man is anxious about the affairs of the Lord, how to please the Lord; but the married man is anxious about worldly affairs, how to please his wife, and his interests are divided" (1 Cor. 7:1, 32–34)—the early Church first recommended the celibacy of the clergy, then gradually legislated to that effect. Tertullian, Origen, and Clement all bear witness to the practice in the early to mid-200s; while Paphnutius, one of the confessor/bishops present at the council, explicitly calls it "the ancient tradition of the Church." It is important to note, however, that even now the Church does not consider a celibate clergy to be a matter of divine law; the ruling has been perpetuated by the bishops as an act of ecclesiastical discipline for the good of the Church's mission, not because there is anything intrinsically disordered about a married clergyman. This is well illustrated by the fact that the laws concerning celibacy differ slightly between the Eastern and Western Churches, yet both practices are legitimate with deep roots in Christian antiquity. The Eastern Churches currently allow for married deacons and priests, enjoining strict celibacy on bishops only; while the Western or Roman Churches allow married men (as a general rule) only to become deacons.

tenth year of every reign. The emperor, therefore, thought it to be opportune, and invited the synod to the festival, and presented suitable gifts to them, and when they prepared to return home, he called them all together, and exhorted them to be of one mind about the faith and at peace among themselves, so that no dissensions might henceforth creep in among them. After many other similar exhortations, he concluded by commanding them to be diligent in prayer, and always to supplicate God for himself, his children, and the empire, and after he had thus addressed those who had come to Nicaea, he bade them farewell.[98]

It was at this banquet that Constantine took Athanasius aside and personally complimented him for the unusual wisdom and courage he had displayed during the debates. Another contemporary described Athanasius as "foremost among those who were in attendance upon the bishops," having "done his utmost to stay the plague." Bishop Metrophanes of Byzantium had been so impressed that he pointed to the young archdeacon and cried out to Alexander, in the hearing of all: "There is your successor! Behold in Athanasius the noble champion of Christ." The defeated Arians, too, had noticed who turned the tide at Nicaea—and would not forget.

6

The Other Woman

"A double minded man is unstable in all his ways" (James 1:5–8 KJV).

Coptic dirges again in Roman Egypt—this time for Alexander, bishop of Alexandria, fading away on a cold, January evening in 326. Scarcely five months have passed since the close of the Nicene Council, and the old shepherd has laid down his crook, taken to his bed for the last time.[LXXVIII] Close around him are his sons in the Lord, all the clergy of the great city—all except for Athanasius who, for reasons that have been lost to memory, is away from Alexandria for the moment, probably on Church business. Happily, however, there *are* songs of the season to be sung this time as well; not yet Christmas carols, but *Epiphany* carols—songs in honor of that great midwinter feast commemorating the first revealing of Christ to the Gentiles, as personified by the Wise Men from the East.[LXXIX] This particular festival has exploded in popularity over the last few decades, now that the ancient Church—founded exclusively by Jews in Jerusalem—has

[LXXVIII] Though other writers suggest a later date, Athanasius himself tells us expressly that Alexander died within five months of the close of Nicaea—probably in January, though certainly not later than April 18, 326.

[LXXIX] Like *ad orientem* prayer, Epiphany originally had a connection to the rising sun; Syrian Christians of the second century called it *denho* (the up-going) and connected it with Zechariah's prophecy at the birth of John the Baptist: "And you, child . . . will go before the Lord to prepare his ways, to give knowledge of salvation to his people in the forgiveness of their sins . . . when the day shall dawn upon us from on high" (Luke 7:76a, 77–78). That Christmas itself was still practically unknown can be deduced by its absence on the preserved listings of early Christian feasts, such as those of Irenaeus, Tertullian, Epiphanius, and Clement of Alexandria (all of which include Epiphany).

become the veritable home of humanity. The Great Unwashed have now become the bulk of the Body of Christ; and that Body finds, apparently, new and special meaning while contemplating the thought of Mary, babe in arms, taking it boldly upon herself to offer Israel's Messiah for the worship of the *goyim*—men with alien, non-Jewish faces, pagans, in fact, and adherents of a strange alien religion (probably Zoroastrians, as many of the Roman Christians had formerly been). New hymns have been written in response to this image, such as this one by Ephraim of Syria, quite possibly sung in Alexander's death chamber, perhaps by one or two of Antony's deep-voiced young monks, as a way to strengthen the bishop for his journey:

> In the birth of the Son light dawned—and darkness fled from the world—and the earth was enlightened; then let it give glory— to the brightness of the Father who has enlightened it!
>
> He dawned from the womb of the virgin—and the shadows passed away when He was seen—and the darkness of error was strangled by him—and the ends of the earth were enlightened that they should give glory.

Yes, the feast of the Magi, who had brought gold, frankincense, and myrrh! Frankincense is probably burned here for Alexander as well, a foretaste of the incense of heaven so close at hand, offered by the angels "with the prayers of all saints upon the golden altar which is before the throne" (Rev. 8:3).

> Mary said, For whom are these?—and for what purpose? And what is the cause—that has called you to come from your country—to the child with your treasures?
>
> They said, Your son is a king,—and he binds crowns and is king of all—and great is his power over the world—and to his kingdom shall all be obedient.
>
> The child is a little one, [said Mary] and lo! He has not—the diadem of a king and of a throne—and what have you seen that you should pay honor to him—as to a king, with your treasures?

A little one, because he willed it for quietness's sake—and meek now until he be revealed—a time shall be for him when all diadems—shall bow down and worship him.

The child is a babe, and how is it possible—he should be king, unknown to the world?—and they that are mighty and of renown—how can a babe be their ruler?

Your babe is aged, O virgin—and Ancient of Days and exalted above all and Adam beside him is very babe—and in him all created things are made new . . .

The ordinary people of Alexandria keep vigil for Alexander as well, gathered around the bishop's residence to hurry his soul to God on their prayers. As darkness comes, a thousand little lamps are lit, a thousand voices joined to the hymnody.

The world on high and the world below bear witness to him—all the watchers and the stars—that he is Son of God and Lord—bear his fame to your lands!

Let the Church sing with rejoicing—Glory in the birth of the highest,—by whom the world above and the world below are illumined!—Blessed be he in whose birth all are made glad![99]

Trembling, failing, his breath coming in short, weak pants, Alexander's eyes grow suddenly bright again somehow, just before the end. For one brief moment, he looks out into space, as if experiencing a vision, an epiphany of his own. He calls out for the absent Athanasius. By chance, another man of that same name is standing nearby and he answers—but Alexander called for his archdeacon, for him who had singled himself out so dramatically at Nicaea in the presence of now seething, now stifled enemies. Alexander cries out again, before realizing finally that the dark little man is not there, that he will, in fact, never see Athanasius again on earth. Settling back with a sigh, the bishop whispers a word of prophecy overheard by his clergy, a report preserved later in Athanasius' own *Apology Against*

Arians: "Athanasius, you think to escape—but it cannot be."[100]
And within a few moments, Alexander of Alexandria is dead.

Alexandria was probably the most important bishopric in
the world in 326, since the episcopal chair of Rome—whose
occupant was undoubtedly due, at the very least, a primacy of
honor, being the successor of Peter—was surrounded by a city
in steep decline, with scarcely a fifth the number of Christians
over which to preside. As the Roman Empire had continued to
be engulfed by wave after wave of barbarian influx from outside
her borders, the state of civilization had fallen much farther in
the West than in the more prosperous East, and her legendary
capital in Italy was already well on its way to becoming the
world's most famous ghost town. Here in Egypt, however, the
patriarch of Alexandria—successor to the chair first founded by
the Gospel writer Mark—acted as archbishop to over a hundred
other prelates in thriving cities all across North Africa, from
Libya to Acadia. Perhaps ironically, these bishops even called
him *papas* or "pope," since this familiar term of endearment
(meaning "dear father") was still used for all the important patriarchs, and not yet narrowed down as it now is in Western
usage to refer to the bishop of Rome only.

In any case, it was this powerful seat that was left vacant by
Alexander's departure—which is what makes it so remarkable
that the office was immediately offered to Athanasius, just now
entering his third decade of life. Dozens of much more senior
clergy were thus skipped over, including many who had sympathized with their now-exiled colleague Arius. Explanation?
Those ordinary people we mentioned seem to have demanded
it. Gathering not only at the cathedral church[LXXX] itself but also
in parishes throughout the diocese, the laity made their wishes
known. Rather than a man with more traditional credentials
(some of whom seem already to have succumbed, once more,
to their Ghetto-era addictions to ease and affluence), the laity

---

[LXXX] A cathedral is a church building in which a Christian bishop has his
official seat, the principal church of a diocese; *cathedra* is Latin for "chair."

of Alexandria called for "the pious, the devout, the true Christian, the ascetic!"—for Athanasius, who would prove, as they believed, "a genuine shepherd" and not just a religious CEO. So Athanasius—still too young even to have cast a vote at the late council he so profoundly influenced—was made "pope" of Alexandria, elected bishop of the most influential see in Christendom, probably on June 8, 326, "and promptly became the principal target of the Arian plots and schemes."[101]

TORN BETWEEN TWO LOVERS

Believe it or not, within a year of Athanasius's election Constantine signed an order recalling Arius and allowing him to continue preaching in the empire. This is perhaps the single most puzzling fact in our whole story, and possibly key to the whole mystery of Constantine's character. Why on earth would he have done such a thing? Dozens of explanations have been offered through the years, hardly any of them at all convincing. Here was a man who, immediately after the council, wrote letters referring to Arius as a "shameless blasphemer . . . an irreverent servant of the devil . . . an enemy of the truth" and perhaps most tellingly, "the sole disseminator of this mischief." In the same correspondence, the emperor sided so thoroughly with the orthodox majority that he called them "my beloved brethren" and expressed the naive opinion that together they had settled the issue so well "that nothing might be henceforth left for dissension or controversy in matters of faith." Yet here, scarcely a year and a half later, he has experienced such a change of heart that he gives his formal permission for the servant of the devil to go back to work.

If Constantine's career had happened in more recent times, we might almost guess that someone had "gotten to" the emperor, in perhaps the same way that Lyndon Johnson persuaded reluctant Southern congressmen to see the light on the Civil Rights Act by presenting them with certain photographs furnished to the president by the small army of detectives he employed. Being an absolute monarch, however, our fourth-century emperor would have been immune to such pressures, not least because imperial amours were such an old, tiresome story by this point. Even so, we might do well to imagine that a woman *was* involved in Constantine's vacillations (which were destined to continue, by the way, for the rest of his life); not so much a literal woman (though the emperor's half-sister does factor in somewhat), but a metaphorical temptress whose hectoring and seductions could go a long way toward clarifying this traditionally obscure matter.

Was Constantine simply a cynical hypocrite all along—the jaundiced conclusion to which so many of his sanctimonious critics have so quickly leapt? That hypothesis clarifies the problem not at all. If that were the case, why not simply establish Arianism by imperial fiat—or at least begin sponsoring the Arian cause immediately? Eusebius of Nicomedia had seen the advantages right away; why not Constantine? That sort of pressure might easily have turned Nicaea's seventeen into a much more sizable minority, perhaps even have won over the "peace party" completely.[LXXXI] No, there is simply too much evidence to show that Constantine had already managed to turn himself into some sort of confused, conflicted, but nevertheless sincere Christian. Peter J. Leithart collected some of these proofs in his book *Defending Constantine*: "In a 314 letter summoning bishops to Arles, he repeatedly referred to 'Christ our Savior' and warned that the 'mercy of Christ' has departed from the hardened Donatists. He expressed surprise that the Donatists had appealed to him in this case, since he himself was under judgment, awaiting the 'judgment of Christ.'" When an expedition to the Holy Land (sponsored by the emperor) returned with what were believed to be actual relics of Christ's saving death (including the nails that pierced his hands and portions of the true cross), "Constantine breathlessly wrote to Macarius about the 'Savior's grace' in giving this 'monument of his most holy Passion.'"

[LXXXI] As we will see, the evidence of later events bears this out absolutely.

And Caesar not only talked the talk, he walked the walk as well. "Eusebius [Pamphilus] recorded that Constantine preached so often in his palace that he virtually turned it into a temple, though he added that the members of the court found the emperor's preaching wearisome." He began to discourage the bloody spectacles of the arena (outlawing death by lions immediately) and threatened those who hastened the demise of their own elderly parents for financial reasons with the prospect of being sewn into a sack full of snakes and tossed into the sea! "Constantine denounced divorce 'for trivial reasons' . . . and also appears to have been the first to legislate against rape . . . [He] promised imperial aid to parents to prevent them selling their children into slavery" and encouraged emancipation of slaves as "a godly work." Constantine was also "a great builder of churches . . . [who] studded Rome with churches and baptisteries."[102]

What, then, should we make of the evidences to the contrary—his hesitancy to accept baptism, for instance, and the "incomplete conversion" suggested by the pagan survivals in some of his laws and personal practices? The delayed baptism, at least, is easily explained: this was actually a pretty widespread minor abuse in the fourth-century Church, indulged in by much more obviously Christian men than the emperor. It arose, at least partially, out of an exaggerated show of reverence for the sacred ordinance, somewhat like the desire in many modern Christian groups to hold Communion very infrequently, lest it be taken for granted. Beyond this, however, we will have to concede that Constantine—official chief of all Roman pagans—had not, in fact, managed to go from zero to sixty in the few short years since Milvian Bridge. As exampled by the sack of snakes mentioned above, the emperor's ideas of crime and punishment remained largely those of a hot-blooded heathen. Such cruelty toward human malefactors often runs side by side in pagans with a sentimental tenderness toward dogs and other animals, and this was the case with Constantine as well. Government officials caught with their hands in the till were sentenced to have both of them chopped off, and tax cheats the emperor threatened with "exquisite tortures"; yet in 316, Constantine went far out of his way to promote a new law forbidding clubs to be used on beasts of burden, decreeing instead that drivers should "employ either a switch or at the most a whip . . . by which the lazy limbs of animals may be gently tickled into action." Probably the most grotesque example of Constantine's lingering heathen outlook also involves a trusted animal: just prior to one of his last battles against a Christian-hating rival emperor, he actually took one of the Crucifixion nails recovered at Jerusalem and superstitiously fashioned it into a bit for his war horse![103]

Nevertheless, the common charges of "syncretism" in the emperor's policy are crudely off the mark. Like the Proto-Christians he championed (and was probably strongly influenced by), Constantine loved his fellow Romans and hoped to "lead them onto the straight path."[LXXXII] He did, indeed, try to slowly shepherd them first into simple monotheism by encouraging existing monotheistic trends in the culture (such as the *Sol Invictus* movement)—allowing the pagans some time, as he had had time, to pass from complete paganism to an ultimate belief in the one God revealed in the Bible. He did not instantly declare a pointless war on traditional Roman folkways, customs for which he himself probably retained nostalgic and patriotic feelings; no, the task at hand was to let the Faith change everything Roman—without simply trampling everything Roman. Constantine grasped this task only dimly at first, perhaps dimly throughout his lifetime, but he went at it instinctively. He composed neutral monotheistic prayers, for example, suitable to both groups—prayers that he and his old army comrades, perhaps, could recite together at official events, even as the emperor himself was hoping for a more complete unity to come. Constantine also allowed an ambiguous sun motif to be imprinted on coins and other government symbols; a motif that could, in fact, bear (in the light of Malachi's "sun of righteousness" prophecy) both

LXXXII These are Constantine's own words as included in the original Edict of Milan.

a Christian and a heathen reading. Yet isn't it true that Constantine was thinking, as G.K. Chesterton once put it, "rather more of saving his empire than saving his soul"? Hadn't he decided (as we imagined Eusebius guessing) to jump on the bandwagon where Christianity was concerned—to salvage Rome's fading fortunes by contracting, as it were, a marriage of convenience with the Bride of Christ?

Here, possibly, is where the image of marital relations becomes really helpful—of those faithful and chaste, and also the temptation to those of a different kind. Imagine, for instance, a man who falls genuinely in love with a good-hearted, beautiful, and very rich woman. Exactly what role will her wealth play—in his own mind and in the suspicions of others—as he decides whether or not to take her as his wife? Does he himself even know? Or will he not always be accused of mercenary motives, not only by unsympathetic outsiders but even, at times, by his own uncertain conscience? Constantine's situation was very much like this. Yes, he found the Christian Church to be uniquely useful toward achieving his goals, as the leaven of Christianity will always be useful to the health of a society. Does that prove that this was his only—or even his primary—reason for getting involved with her? How could we ever know, if even the emperor himself might not have been entirely sure?

Yet Constantine quickly discovered something else about his new Bride: she was no pushover. The emperor may well have expected, as many young husbands expect, to wear the pants in his new family—but once the honeymoon was over, he found that he'd actually married a strong, willful woman, not easily bossed.

This may not have been his only disappointment at Nicaea; he may well have had the last of his "new convert's zeal" kicked out of him there as well. Yes, he accepted the fact that the council had ruled out Arius's false understanding of the nature of Christ; but what was the true understanding? Likely he gathered up analogies, as many Christians do, in an effort to understand the mysterious subject—only to be told by his contentious Bride that all of them were wrong.

Was the Trinity (as the Godhead was now beginning to be called) like *water*, which remains the same substance even though it can appear as a liquid, a solid, and a gas? No, this was rank modalism, blurring the individual reality of the three divine Persons, since water cannot exist in all three forms at once. Perhaps a *shamrock* is a better image, then; three distinct and equal parts, yet only one leaf.[LXXXIII] No, this was the error of Paulus—a God who has three detachable "pieces," a dalliance with tritheism. All right, how about comparing God to a family man; one individual human being, yet a father to his children, a son to his own father, and a husband to his wife? Alas, the emperor was told, this represents another descent into modalism, "God's three hats" again. Constantine had never imagined that such subtle, maddening differences in theology could exist. He'd been drawn to the Church for her grandeur, unity, and common sense (certainly as compared with the tangled pantheons of paganism). He'd joined her ranks as a recruit joins a noble cause, and his sponsoring of her interests had been equally straightforward, the act of a soldier.

At Nicaea, however, he'd seen (an overreaction, to be sure) nearly as much pedantry, pomposity, and lawyerly logic as at any other confab of politicos—and over an issue impossible to understand, apparently, no matter how hard one tried. The sad discovery that the Church does have a merely human and political side—that it is not, in fact, heaven on earth as it may have first appeared—has thrown more than one convert into disillusionment and letdown. And Constantine was not the first, either, to have

---

[LXXXIII] Though many of us have heard this analogy attributed to St. Patrick of Ireland (fifth century), there is no real evidence that he actually employed it. The story does not appear in writing until 1726, when English botanist Caleb Threlkeld uses it to explain the Irish custom of wearing shamrocks on St. Patrick's Day—adding an insulting anti-Catholic remark to boot. Still, it might be best to describe this old simile as defective, rather than actually heretical; like all analogies, it breaks down if carried too far.

his mind boggled by the deeper things of God. But these discoveries must, surely, have taken a lot of the wind out of his sails as he thought about moving forward with his new "marriage."

And now the temptations could set in—the lure of "the other woman." Once Constantine found that he had married himself to a difficult, even bossy woman, the appeal of Arianism—of shooting for the moon with Eusebius—must have become palpable. This beckoning partner was pliant, easy, and all too ready to offer her services on Constantine's terms. She had almost everything, in fact, the emperor wanted from his lawful wife but without all the damn silly hoops to jump through. And in his darker, more discouraged moments, the thought of using Arianism in this way—the way that a discouraged, unhappy husband has all too often used an easy woman—must have hissed in his heart like a poisonous snake. The record shows that he put the temptation down—manfully, as a Christian would. But he did it repeatedly, over and over in the years ahead, and not always with complete success.

It is important to consider the chronology involved as well: Arius's rehabilitation came right in the middle of the most trying, the most stressful, and (ultimately, as we shall see) the darkest part of Constantine's life. First of all, he turned immediately from the council to the planning of one of the most gigantic and audacious projects of all antiquity—the moving of his empire's capital city from ancient Rome on the Tiber to a completely new city in the East. Old Rome was growing "weeded and stagnant." Her municipal economy had well-nigh collapsed and her thinly populated streets were stained, in Constantine's mind, by centuries of dark deeds, committed in the name of false gods. The imperial government needed a fresh start. So this one man, who had already changed the unchangeable religion of Rome, now proposed to move Rome itself!—and, as one might imagine, the effort was stupendous. The task required his full attention and he took a "hands-on" approach. He reviewed plans and models late into the night, worked with surveyors, got his feet muddy on construction sites. And though it was never called

Constantinople during the emperor's lifetime (he christened it "New Rome" and it continued to be called that for many years), Constantine's fresh start on the Bosphorus fully merited that name in every respect.[LXXXIV]

Secondly, domestic troubles erupted during this same period in Constantine's own palace. His wife, Fausta, suddenly claimed to have been raped by the emperor's grown son (and her own stepson) Crispus. Not only would this have been emotionally troubling to Constantine, but it also put him under pressure to act, since his own laws now called for the death penalty on Crispus. In the end, he decided to exile him instead to the remote island of Pola where, not long afterward, the young man was found dead of poisoning. Though the most likely explanation was suicide, Caesar's still-pagan enemies (along with not a few modern critics) instantly accused him of ordering his son's death; indeed, of having engineered the whole affair in order to remove a potential rival to the imperial throne.

This is the point at which the Empress Constantia comes into the story. She was Caesar's sibling by way of his father's second wife, also living at the palace in Nicomedia. She was also the widow of Licinius, the last holdout amongst Constantine's four original rivals; a man who had gone to war against the emperor, been defeated by him and then forgiven, but executed after all when he used this forgiveness as a smokescreen for additional intrigues. And Constantia had taken her husband's side against Constantine. She was not only a close friend of Eusebius of Nicomedia then, she was most likely sore, as well, over the loss of her late husband on Constantine's orders. Eusebius would have known this very well—and perceived an opportunity.

[LXXXIV] "Constantine's new capital, Constantinople, constructed on the site of the old Greek city of Byzantium in what is now Turkey, was intended as a replica of Rome, even to the seven hills . . . many of its buildings were exact reproductions of Roman originals. There, the Roman emperors continued to rule for another 1,100 years, long after the Western Roman Empire was lost to barbarians." Broughton, *Imperial Rome*, 146.

"This princess," according to Socrates, "maintained in her household establishment a certain confidential presbyter, tinctured with the dogmas of Arianism; Eusebius and others having prompted him, [this Arian priest] took occasion in his familiar conversations with Constantia, to insinuate that the Synod had done Arius injustice, and that the common report concerning him was not true." Not only had the slippery Eusebius quickly finagled his own return to the see of Nicomedia (after having been briefly exiled for withholding his consent to the banishment of Arius), he was now pulling strings in the emperor's own household, whispering in the ear of the empress:

> [Later, this Arian] presbyter became one of the most confidential persons about the emperor; and having gradually increased in freedom of speech, he repeated to the emperor what he had before stated to his sister, affirming that Arius had no other views than the sentiments avowed by the synod; and that if he were admitted to the imperial presence, he would give his full assent to what the synod had decreed: he added, moreover, that he had been unreasonably slandered. The presbyter's words appeared strange to the emperor, and he said, "If Arius subscribes with the synod and holds its views, I will both give him an audience, and send him back to Alexandria with honor."

As can be imagined, Eusebius jumped into this opening with both feet. He and Arius quickly cribbed together a creed of their own, meant to resemble the Nicene closely—but minus (at least in its surviving form) the critical word *homoousios*. To this document, the two affixed their signatures with pleasure, adding an oath for emphasis: "If we do not so believe and truly receive the Father, the Son, and the Holy Spirit, as the whole Catholic Church and the holy scriptures teach (in which we believe in every respect), God is our judge both now, and in the coming judgment."[104]

It is difficult to believe that Constantine could have been deceived by so simple a scheme as this. There *are* existing records, however, that claim that some of the Arian seventeen at Nicaea had surreptitiously added an extra iota to the benchmark word in order to slip past the test: with the extra character *homoousios* becomes *homoiousios*, meaning "of like substance" rather than "of the same substance," something the Arians could live with. Is it possible that Eusebius took advantage of the emperor's defective Greek to deceive him here with the same trick? It may very well be, though we will probably never know for sure. Possibly Constantine had simply grown careless through despondency and consternation, and rubber-stamped Arius's phony creed in a moment of vexation with the Church, or simply of despair. At any rate, the order was given—and the work of Nicaea largely undone.

Within a few months of his election as bishop, Athanasius received word that his colleague Eustathius, lately the Eastern president at Nicaea, had been brought down by the Eusebians (as partisans of the Nicomedian were now commonly known). "It was most generally believed that he was deposed merely on account of his adherence to the faith of the council of Nicaea, and on account of his having accused Eusebius, Paulinus, bishop of Tyre, and Patrophilus, bishop of Scythopolis . . . of [continuing to favor] the heresy of Arius. The pretext resorted to for his deposition, however, was, that he had defiled the priesthood by unholy deeds." The ordinary Christians of Antioch knew Eustathius better and realized right away that the trumped-up charges were false. "His deposition excited so great a sedition at Antioch, that the people were on the point of taking up arms, and the whole city was in a state of commotion. This greatly injured [Eustathius] in the opinion of the emperor; for when he understood what had happened, and that the people of that church were divided into two parties, he was much enraged, and regarded him with suspicion as the author of the tumult. The emperor, however, sent an illustrious officer of his palace, invested with full authority, to calm the populace, and put an end to the disturbance, without having recourse to violence or injury"[105]—but also, we must add, without restoring Eustathius to his bishopric. Disturbing the peace had always been a fast way to get on the emperor's bad side, and even more so now that he was tired and distracted. Constantine nominated another man to replace him.

Emboldened by success, the Eusebians now turned their sights directly upon Athanasius, "being instigated to this by two causes—on the one hand the Arian heresy with which they had been previously infected, and bitter animosity against Athanasius on the other, because he had so vigorously withstood them in the synod while the articles of faith were under discussion."[106] He was "small in stature, and young in years . . . the head of a singularly united body of nearly a hundred bishops, and his energy and vivacity, his courage and determination marked him out as the one foe the Eusebians had to dread."[107] Eusebius wrote to Athanasius, seeking to have Arius and his followers re-admitted to the Church. Constantine could recall Arius from exile, to be sure—but he had not yet persuaded the bishop of Alexandria to allow him back into Roman Egypt. "And as Athanasius would by no means accede to this, [Eusebius] endeavored to induce the emperor to give Arius an audience, and then permit him to return to Alexandria."[108]

It seems to have been right about this time that the other shoe dropped in the matter of Crispus and Fausta. Palace insiders had their own account of what had happened between the two: there'd been no rape at all, according to them, but rather a consensual love affair—initiated by the empress. And not long after this version got back to Constantine, Fausta herself was dead; stifled to death in an overheated steam bath. Once again, his detractors leapt quickly to the assumption (as they still do) that the emperor had his wife killed, which, incidentally, he would have been perfectly within his rights to do, according to the old pagan ways. More patient critics have suggested what seems a likelier scenario: that the rape charge was a cover story for an inconvenient pregnancy and that Fausta, after the unexpected death of her lover, tried to abort his child by means of the steam bath (a common expedient in those days), inadvertently killing herself in the process (also not uncommon). The actual truth may never be known. Perhaps Constantine did, in his anger and humiliation, backslide during a moment of weakness, either demanding the abortion or even insisting on his old pagan rights over life and death. At any rate, the horrific situation cannot have left him much leisure to consider the most recent Arian flare-up with any care or equanimity.

Due, at least in part, to the emperor's inattention, "the dispute concerning the doctrines of Arius was rekindled once more in other cities, and particularly in Bithynia and Hellespontus, and in the city of Constantinople. In short, it is said that Eusebius, bishop of Nicomedia, and Theognis, bishop of Nicaea"—whose exile, by the way, Eusebius had papered over by means of another tricky recantation, leaving Secundus the sole remaining Nicene heretic—

> bribed the notary to whom the emperor had entrusted the custody of the documents of the Nicaean Council, effaced their signatures, and attempted openly to teach that the Son is not to be considered consubstantial with the Father. [When] Eusebius was accused of these irregularities before the emperor, and he replied with great boldness [by showing] part of his clothing. If this robe, said he, had been cut asunder in my presence, I could not affirm the fragments to be all of the same substance. The emperor was much grieved at these disputes, for he had believed that questions of this nature had been finally decided by the council of Nicaea, but contrary to his hopes he saw them again agitated.

The two Arian bishops went on to accuse Athanasius, "of being the author of all the seditions and troubles that agitated the Church, [by] excluding those who were desirous of joining the Church; and alleged that unanimity would be restored were he alone to be removed. The accusations against him were substantiated by many bishops and clergy . . . imputing to Athanasius and the bishops of his party all the bloodshed, bonds, unjust blows, wounds, and conflagrations of churches." Informed of this, Athanasius wrote patiently back to the emperor refuting the charges. When he carefully "demonstrated . . . their innovations of the decrees of the Nicaean Council, and the unsoundness of their faith, and the insults offered to those who held right opinions about God, Constantine was at a loss to know whom to believe."

Here, the emperor's mental exhaustion on the subject becomes apparent; he simply throws up his hands in exasperation. "Since there were such mutual allegations, and many accusations were frequently stirred up by each party, and since he was earnestly anxious to restore the like-mindedness of the people, [the emperor] wrote to Athanasius that no one should be shut out." Frustrated as a lion in a cage, Constantine abandons, for the moment, his own principle of peace through unity and simply falls back into pagan indifferentism: okay, let 'em all in, then, and let God sort it out. Does this mean he was in serious doubt all of a sudden about which side was in the right? That he'd forgotten the 316–2 vote at Nicaea? Probably not. This was a feeling, not a thought. He just wanted to hit back a little at this thing that had cost him so many sleepless nights, whose doctrines were making his head hurt, that left him pining almost for the simpler days of Nero or Claudius. So in his letter to Athanasius, Constantine finally does for the first time what he had not done at Nicaea but is so often accused of doing—he interferes in Church matters directly: "You are now acquainted with my will, which is, that to all who desire to enter the Church you should offer an unhindered entrance. For should I hear that any who are willing to join the Church, have been debarred or hindered therefrom by you, I shall send at once an officer who shall remove you, according to my command, and shall transfer you to some other place."[109]

Persistent as Potiphar's wife, the "other woman" now has Constantine firmly by the cloak—and from now on Athanasius and company will have to deal with an emperor whose attitude toward Christianity will depend greatly upon which type of Christian happens to have his ear at the moment.[LXXXV]

[LXXXV] "The fickle Constantine banished Arius and recalled him, silenced Alexander, then gave him a hearing, expelled Athanasius and restored him, sat in silence and awe before the assembled Fathers at Nice, and yet [later, took spiritual guidance] from Eusebius, whose faith was as uncertain as his conduct was blame-worthy." P.J. Harrold, "The Alleged Fall of Pope Liberius," *American Catholic Quarterly Review*, vol. 8, 1883, 529–49.

BLAST FROM THE PAST

Antony of the Desert got very few letters—not because he had no friends or wasn't well worth writing to, but simply because (as we mentioned earlier) he couldn't read. He did have plenty of helpers, though, and several of them could; and these did occasionally bring the old man a dispatch or two, while he was digging the turnips in the community patch or some such, and read them aloud to Antony on the spot, sometimes translating into Coptic on the fly if the originals happened to be in Greek or Latin or some other high-toned foreign tongue. Actually, there had been several from the emperor in recent years, who knew all about the monks of the desert and seemed to be interested in gaining their friendship.[LXXXVI] The younger boys (and most of the monks were younger, since their father in the Lord was now over eighty) seemed much more impressed by these than Antony was.

One particular letter from Constantine did finally prick up his ears, however: apparently the emperor had heard some of his Arianizing sycophants imply that Antony himself thought as they did concerning the Father and the Son. To this libelous rumor, the tough, goatlike old saint replied right away: "[He had always] detested the heresy of the Arians, and exhorted all not to approach them, nor hold their misbelief. In fact, when certain of the Ariomanites came to him, having discerned them and found them impious, he chased them out of the mountain, saying that their words were worse than serpent's poison."[110] What, then, *was* Antony's doctrine concerning the divine substance? Illiterate as he was, he had written it for all to see—on the heart of his son Athanasius.

One day a letter arrived from Athanasius, bearing the impossible return address of Treves in the Far West (what is today the city of Trier in the thickly wooded Rhineland portion of Germany). The foremost bishop of Egypt, 2,700 miles from home,

---

[LXXXVI] "His fame was so widely spread throughout the deserts of Egypt, that the emperor Constantine, for the reputation of the man's virtue, sought his friendship, honored him with correspondence, and urged him to write about what he might need." Sozomen, *Ecclesiastical History,* I:13.

was now living, apparently, at the castle of Constantine II, the emperor's eldest son (now that Crispus was gone) and imperial commander of Gaul. The story of how Athanasius got there— and why—made for interesting reading indeed.

The emperor had backed down, it seems, almost right away, from his order to admit Arius or face banishment. Athanasius had asked him, rather simply, how the same Church can possibly worship two different Christs, and Constantine saw his point. The Eusebians, however, had seen their moment. They immediately assembled a wild potpourri of discordant accusations and flung it at Constantine's wall, hoping something would stick: Athanasius had given a purse of gold to a rebel named Philomenus; he had stopped grain shipments to the capital in hopes of putting pressure on the emperor; one of his presbyters had smashed a holy Communion vessel while suppressing a tiny, schismatic cult. All of these largely unsupported charges had been easy to refute.

Yet just when Constantine was about to dismiss the whole transparent business for good, the Eusebians saved their cause by striking at his superstitious side, at his lingering pagan credulity. Someone produced a repellent black talisman—the withered hand of an Egyptian mummy—and told the emperor that it was the dried hand of a murdered man, a minor Arianizing bishop named Arsenius. Athanasius had killed him (or so the horror story went) and dismembered the corpse in order to create a "Hand of Glory"—one of the weird, magical artifacts commonly used by practitioners of the Dark Arts. Since such charms were believed to have played a role in the overthrow of rulers in the past, the yarn was just absurd enough to give the emperor pause. Evidence to the contrary could do little to assuage irrational fears of this type: a letter even appeared, purporting to be from Arsenius, insisting that the rumors of his death had been exaggerated and that he was, rather, doing fine and living in an isolated monastery on the eastern bank of the Nile. While this did calm things down for a while, officers sent to find Arsenius had trouble verifying the story, raising suspicions that the letter had been forged. The emperor finally ordered a synod to be held at Tyre in Lebanon for the purposes of sorting the whole matter out and reviewing Athanasius's leadership generally.

Athanasius refused to attend at first; in fact, he resisted the emperor's calls for thirty whole months—more than two-and-a-half years. He did this not so much out of fear for his own freedom or safety, but because he worried that the opening of another council would become an excuse to revisit the decisions of Nicaea, under much more unstable conditions. When he could resist no longer, Athanasius rode to Lebanon accompanied by fifty of his brother clergy, ready to defend his episcopacy and refute all slanders. Yet when they reached Tyre it became obvious that Athanasius was to be treated there as a prisoner in the dock. He was shocked to discover that the so-called synod amounted to little more than a courtroom, and that the court was heavily packed with Arians.

Yet just before the matter of Arsenius's hand was to have been tried, Athanasius was contacted privately by Archelaus, governor of the district. His servants, it seems, had overhead some talk at an inn to the effect that Arsenius, supposedly murdered by the bishop of Alexandria, was not only alive and well, but was actually present in Tyre, concealed in the house of one of its citizens! Archelaus had him searched out and apprehended. The weak-kneed fellow confessed right away: he'd been contacted by Eusebians not long after writing his original letter and bribed to disappear for a while. He had, however, been unable to resist the spectacle of Athanasius's trial, so he snuck into Tyre in a disguise, hoping to secure a seat in the public galleries. The governor, at any rate, had Arsenius safely in hand and was ready to produce him at any time.

Athanasius considered this a special providence of God and, obviously, went back into the courtroom in a much more cheerful frame of mind.

As soon as he presented himself, his traducers exhibited the hand, and pressed their charge. He managed the affair with great prudence, for he enquired of those present, as well as of his accusers, who were the persons who knew Arsenius? And several having answered that they knew him, he caused Arsenius to be introduced, having his hands covered by his cloak. Then he again asked them, "Is this the person who has lost a hand?" All were astonished at the unexpectedness of this procedure, except those who knew whence the hand had been cut off; for the rest thought that Arsenius was really deficient of a hand, and expected that the accused would make his defense in some other way. But Athanasius turning back the cloak of Arsenius on one side showed one of the man's hands; again, while some were supposing that the other hand was wanting, permitting them to remain a short time in doubt afterward he turned back the cloak on the other side and exposed the other hand. Then addressing himself to those present, he said, "Arsenius, as you see, is found to have two hands: let my accusers show the place whence the third was cut off."[111]

Unfortunately, the letter to Antony did not have the happy ending one might expect after such a stunning vindication; Athanasius had been exiled anyway, not long after the trial. Though the exposure of Arsenius allowed him to walk free from Tyre, the council continued to sit without Athanasius and right away set about drumming up some additional dirt. He decided to sail directly to the new palace at Constantinople and demand an audience with the emperor. Under the shelter of Constantine's reckless rehabilitation of their progenitor, Arians were apparently proliferating like mushrooms now. Athanasius had found them large and in charge at Tyre, where, due to the misguided tolerance of the regional patriarch Eusebius of Caesarea (still naively styling himself as head of the "peace party"), the sound of the Thalia was again being heard in the streets.

Constantine was either grossly negligent or else flirting with the heresy himself to have allowed such an obvious kangaroo court to sit in judgment over him—and Athanasius wanted to know which it was. The emperor heard he was coming . . .

and was thereafter indisposed whenever the Alexandrian bishop came knocking. Finally, Athanasius took a meager flat on the street leading to the palace. He lived there several weeks, waiting for just the right moment. At last, Constantine came riding by on horseback and a tiny black man with an auburn beard stepped boldly from around a corner and took hold of the bridle. The emperor was irate; perhaps he thought at first that this was an assassination attempt. But when Athanasius cried out, "God will be the judge between you and me, for you have joined the ranks of my calumniators!" Constantine realized who it was well enough. Athanasius demanded a new trial, and eventually a new one was granted. The second proceeding, though somewhat less biased than the first, was held at Constantinople, where Arians were almost as strong now as at Tyre. Though they obviously dropped the affair of Arsenius's hand from the docket, they replaced it with several other baseless charges, most of them highlighting the wealth of the Alexandrian diocese and designed to raise in the emperor suspicions that the hugely popular Athanasius might someday become a rival.

Eventually, however, Constantine grew tired of listening to the "evidence" and ended the circus abruptly with a preemptory sentence of banishment for Athanasius. This decree, nevertheless, revealed the divided state of Constantine's heart better than just about anything so far: Athanasius was sentenced to live in a palace, under the supervision of the emperor's mildest and most amiable son, who happened to be an orthodox Christian and a personal admirer of the little champion of Nicaea. Constantine didn't even replace Athanasius as patriarch of Alexandria, though the Arians loudly insisted that he do so, but simply allowed his vital see to remain vacant—and thus ended the letter from Athanasius.

Antony of the Desert, now fully up to date, responded with action and determination of his own, as Athanasius undoubtedly expected he might; someone else would have to finish harvesting the turnips. It is true that the old man hated to leave his wilderness. He'd often expressed his belief that "as fishes are nourished in the water, so the desert is the world prepared for monks; and as fishes die when thrown upon dry land, so monastics lose their gravity when they go into cities."[112] Even so, duty called, as the new information from Athanasius so clearly indicated.

And so Antony

went down from the mountain, and entering Alexandria he denounced the Arians, saying, that that was the last heresy, and the forerunner of Antichrist; and he taught the people that the Son of God was not a created thing, neither made from naught, but that he is the eternal Word and wisdom of the essence of the Father; wherefore also it is impious to say there was a time when he was not, for he was always the Word co-existent with the Father. Wherefore he said, 'Do not have any communication with these most impious Arians; for there is no communion between light and darkness. For you are pious Christians: but they, when they say that the Son of God and the Word, who is from the Father, is a created being, differ naught from the heathen, because they worship the creature instead of God the Creator. Believe rather that the whole creation itself is indignant against them, because they number the Creator and Lord of all, in whom all things are made, among created things.

All the people therefore rejoiced at hearing that Christ-opposing heresy anathematized by such a man; and all those in the city ran together to see Antony, and the Greeks [i.e., the pagans], and those who are called their priests came into the church, wishing to see the man of God; for all called him by that name, because there the Lord cleansed many by him from demons, and healed those who were out of their mind. And many heathens wished only to touch the old man, believing that it would be of use to them; and in fact as many became Christians in those few days, as would have been usually converted in a year.[113]

7

Plantations of Tares

"Another parable put he forth unto them, saying, The kingdom of heaven is likened unto a man which sowed good seed in his field: But while men slept, his enemy came and sowed tares among the wheat, and went his way. But when the blade was sprung up, and brought forth fruit, then appeared the tares also" (Matt. 13:24–26 KJV).

How had it happened? How had Arianism gone, over the course of some twelve to fifteen short years, from a fringe theory preached in one church by one wild-eyed presbyter to the roaring brushfire that had now pushed the "pope" of Alexandria himself into exile? Arianism, in fact, actually seemed to have been strengthened somehow by its initial defeat at Nicaea. Why? The simplest answer, perhaps, is that after the council, Arius suddenly found himself selling, almost by chance, exactly what a good portion of the Roman population happened to want at the moment. It had been the last thing on *his* mind, to be sure, but the Egyptian heresiarch had succeeded in perfecting a kind of "Christianity Lite," a diet substitute—a way to accept Constantine's great revolution without really accepting it, a method for being "Christian" without actually putting the Christians in charge. The poor deluded fellow himself (who died not long after Athanasius was sent to Treves) must have gone to his grave believing that the whole world had suddenly developed a burning interest in his woolly-headed Christology.[LXXXVII] But the

LXXXVII "The death of Arius was productive of no important consequences in the history of his party. They had never deferred to him as their leader, and since the Nicene Council had even abandoned his creed [switching for a while instead to a subtler semi-Arianism]." Newman, *Arians of the Fourth Century,* 271.

truth is that Arius had built the world something else altogether, something it really was interested in: he'd made a fallback position in which to retreat, *a refuge for the reluctant.*

Nicaea had been quite the spectacle to pagan observers. Many of them must have felt that the council "got away" from Constantine. Here, after all, was an emperor who began by threatening the bishops in the good old Roman style, insisting on "peace" in their churches in the crudest, most political sense or consequences to follow. Yet by the end, Constantine had risen from his low stool to give Hosius, Alexander, and (the now-banished) Eustathius exactly what they had wanted from the beginning: his stamp on their leadership. So it must suddenly have felt, for the nonbeliever, as if your father had got mixed up in a cult somehow and started signing all his property over to the head gurus. Eusebius of Nicomedia had not been alone in suspecting Constantine of converting "for the greater good." Probably most of the pagan population suspected this; and it was, in fact, even true in a certain sense—at least to begin with.

But his behavior since then had only grown more and more puzzling. Surely the emperor could see that if his plan was going to work, it depended greatly upon the Church's ability to absorb almost everyone—or perhaps we should say its *willingness* to do it. That, after all, is what unity means. His nascent cult of solar monotheism had shown promise, from the pagan point of view, because it would have allowed all but the most stalwart polytheists to avow themselves "Christians" in at least some vague sense—to go ahead and accept baptism in many cases (perhaps with mental reservations) or, at the very least, to participate in the broad sweep of Roman religious life at civic events and so forth. An "out" would have been provided, in other words. Yet if it had shown anything at Nicaea, the Church had shown its *unwillingness* to accept everyone on this kind of a basis. After all, the system of Arius was, at the very least, a great deal closer to orthodoxy than sun worship—and yet Arius had been drummed out of the building like a dog, with the emperor's approval! If a man could be banished over the difference between *homoousious* and *homoiousious,* what sort of treatment could the rest of the populace expect? Were the tables to be turned as completely as that—with the Christians on top now and anyone not completely in sync with their leadership fated to become the new persecuted underclass?

It was panicky thoughts such as these that began turning some portion of those who had merely looked on in curiosity before into staunch, enthusiastic Eusebians. Which portion? Perhaps it would be well to step back and review how the lines had originally shaken out. First, there was the initial core of committed Christians—those who had come out of the Great Persecution smelling so much like a rose—and these were rock solid, of course. To their number had been added since, untold millions of the Proto-Christians, also solidly orthodox, in a process that had been well under way before the emperor ever got involved. Then a great many more Romans had come in, simply taking their cue from Constantine; either inspired by the dramatic story of his conversion and the deliverance it had wrought over the tyrant Maxentius, or simply trusting that the emperor knew best. Were these the "half-converted" heathens one hears about, so often suspected of polluting the pure early Church with their presence?

Not really. They were just the ordinary people of the empire, the common herd, the plebs—and no doubt some of them really were just "going along to get along," as most humans do with regards to the political or religious arrangements in their families or homeland. True, this sort of adherence may have done them little spiritual good as individuals, but to the extent that they supported the emperor's initiative rather than resisting it, we must continue to class them on the "pro-Christian" side of the emerging divide. A surprising percentage of these, however, approached the new arrangement with a much more active goodwill. The records show a genuine popular enthusiasm for Constantine and what he was attempting. One might compare the relationship to scenes one often sees in old films from the 1930s, where struggling Okies in ramshackle dust bowl farmhouses kept a portrait of FDR over the mantelpiece and prayed for him every night. Certainly it is true that most of these additional millions understood little about Christian theology and wouldn't have known Arius or Athanasius from Adam, any more than President Roosevelt's millions of admirers knew anything about the economic principles of John Maynard Keynes or the social theories of Rexford Guy Tugwell.

Yet they came in with much more than their "mere external baptisms"; they came with a docility akin to the emperor's own—a willingness to leave the theology to the professionals, or, to put it more sympathetically, a willingness to take on the yoke of Christ even with many of their questions still unanswered. And how, really, could it have been otherwise?—when the number of Bibles in existence probably numbered in the hundreds rather than the millions, and only unusually educated people could read them? By the very nature of the circumstances, converts were the sheep and the Christian bishops were the shepherds—and like sheep, these new throngs came in to learn, rather than learning first and then coming in.[LXXXVIII]

How do we know that they came with this kind of docility? We know it because all those who lacked this quality now ran to Arius (or, more accurately, to Eusebius). As Hilaire Belloc once put it, "Arianism became the nucleus or center of many forces which would be, of themselves, indifferent to its doctrine. It became the rallying point for many strongly surviving traditions from the older world: traditions not religious, but intellectual, social, moral, literary and all the rest of it."

[LXXXVIII] Most important to note: the Church's officers certainly *were not* content with baptism alone, except as a starting point, nor indifferent to the content of a man's religion, as they had so recently proved at Nicaea. The distinction, however, between clergy and laity must be kept firmly in mind; *teachers* were to be vetted with various tests, but the rank and file were given time to grow into their new Faith slowly—just as they are in most churches today, of whatever affiliation, where ordinary individuals are seldom asked to sign a creed or statement of belief.

Everyone willing to embrace actual Christianity had done it, even if the embrace was incomplete. Those who resented the change (and their numbers were skyrocketing since Nicaea) had to find someplace to land.

Many regretted the old gods, but thought it not worthwhile to risk anything in their defense. Very many more cared nothing for what was left of the old gods . . . but they had pride of culture. They remembered with regret the former prestige of the pagan philosophers. They thought that this great revolution from paganism to Catholicism would destroy the old cultural traditions and their own cultural position. . . . We might put it vividly enough in modern slang by saying that Arianism . . . attracted all the "high-brows" . . . [while] the Church relied upon and was supported at the end by the masses. Men of old family tradition and wealth found the Arian more sympathetic than the ordinary Catholic and a better ally for gentlemen.

Eusebius of Nicomedia must have known, going into the Nicene Council, that his side couldn't actually win out there; he was far too shrewd a politician not to have run the numbers in advance and seen defeat for out-and-out Arianism coming a mile off. What he had actually been doing, surely, was playing for time, hoping to hold out long enough and raise enough doubts for Eusebius of Caesarea's gullible peace party to grow stronger. Then, if the Nicomedian could have combined his seventeen with a few dozen of the waverers, perhaps another score or two of those paralyzed by his "Bible words only" argument, he might have produced a voting block substantial enough to insist upon a vaguely worded creed, something squashy enough to allow Arianism to survive as a minority opinion within the Church. Having seen this attempt fail, however, the obstinately unchristian portion of the public was now turning, as had the Nicomedian himself, to straightforward Arian partisanship. If the Church couldn't be made to tolerate Arianism in its ranks, then the Church would have to be made Arian and tolerate the orthodox—or not, if that should happen to prove the more expedient.

Yes, as Belloc concludes,

> Arius was condemned [at Nicaea, and] the creed which his followers had drawn up was trampled under-foot as a blasphemy, but the spirit behind that creed and behind that revolt was to re-arise . . . Arianism, founded like all heresies on an error in doctrine—that is on something which can be expressed in a dead formula of mere words—soon began to live, like all heresies at their beginning, with a vigorous new life and character and savor of its own. The quarrel which filled the third century from 325 onwards for a lifetime was not after its first years a quarrel between opposing forms of words the difference between which may appear slight; it became very early in the struggle a quarrel between opposing spirits and characters: a quarrel between two opposing personalities, such as human personalities are: on the one side the Catholic temper and tradition, on the other a soured, proud temper, which would have destroyed the Faith.[114]

The New Order

The single best proof of where Constantine really stood in relation to that Faith is to be found in what happened immediately after his death: the emperor's third son Constantius ascended quickly to the throne and then leapt instantly and enthusiastically into the arms of his father's old temptress. Not only did Constantius become an Arian himself, he quickly partnered with the Eusebians and began to persecute Athanasius and his allies with all the prestige and mighty resources of his office. Unhindered by any emotional or religious attachments to the Faith as his father had found it, Constantius set about customizing Christianity to fit the perceived needs of his empire with the coldness and efficiency of a court-appointed bankruptcy judge.

Constantine had grown fat and sick as the end approached, disillusioned and worn out from cares, yet he still buckled on his armor and prepared to lead his men into battle when Sapor II of Persia declared war on the Roman Empire late in the year 336. He never made it to the battlefield. The emperor was taken instead to Helenopolis in a vain effort to restore his health by means of the famed mineral waters there. When this failed, Constantine was carried to his deathbed at his old palace near Nicaea where, at long last, he was baptized by the local bishop—none other than (sad irony!) Eusebius of Nicomedia. "After the ceremony he was filled with joy," writes Sozomen,

> and returned thanks to God. He then confirmed the division of the empire among his sons, according to his former allotment, and bestowed certain privileges on old Rome and on the city named after himself. . . . After making these arrangements, Constantine survived but a few days; he died in the sixty-fifth year of his age, and the thirty-first of his reign [337]. He was a powerful protector of the Christian religion, and was the first of the emperors who began to be zealous for the Church, and to bestow upon her high benefactions. He was more successful than any other sovereign in all his undertakings; for he formed no design, I am convinced, without God.[115]

Many detractors have read a dark significance into the location of Constantine's burial place: the emperor is said to have been interred in the sacred vault of the Church of the Holy Apostles at Constantinople, surrounded on all sides by tombs for each of the original Twelve—a kind of grotesque recapitulation of the Last Supper, with Constantine himself taking the hallowed thirteenth place. The facts, alas, are just a touch less perfect when it comes to creating a juicy, conspiracy-confirming mental image. Although it is true that the emperor did commission this church and also initiated the search for apostolic relics, there's no evidence at all that Constantine himself—he who had spurned a golden throne at Nicaea—intended it to be his mausoleum. Indeed, Socrates, Sozomen, and Theodoret all credit Constantius with this design, not his father—Constantius, who was, as we shall see, entirely under the thrall of the two Eusebii, those of both Nicomedia and Caesarea. Eusebius Pamphilus (whose idolatrous passion for peace at any cost had led him to become what is known as a "soft Arian" by this time[LXXXIX]) had been calling Constantine "the New Moses" for years, "and regarded his monarchy as the fulfillment of the highest Christian hopes."[116] He and the Nicomedian presided over the emperor's funeral personally, with Constantius present as well, intending (according to the express testimony of Socrates) "that the emperors and prelates might receive a degree of veneration but little inferior to that which was paid to the relics of the apostles."[117] The alarming picture of "Constantine usurping the place of Christ" is also spoiled by the fact that only one of the apostles was actually present at the time (the body of Andrew, the brother of Peter) and that the other two saints interred in the crypt thus far (Timothy and Luke) weren't part of the original Twelve at all—a detail that casts doubt, surely, over the entire absurd conception.

The "former allotment" Constantine made was done in the same quixotic spirit that motivated Diocletian at the beginning of our story: haunted by memories of the free democratic Republic they had lost to dictatorship three and a half centuries earlier, the Romans were loath to confess that one-man rule had now become permanent among them and the only way to keep their fractious

---

[LXXXIX] Soft or Semi-Arianism was the position of those who thought the crisis could be weathered by compromise: compromise between two inherently exclusive propositions. Compromise, therefore, came to mean, in this context, trying to force everyone to confine themselves to terms "we can all agree on"; words, that is, which would defer or delay the issue indefinitely. Yet Christ either is or is not coeternal with his Father and no mere form of words could paper over this central, unavoidable test. "To attempt comprehensions of opinion," as Newman writes, "amiable as the motive frequently is, is to mistake arrangements of words, which have no existence except on paper, for habits which are realities; and ingenious generalizations of discordant sentiments for that practical agreement which alone can lead to co-operation." Ultimately, the long attempt to make room in the same Church for the worship of two different Christs only embittered the affair even more than necessary.

collection of vassal states in order. Motivated, then, by this badger-
ing idealism, Constantine chose, as death approached, to re-divide
the imperial sovereignty he had spent his whole career uniting and
to designate his three sons as his heirs: Constantine II to rule the
extreme West; Constantius to govern Asia, Syria, and Egypt; and
his youngest son, Constans, upon reaching majority, to rule Illyricum, Italia, and Africa.[XC] And over the next twelve years or so, this
arrangement led (to the surprise of practically no one), to backstab-
bing, bloodshed . . . and then back around to one-man rule again.
Nevertheless, the change did have at least one positive effect—it
led to the release of Athanasius of Alexandria from his comfortable
"prison" in Germany. About three weeks after his father's death,
Constantine II sent the diminutive bishop back to his home church
in Egypt with a rather disingenuous letter of pardon built around
the face-saving theory that he'd only been exiled to begin with "in
order to shield him from his enemies." Athanasius was, at any rate,
once more established in his episcopal see by the end of November
337—at the age of forty-two.

Just as his flight into the Egyptian desert as a small child had
been rich in biblical analogy, so does his return to Alexandria
seem to evoke a Gospel parallel—this time with echoes of Palm
Sunday. Payne describes the scene memorably in *The Holy Fire*:

> In his absence Athanasius' name had been kept green by the
> desert fathers. When he returned, it was in triumph. Grego-
> ry Nazianzen, who seems to have been present on the occa-
> sion, speaks of the whole city waiting to receive the man who
> had retained the papacy of Alexandria while living far away
> in Gaul. There was no sudden outburst of greeting. A formal

---

[XC] Though odd and confusing to modern readers, all of these many Con-
stantine-based names aren't entirely outside our own experience; Hill-
ary Clinton, for instance, quickly stopped emphasizing her "Rodham"
maiden name as she acquired presidential ambitions of her own, and of-
fice-seekers by the name of King and Kennedy have had the inside track
for decades when it comes to getting elected in Atlanta or Massachusetts.

entry was agreed upon. There was a solemn stateliness in the arrangements. The men and women were apart, and children formed a group by themselves, all waving green branches. The tradesmen formed compact groups; so did the church officials. Athanasius stepped off the ship, was lifted onto an ass and led the procession through the city, with gay carpets spread before his feet, and more carpets hung from the windows of the houses. Little cups filled with fragrant oil hung at the doorposts. At night there were illuminations, and the richer householders provided entertainment outside their houses.

It was a time of feasting and hymn singing. "Nothing can separate us from Christ," Athanasius had written in a festal letter celebrating his return. In Alexandria there appeared very briefly one of those rare manifestations in which whole cities are given over to worship. In their enthusiasm for Athanasius hundreds and perhaps thousands of Alexandrians became monks; the hungry and the orphans were sheltered; and every house became a church . . . Athanasius had returned; Alexandria adored him; and only Constantius, the emperor of the East, detested him.[118]

No doubt about it—Athanasius had now become a folk hero in the empire, nothing less, and not only to the Christians. Believers, of course, still found inspiration in his gallant stand at Nicaea and more recently, in the grace he had shown while under the sentence of exile. Just as when they'd made him a bishop some ten years ago, calling for "the real Christian, the ascetic," they'd learned to identify the austerities Athanasius had picked up from Antony (and still practiced every day) with sincerity and authenticity of Faith. These practices stood, at any rate, in marked contrast with those of the Arianizing clergy now being sent out so frequently to their parishes. Rarely found praying or fasting by their congregants, these men were always respectable and stylishly dressed and seemed to think that the main content of the Christian life consisted of theological debate and political advocacy. They were "all talk," in other words—and many of

them seemed, in the eyes of the ordinary folk, to have aspired to
the life of a Christian minister mainly because they wouldn't do
a day's work. The general populace had also had a good enough
look at Arians by now not to like what they were seeing. Whatever else one might think of Athanasius and his brand of Christianity, he did certainly put his money where his mouth was.
The desert monks fed the poor, clothed the naked, sheltered
the homeless whether Christian or pagan, and they taught their
admirers to do the same.

Those of the Arian stripe, on the other hand, were not only
idle, they were shifty and dissembling. Eusebius Pamphilus,
bishop of Caesarea, had (as even the pagans knew) originally
voted with the Arians at Nicaea—before, upon further review,
saving his job with a tricky recantation. He then spent the rest
of his career earning Constantine's contempt through his everlasting eagerness to kiss the imperial backside. Another Arian
prelate, Leontius, was also the subject of a now-famous story,
familiar even to unbelievers; to wit, that during the communal
recitation of the public doxology on Sundays—not even those
nearest to him in the congregation could ever hear Leontius say
anything more than the final words, "for ever and ever." Athanasius, on the other hand (though respectful to the emperors and
granting them their proper due), had been willing to suffer for
his convictions. He'd assembled with the others at Nicaea, for
instance, in meek obedience to the emperor's directive; yet he
had also disobeyed Constantine outright when commanded to
rescind Alexander's excommunication of Arius.

"If a decision was made by the bishops," Athanasius later wrote,

> what concern had the emperor with it? . . . When did a deci-
> sion of the Church receive its authority from the emperor? Or
> rather, when was his decree even recognized? There have been
> many [local] councils in times past, and many decrees made by
> the Church; but never did the fathers seek the consent of the
> emperor for them, nor did the emperor busy himself in the af-
> fairs of the Church. . . . The Apostle Paul had friends among

those who belonged to the household of Caesar, and in the writing to the Philippians he sent greetings from them: but never did he take them as associates in his judgments.[119]

Though the actual subject of his struggle may have been of little interest to them, the pagans, many of them, liked this stance toward imperial overreach and absolutism. And besides, the symbolism of the whole thing was just so perfect! Like Athanasius, the new emperor Constantius was a redhead—but there any similarity ceased. Constantius wasn't the runt, he was the pick of the litter; tall like his father, beautiful and fit, with the physique of a Greek boxer. The sickly little black man, by contrast, was (to use a metaphor picked up from the Jewish holy books) a David without even a slingshot, rising to do battle with this Goliath of pride and privilege. In other words, a good fight was brewing—something the Romans had *always* enjoyed—and a man didn't have to be a practicing Christian himself to savor the prospect and to start taking bets on the coming donnybrook.

What motivated Constantius? Belloc, once again, gets close to the truth:

> Arianism . . . had for ally the tendency of government in an absolute monarchy to be half afraid of emotions present in the minds of the people and especially in the poorer people: emotions which if they spread and became enthusiastic and captured the mass of the people might become too strong to be ruled and would have to be bowed to. . . . It does not like to feel that there is in the state a rival to its own power. It does not like to feel that great decisions may be imposed by organizations other than its own official organization. That is why even the most Christian emperors [such as Constantine and Constantine II] and their officials always had at the back of their minds, during the first lifetime of the Arian movement, a potential sympathy with Arianism, and that is why this potential sympathy in some cases appears as actual sympathy and as a public declaration of Arianism on their part.[120]

Digging a little deeper, Orthodox writer Vladimir Soloviev uncovers the subtle connection between this kind of jealousy and heretical theology:

> Heresy attacked the perfect unity of the divine and the human in Jesus precisely in order to undermine the living bond between Church and state, and to confer upon the latter an absolute independence. Hence it is clear why the emperors of the Eastern Empire, intent on maintaining within Christendom the absolutism of the pagan state, were so partial to all these heresies, which were but manifold variations on a single theme: Jesus Christ is not the true Son of God, consubstantial with the Father; God has not become incarnate; nature and mankind remain cut off from divinity and are not united to it; consequently, the human state may rightly keep its independence and supremacy intact. Constantius . . . had indeed good reason to support Arianism.[121]

One of the new emperor's first official acts was to have Eusebius of Nicomedia made bishop of Constantinople. The Nicomedian then quickly revived his old charges against Athanasius, along with some new ones, including the accusation that his return from exile had not been legal, since it was done without the consent of Constantius (in whose realms Alexandria lay). All this drove the dispute onto the streets again, where the people became, once more, "divided into factions and the whole city [of Alexandria] was thrown into confusion: some insisting that the Nicene Creed should be by no means infringed on, while others contended that the opinion of Arius was consonant to reason."[122]

> Moreover, the mischief quickly extended to other provinces and cities, the controversy, like a spark, insignificant at first, exciting in the auditors a spirit of contention: for every one who inquired the cause of the tumult, found immediately occasion for disputing, and determined to take part in the strife at the moment of making the inquiry. By general altercation

of this kind all order was subverted; the agitation, however, was confined to the cities of the East, those of Illyricum and the western parts of the empire meanwhile were perfectly tranquil, because they would not annul the decisions of the Council of Nicaea. As this affair increased, going from bad to worse, Eusebius of Nicomedia and his party looked upon popular ferment as a piece of good fortune. For only thus they thought they would be enabled to constitute someone who held their own sentiments bishop of Alexandria.[123]

At this point the gloves came off. Up to now, the persecutions on behalf of Arianism had been done at least quasi-legally, under the recognized forms of ecclesiastical law. Actual charges had been proffered (however bogus) and trials conducted. With these techniques, Eustathius had been banished, and Arian or Semi-Arian bishops installed at Hadrianople, Heraclea, Ephesus, Ancyra, both Caesareas, Laodicaea, Antioch—practically all of the important churches of the East. But now, with a fully supportive monarch on the throne, naked force was resorted to for the first time—with the excuse, naturally, that law and order must obviously be restored. Less than three years then, after his return from Treves, Athanasius was commanded to vacate his position and make way for a new bishop—an Arian bishop—or face summary execution on the spot.

This new bishop, a meekly submissive party man by the name of Gregory of Cappadocia, arrived on March 23, 340 . . . along with a cohort of 5,000 soldiers. "Sensing the horror of the people," writes Payne, "he immediately set about creating a reign of terror. Orthodox churches were desecrated, and their altars polluted. Monks and virgins were arrested, thrown into prison and tortured for the amusement of the guards. Orthodoxy became criminal."[124]

Athanasius, eager to protect his people,

assembled them by night in the church, and when the soldiers came to take possession of the church, prayers having been concluded, he first ordered a psalm to be sung. During the chanting of this psalm the soldiers remained without and quietly awaited its conclusion, and in the meantime Athanasius passed under the singers and secretly made his escape, and fled to Rome. In this manner Gregory possessed himself of the see of Alexandria. The indignation of the people was aroused, and they burnt the church which bore the name of Dionysius, one of their former bishops [but now occupied by an Arian pastor].[125]

ORTHODOXY ALIVE

Once again the little patriarch of Alexandria, hero of perhaps millions by now, was a homeless refugee. Yet when he sailed into Centumcellae, the port of Rome, under a sky of Tyrrhenian blue, he was likely welcomed at the dock by the pope of Rome himself, Julius I. Julius had succeeded Sylvester, bishop of Rome at the time of Nicaea, back in 337, and had, since that time, followed the career of Athanasius closely—albeit from a distance. Such a welcome was, in itself, a very serious step, since it signaled right away Julius's willingness to revisit the conviction of a clergyman already formally sentenced by his episcopal brethren in the East. This was irregular, to be sure, and yet having gotten a taste of what passed as "evidence" at these recent synods— particularly in the story about the "Hand of Glory"—Julius was, shall we say, disinclined to take Athanasius's condemnation entirely at face value. For his own part, Athanasius held his conviction to be invalid simply and solely because his accusers were heretics and traitors to the Nicene Faith; but, as Chadwick mildly puts it, "the proposition did not seem self-evident at the time in the East."[126]

With Athanasius safely under his protection now, Julius suggested a new trial, a fair trial to be conducted in Italy, far from the charged political atmosphere that had made such a hearing so difficult to obtain in the East. The Eusebian bishops quickly replied to this proposal with a haughty letter of refusal; insulting the pope's intelligence, particularly, by the way in which they refuted his insinuation that the influence of Arius might still be felt among them: "How should we, as bishops, be subject to a mere presbyter?" And, in fact, the Eastern churches did have at this time, on the whole, a rather low view of the pope's intelligence—not just his, but that of the entire Christian West. As we previously noted, Julius was bishop of a fading city: Rome had already lost (since her glory days under the Antonines) more than half her population of one million souls and would dwindle, eventually, to a mere town of fewer than 40,000 people. The rest of the West had reverted to semibarbarism as well, and was hamstrung, theologically speaking, by its continued use of the increasingly irrelevant Latin tongue—a Christian population unable even to read the Bible without employing a Greek translator, much less to discern the true import of a subtle word like *homoousious*. G.K. Chesterton encapsulated these Eastern attitudes rather well: "You must not be too angry with the poor Romans; they are rude and ignorant and have never had our advantages; it is not as if you were arguing with educated people."[127]

And, to be sure, the undoubted acumen of the more civilized end of Christendom was not to be dismissed lightly. Still, as Julius must have reflected, it was mainly *Eastern* bishops who had adopted *homoousious* at Nicaea, not we rustics from the hinterlands—and the vote had been lopsided, to say the least. What had changed in the meantime? Nothing, surely, but the political climate of Byzantium, where "soft Arianism" ("the Son is *like* the Father") had now become the "moderate" position, the sweetly reasonable compromise between real Christianity and straight-up heresy.

In any event, Julius, having been rebuffed, decided to hold his fair trial anyway—a new synod at Rome open to any bishop willing to attend, and this council promptly exonerated Athanasius completely and reestablished him in his episcopal rights. Julius sent the verdict East, along with a letter of undisguised rebuke:

[Even if it had been] entirely as you say, that some offense was committed by those persons [Athanasius and his supporters], judgment ought to have been made, not as it was, but according to the ecclesiastical canon. It behooved all of you to write to us, so that the justice of it might be seen as emanating from all. . . . Are you ignorant that the custom has been to write to us first, and then for a just decision to be passed from this place? . . . If, then, any such suspicion had rested upon the bishop there, notice of it ought to have been written to the Church here. But now, after they have done as they pleased [by substituting Gregory for Athanasius at Alexandria], they want to obtain our concurrence, although we never condemned him. . . . This is another form of procedure, and a novel practice.[128]

Though this letter undoubtedly infuriated the Eusebians, they didn't dare resort to an open breach with Rome. The long tradition of deference to the storied See of Peter could not be simply spurned, since public opinion in the churches would not have stood for it. Julius knew this very well when he ended his letter by saying, "what we have received from the blessed Apostle Peter, these things I signify to you."[XCI] Eusebius and his cronies were forced instead to content themselves with the complaint that this, surely, was Roman guidance in a new and aggressive form. "As for the claim of Rome to act as a court of appeal," writes Chadwick, "the Greeks retorted that it was a new thing for a western synod to judge eastern decisions"[129]—which, one supposes, it may well have been, just as it was a new thing for the whole East to go suddenly heretic.

Much as Abraham Lincoln, faced, in 1861, with an eleven-state secession unprovided for by the constitutional framers, found himself forced to chart new waters for the presidency, so the bishop of Rome was compelled, by the brewing revolution in the East, to stand pat for Nicaea and for Athanasius in ways theretofore

---

[XCI] Even Cyril of Jerusalem, flirting with Semi-Arianism himself at this point, could write, about this time, of "Peter, both chief of the Apostles and the keeper of the keys of the kingdom of heaven," acting "in the name of Christ" and "in the power of the Holy Spirit."

unenvisioned.[XCII] Though he had certainly been out of sight and out of mind for a while, there in his "dead city of the Tiber," as Chesterton calls it, "the pope had never in theory lost the power to protest or even to condemn . . . but his practical position was weak; and the practical position of the great Patriarchs surrounding the golden throne of Caesar was very strong."[130]

Unable to just ignore Julius, however, the Eastern bishops determined instead to convince him of their orthodoxy—or, at any rate, to set about trying to put this over to the public. They held a new council of their own (something they had, significantly, been unwilling to try while Constantine lived), at Antioch, during the summer of 341, where they immediately began to churn out new creeds at a bewildering pace. They made four, even five attempts, each longer than the last (one, in fact, is still called today "the Lengthy Creed") all of them aping the Nicene language as much as possible, while still avoiding, of course, the hated *homoüsion*. Some of these, in fact, when read today alone and out of context, sound perfectly orthodox—would really *be* perfectly orthodox, were we unaware of their origin. Yet here was just the trouble: Julius, Hosius, Marcellus, and the rest of the orthodox champions *were* aware. No matter how mild and inoffensive may have been the creeds they sent out, the Eusebians always spoiled their cause at the last moment by attaching strident, hysterical demands that Athanasius be delivered to them for condemnation.

"In truth," writes Newman,

> no such exposition of the Catholic faith could satisfy the Western Christians, while they were witnesses to the exile of

---

[XCII] We should add, however, that the first such Roman "interference" in the affairs of a Greek church came early indeed: Clement I of Rome, who became pope about the same time that the apostle John was writing his Gospel, warned a rebellious clique at Corinth that "should any disobey what has been said by [the Holy Spirit] through us, let them understand that they will entangle themselves in transgression and no small danger."

its great champion on account of his fidelity to it. Here the
Eusebians were wanting in their usual practical shrewdness.
Words, however orthodox, could not weigh against so plain
a fact. The Occidentals, however unskilled in the niceties of
the Greek language, were able to ascertain the heresy of the
Eusebians in their malevolence toward Athanasius. Nay, the
anxious attempts of his enemies to please them by means of
a confession of faith were a refutation of their pretenses. For,
inasmuch as the sense of the Catholic world had already been
recorded in the *homoüsion*, why should they devise a new formulary, if after all they agreed with the Church? or, why
should they themselves be so fertile in confessions, if they had
all of them but one faith? It is brought against them by Athanasius, that in their creeds they date their exposition of the
Catholic doctrine as if it were something new, instead simply
of its being declared, which was the sole design of the Nicene
Fathers; while at other times, they affected to acknowledge
the authority of former Councils, which nevertheless they
were indirectly opposing.[131]

Acquitted by Julius, yet unable to return to his own see of
Alexandria, Athanasius began to wander the cobbled roads of
Western Europe, an outlandish little Oriental whose Latin was
likely rudimentary at best, stranger in a strange land. Yet, as
Payne writes, "Athanasius was orthodoxy alive, greeted everywhere in Italy with deep respect, the friend of Antony, the
apostle of orthodoxy, the inheritor of the ascetic traditions of
Egypt."[132] He was welcomed at every church, preached hundreds of guest sermons, and had a free meal or a house in which
to sleep wherever there were Christians. He returned, briefly, to
Treves, to confer with Hosius personally, though the Spaniard
was quietly retired now and getting along in years.

And everywhere he went, young European men were inspired to imitate his example, just as his own role model Antony
had inspired the earliest Eastern monks more than fifty years
previous. It is possible that he inspired Hilary of Poitiers to take

up the ministry during this period, and to grow into the great champion against Arianism he later became. At one point, Athanasius was summoned to Sardica, where Pope Julius had planned a great unifying council in hopes of healing the widening rift between East and West. Yet when Athanasius arrived he learned that the Easterners, having been alerted to his coming, had balked at the news and refused to sit under the same roof with their nemesis, sabotaging the whole project.

In any case, Athanasius was exiled, all in all, three years in Western Europe, years during which Gregory the Arian shepherded his flock back home in the East. The reports of Gregory's leadership, which Athanasius sometimes received in letters from his old parishioners, were nothing short of heartbreaking, as the little patriarch himself recounts:

> [Gregory] accuses before the governor those who pray in their own homes; and he takes every opportunity to insult their ministers. His conduct is of such violence, then, that many run the risk of not being baptized, and many have no one to visit them in sickness and distress, a circumstance which they regret even more bitterly than their illness. For while the ministers of the Church are under persecution, the people condemn the impiety of the Arian heretics, and choose rather to be sick and to run the risk, than to permit a hand of the Arians to come upon their head.[133]

This peaceful resistance the emperor chose to regard as simple rebellion against his lawful authority.

> Constantius writes letters, and commences a persecution against all. Gathering together a multitude of herdsmen and shepherds, and dissolute youths belonging to the town, armed with swords and clubs, they attacked in a body the Church of Quirinus: and some they slew, some they trampled underfoot, others they beat with stripes and cast into prison or banished. They haled away many women also, and dragged them openly

into the court, and insulted them, dragging them by the hair. Some they proscribed; from some they took away their bread, for no other reason but that they might be induced to join the Arians, and receive Gregory who had been sent by the emperor.[134]

ATHANASIUS BEWARE!

Finally, rioting broke out in the streets of Alexandria. More buildings were set ablaze and hotheaded young men on both sides leapt into the fray. Before it was over, "Bishop" Gregory himself had been dragged from his house (actually, *Athanasius's* house) and killed outright. Numerous historians since that time have expressed astonishment that human beings could ever have rioted and slain over an arcane piece of Christian theology— over a single iota in the middle of a single Greek word. Their astonishment, however, seems to come mainly from antipathy to the subject matter at hand or, at least, a tone deafness to the context of the times. Cities have certainly risen up over a few short words since then—one may recall that *Liberté, Égalité, Fraternité* set all of Europe ablaze a few years back—and likewise *homoousious* and *homoiousious* had become symbolic of a larger war between worldviews as well.

To begin with, it was not simply Arians and the orthodox fighting in these streets—not even primarily, in fact. Probably some genuine Christians (recent and immature converts, for instance) did engage in violence in contradiction of their principles; troubled times bring out the worst in everyone. Yet the fact remains that there's not a word of encouragement to this sort of thing in any orthodox writing from the period. If a certain portion of the faithful did falter through weakness and "hit back" in opposition to the edicts of their Faith, it was in spite of their leaders, not because of them. Many of their clergy continued to resemble that "army of martyrs" seen at Nicaea—striped, lame, and one-eyed—the visible symbol of a 300-year tradition of turning the other cheek.

And, in fact, it was only Christian forbearance that made the whole episode possible anyway: Tertullian's old guess that Christians had already become numerous enough to impose their will on the empire was now 150 years in the past and things had only improved for the Church in that regard since then. In other words, if the violent attitudes seen in these Alexandrian riots had been at all widespread among believers, not only Gregory but Constantius himself would have been assassinated. Genuine Arians, likewise, were probably few and far between during the riots as well. Real theoretical Arianism was confined largely to the upper classes, to the rich and the cultured—the sort of people who always allow others to brawl in the streets on their behalf.

Who did rise up, then, and kill Gregory of Cappadocia? Surely it must have been those plebs and "pro-Christians" we referenced earlier; those who had kept a portrait of Constantine, so to speak, on the mantelpiece above the home fires. For whatever reason—perhaps a man had a mistress he was too fond of to renounce, or some other old vice that kept him away from the baptismal font—many of these admired Christianity but were content to do so from afar, not yet ready to jump in with both feet. Nicaea, nevertheless, had been a spectacle to these as well. There they had seen an emperor who had earned through his deeds more power than any Caesar since Augustus but who had, nevertheless, deliberately curbed his own power in service to an ideal. Less worthy Caesars than this had proclaimed themselves gods and demanded the most abject submission from their subjects, but Constantine the Great had "sat quietly" and deferred his own will to that of the Christian bishops, successors to twelve Jewish fishermen from Galilee. By Jupiter, it was like the legendary Cincinnatus come back to life!—that humble Roman farmer in the days of the Old Republic who accepted dictatorial powers to meet a war emergency, then went voluntarily back to his fields after the crisis had passed.

Constantius, on the other hand, had shown every sign of wanting to go back to business as usual. If he could exploit the Christian movement to further his own ends, he would allow it to continue, to be sure—provided it would permit itself to be tamed and domesticated and made subservient to him. If not—if the Arian strategy were to fail, for instance—these pro-Christians had little doubt that Constantius would turn quickly to killing the Christian Church, to slapping down the one worthwhile thing that had come along in their empire for centuries rather than allow it to exist without his leave. Already he had invited in a lot of wolves to cut the thing up from the inside— veritable "plantations of tares," as Theodoret would later call them. Now he seemed fixated on their pathetic little hero Athanasius, ready to put all public business aside in his obsession with punishing a single harmless individual whose only crime, as far as they could see it, was in showing up a pack of power-hungry hyenas at the council. The late emperor Constantine, at any rate, had not acted like this.

Surely then, it must have been these rude, passionate patriots—the type of men who tarred and feathered the officers of King George in the streets of Boston a millennium-and-a-half later—who rose up to throw the rascals out in Athanasius's Alexandria; and they did it less in defense of the little patriarch than for the memory of Constantine. It was, in a sense, the emperor's last service to the vast commonwealth he loved so much. Though they may not have been ready to take the pledge themselves, his half-Christian admirers certainly knew, as the old soldier himself had known deep down, which side the "gentlemen" were on—and which side was friend, like its Founder, "to publicans and sinners."

Constantius, as one might expect, was enraged by the death of Gregory, yet he responded in a surprising way. He recalled Athanasius and guaranteed him safe conduct back to Egypt. "Constantius, yielding to fear what he denied to justice, consented to restore to Alexandria a champion of the truth, who had been condemned on the wildest of charges, by the most hostile and unprincipled of judges."[135] The war started by Sapor on the borders was going badly thus far; and reports that the Persians were executing thousands of Christians as they advanced were softening Arian resolve in some quarters, reawakening uncomfortable memories of Galerius and of the methods he had used to aggrandize imperial authority. Constantius had also received a threatening letter from his last remaining rival, his youngest brother Constans, who was now old enough to make trouble. Constans had become friendly with Julius, who persistently recommended that the young Caesar intercede with his brother on behalf of the orthodox. With little luxury, then, to deliberately foment unrest in his own dominions, Constantius decided that a brief feint seemed to be called for. The letter he wrote to Athanasius, announcing this sudden change of heart, is comic in its insincerity: "Our clemency no longer allows us to see you tossed by the wild waves and tumultuous seas, driven from your home and spoiled of your goods." The offer of peace, however, was genuine.

Athanasius, schooled in the strictest Christian poverty since his days in the desert, probably owned nothing, needed to pack nothing as he took his leave of Julius for his return to the East. Julius, however, likely had one final word of warning to convey as the two men parted for the last time—Julius, who knew Rome and Roman politics like few men alive, and who, as a result, could doubtless see the future coming from afar. Beware, Athanasius! Beware of the Roman army, maker and breaker of emperors from the start, and the real rulers of the empire.

The army is everything.

8

The Devil's Advocate

"Strive for peace with all men, and for the holiness without which no one will see the Lord. See to it that no one fail to obtain the grace of God; that no 'root of bitterness' spring up and cause trouble, and by it the many become defiled . . . like Esau, who sold his birthright for a single meal" (Heb. 12:14–16).

THE STUDENT PRINCE

"Hail, Caesar!" proclaimed the big, barrel-chested Cappadocian, raising a glass suddenly in the golden afternoon. "Hail, Flavius Claudius Iulianus!" Snapping quickly to their feet, the dozen or so other university students at the symposium (fancy Greek name for a banquet of wine) joined their unofficial captain with an impressive gusto of their own. "Hail, Caesar! Hail, thou governor of Gaul!" The toastmaster, ever the showman in their presence, held his moment for just a few solemn seconds—then joshed the man standing next to him in the ribs with his elbow, breaking the entire party up into happy laughter. And the man who laughed hardest was the man who had just been joshed, the newly minted Caesar himself, whom these happy old friends all called simply *Julian*.

The place was a pleasant *taberna*, a wine garden in a grove overlooking the city of Athens; the year was 355—mid-October, to be exact. The occasion was a send-off, a bachelor party, so to speak, for young Julian, not only deputy-emperor now under Constantius but engaged to marry the lady Helena as well—daughter of the late emperor Constantine and named after her grandmother. It was an arranged affair, of course, a matter of state; but Julian was content with the arrangement, part and parcel as it was with his surprising promotion. Just now twenty-three, with bright, beautiful eyes and a natural charm, Julian was

Constantine's nephew, son of the emperor's half-brother; and his sister was the wife of Constantius. Yet few had ever expected him to rise to imperial honors himself. Indeed, Constantius had, for most of the young man's life, been actively undermining such a potentiality. One of Julian's earliest memories—burned deep into his mind as a defining moment—was receiving the news, at age seven, that most of his closer kin had been purged in the wake of Constantine's death. Though there was some question at the time about whether the soldiers who murdered them might have been acting on their own initiative to remove more distant relatives whom they did not recognize as legitimate future claimants, Julian later learned to put the blame squarely onto the shoulders of Constantius:

> [I]n the paternal line both Constantius and I are descended from the same stock. Our fathers were brothers, sons of the same father. And what this most beneficent emperor did for us who were so closely related to him! Six of our common cousins, his uncle, my father, and another uncle on our father's side, and my eldest brother, he put to death without a trial. My brother and I, whom he had intended to kill, were eventually sent into exile.[136]

Initially, this exile took the form of an extended residence at an imperial hunting lodge in Cappadocia, the rustic mountain region of eastern Anatolia, to receive his elementary education from a series of tutors; and it was there that Julian seems to have made the acquaintance of our gregarious, black-bearded toast-master, Basil of Cappadocia.

Basil's background was far more humble, socially speaking, but he, too, came of royal stock in the eyes of the Christian world: his mother, Emmelia, was the daughter of a well-known martyr, his older sister had founded a famous convent, and his father (also named Basil) was the son of Macrina the elder, a disciple of the third-century saint Gregory the Miracle Worker. So Basil, obviously, received a thoroughly Christian upbringing in

Cappadocia (it is possible that he and Julian were lectors together at church there), yet it had, perhaps, been a bit too Christian, so to speak, for he had shown himself something of the "preacher's kid" up to this point in his life. Rather casual toward the Faith in which he had always been immersed, Basil was, at this stage, far more devoted to the secular studies at which he excelled: philosophy, astronomy, medicine, and geometry. Here at Athens now, at any rate, center of such learning for nearly a thousand years, Basil had been the proverbial kid in a candy store.

Standing to his left at Julian's symposium was Basil's inseparable companion during these university years, young Gregory Nazianzen (so named later because he eventually succeeded his father as bishop of the city of Nazianzus). Another native of Cappadocia (though not to be confused with the phony bishop of Alexandria who had been killed by the mob), Gregory had always been in awe of Basil, ever since the two of them had been teens together. "[We were] sent by God," he recounted, when preaching Basil's funeral many years later,

> and by a generous craving for culture, to Athens the home of letters. Athens, which has been to me, if to any one, a city truly of gold, and the patroness of all that is good. For it brought me to know Basil more perfectly. . . . Philosophy was our aim, we were all in all to one another, housemates, messmates, intimates, with one object in life, or an affection for each other ever growing warmer and stronger. . . . We struggled, not each to gain the first place for himself, but to yield it to the other; for we made each other's reputation to be our own. We seemed to have one soul, inhabiting two bodies.[137]

Even so, Gregory was quieter, more reflective than Basil and inclined toward poetry and literature rather than science and math. Yet he, too, had allowed his Christian observance to slip while here at school, something that happens to most college students, it would seem—though his devotion had recently been reignited somewhat by a near-fatal experience during a rough sea crossing. When Julian joined them at Athens, earlier in 355, to study rhetoric under the famous Libanius of Antioch, they became "the Three Cappadocians"—for Julian, having grown to manhood there, had surely gained an honorary citizenship, at least in the eyes of his fellow students.

The feasting at such an event was usually restrained; the Greeks admired dignity and simplicity in all things, so Julian's bachelor party was less the bacchanal we might expect today and more the quiet, sentimental parting of friends. Food there certainly was, however, a delightful foretaste of the big fat Greek wedding to come: baked cod served with *skordalia* (garlic sauce), and other seafood dishes such as fried squid and baby octopus; cabbage, onions, fasolada, chickpeas, broad beans, and lentil soup; with honey-laden pasteli for dessert. The second part of an evening like this, during which guests would divide up into smaller groups for conversation or table games such as *kottabos*, was traditionally inaugurated with a libation: a ritual drink offering poured out onto the ground, usually in honor of Dionysus. Though the practice originated, to be sure, as a serious act of pagan worship, it had become, for most Romans, a simple matter of custom by this time—akin to our own shaking of hands or peck on the cheek under the mistletoe (both of which have similar pagan origins).

Gregory, however, in the newfound zeal of his Christian reconversion, chose to abstain—a common (since Constantine) but slightly ostentatious act of conscientious objection. As he did, Gregory watched his companions very closely. Though there were one or two others who, like himself, withheld participation, the majority was still pagan, as was most of the educated class; or, to put it more accurately, was still skeptical of all religion, pagan or Christian, but perfectly willing to observe societal conventions. Basil, too, poured some of his glass onto the earth—to Gregory's slight disappointment, if not very great surprise. Julian, however, paused significantly with his cup held out before him. He waited until practically all faces were turned in his direction (some of them wearing expressions of the keenest interest) before he, too, lowered his drink like Gregory—and abstained.

Later, when the campfires were lit and the new Caesar was asked to play for the group, taking out his exotic Eastern *kitara* (ancient forerunner of the modern guitar) and casting a spell over everyone with his music, Gregory began to ponder over his abstention. Certainly, Julian was a Christian—though Gregory sometimes wondered how, given the circumstances. His mother, Basilina, was the cousin of Eusebius of Nicomedia; and when Julian's relatives were assassinated it was, initially, to Eusebius that he was sent for raising. Eusebius, however, soon left to become bishop of Constantinople; and Constantius, who had probably spared Julian's life (along with that of his brother, Gallus) solely because the deed could not be plausibly attributed to others, kept him out of politics via his exile to Cappadocia, where Julian learned his Bible and creeds from an exclusively Arian set of catechists. In fact, he seemed to have been allowed to learn little else, as Julian himself once avowed: "No strangers came near us, nor could any of our old friends visit us. We passed the time shut off from every liberal study and from all free intercourse, being reared in the midst of a brilliant servitude, and sharing in the activities of our slaves as though they were our equals. For no one of our own age came near us, nor were they allowed to do so."[138]

At some point, however—perhaps at a time when Constantius was too busy persecuting the great Athanasius of Alexandria to keep his eye so carefully on his prisoner—Julian made the acquaintance of a local Arian clergyman, George of Cappadocia. George had an extensive library at his villa, of both Christian and pagan works, and he allowed the emperor's adolescent brother-in-law full access to them. Forbidden fruit up to this point, it was, of course, the pagan books to which Julian was most strongly drawn: Homer, Hesiod, Plato, and Porphyry. The stirring myths and legends contained therein must have stood in stark contrast to the cheerless pedantry of the Arian spirit; and the wild, lawless mysticism of Neoplatonic theurgy would have offered an enticing alternative spirituality to a young man far too temperamentally religious to embrace mere atheism.

Yet Julian had, at least as far as Gregory knew, remained not only Christian but punctually and carefully Christian. He never missed Sunday service (which was better than either Basil or Gregory could themselves say, at this point) and he could quote Scripture like a scholar.

Yes, Julian was a puzzlement—but, like practically everyone else here at Athens, Gregory was very fond of him. He recalled, particularly, being charmed by Julian's mystical love of nature (expressed later in one of his writings) a quality that he himself strongly shared:

> From my childhood a great longing for the rays of [the sun] encompassed me, and from my earliest years my mind was so completely enthralled by the ethereal light that I not only longed to gaze steadfastly at the sun but also, whenever I walked forth at night under a clear and cloudless sky, casting aside all else, I gave myself up to the beauty of the heavens, paying no attention to what anyone said of me or what I was doing myself.[139]

Libanius, their mutual teacher, once reported that whenever Julian finished expressing an opinion "he quickly blushed at whatever he said, and this bashfulness was a source of delight to all."[140] People hated to part from him and could not say goodbye without distress. Yet even his warmest admirers knew that Julian had a dark side as well—an angry side that often revealed itself unexpectedly. Any mention of Constantius, for instance, set his beautiful eyes to flashing:

> Nothing of my father's estate came to me. I acquired nothing of the great wealth which had naturally belonged to my father, not the smallest clod, not a slave, not a house. For the noble Constantius had inherited in my place my father's entire substance, and he left me, as I have said, not even the least trifle of it. Further, though he gave my brother a few things that had belonged to our father, he deprived him entirely of his mother's estate.[141]

When Constantius, after the deaths of his own brothers, felt himself forced to make new Caesars to take their places, he had first chosen Gallus, this older brother of Julian's; yet Gallus acted the fool and eventually had to be removed, necessitating the recall of Julian as well. Even Gallus's folly, however, had actually been, in Julian's eyes, the fault of Constantius: "If there was anything rude or harsh in his disposition it was aggravated by his having been educated among those mountains. Consequently, the emperor is to blame for this also, since he provided such a bringing up for us against our wills." At times like these, a shadow seemed to pass over Julian's face, a subtle combination of pain and suppressed rage, and even violence did not seem out of the question. As for the ongoing dispute between Arian and orthodox Christianity, Julian's prevailing attitude was to put a pox on both their houses: "There are no wild beasts so hostile to mankind as are most Christians in their hatred for each other."

At this point, Libanius himself joined the party, ready to toast his now-famous student off to his new governorship in the West. Julian looked up from his playing and smiled at the teacher's arrival, sweetly and genuinely. Libanius, the celebrated—and still pagan—professor of Greek rhetoric, returned the welcome with a small, tight-lipped smile of his own, and (as Gregory thought) with a knowing look. When Constantius had finally allowed Julian to leave Cappadocia for the school at Athens, it was primarily so that he might continue innocent of all political aspirations by becoming more and more the harmless bookworm instead. Nevertheless, the emperor had, before granting his permission, made Julian swear not to attend Libanius's lectures for fear that he would lose his (Arian) Christianity.

Gregory and Basil knew for a fact, however, that Julian had followed Libanius's lectures anyway, by secretly paying other students to take notes for him. The two of them, in fact, often joked that their friend had acquired in this way a much more exalted opinion of Libanius than any of the students who had actually sat through his course! Yet now—perhaps it was the new (though admittedly remote) possibility that Julian might actually succeed

Constantius as sole emperor one day—all this didn't seem quite so funny to Gregory. He had, in fact, begun to connect it with what could only be described as "squirrelly behavior" from Julian as of late: irregular habits, shifty eyes, odd bursts of unexplained laughter, mysterious comings and goings during the night.

Lost in these reflections, Gregory hardly noticed at first when someone called for a debate. Ever since the days of Plato and Xenophon, no Greek symposium had been complete without a trial of rhetorical skill. The symposiarch, or wine master, had already mixed the wine in such a way as to sharpen the wits rather than indulge the senses, and even now, two young slaves were rounding the garden filling cups with it from their ceremonial *oenochoe* or wine pitchers. Libanius was urged to select the topic for dispute. At some slight risk of bad taste, he elected to cut right to the chase: "Is the Christian religion of God or of men only?" Gregory watched as this announcement sent a ripple of hesitation through the assembled group; yes, they seemed to grant, this topic had been fair game before, just as any subject could be debated among open-minded men of seriousness and good manners—but wasn't it, tonight at any rate, perhaps a bit too "on the nose"? All the same, Libanius proceeded to choose the two disputants as well: Basil of Cappadocia (long recognized as the ablest debater of the group) to take the pro-Christian position . . . and his old friend Julian Caesar to take the anti-Christian.

Basil rose willingly, confident of his skills, smiling and waving off the many proffered words of admiration, all to the disappointment of Gregory who (ever since the storm at sea) had grown more traditionally Christian in his dislike of seeing the things of the Lord handled with this kind of familiarity. One would have thought that Julian might be averse to such an assignment as well—not merely because he was a Christian himself (Libanius's debating students were taught to defend any intellectual position they were assigned, regardless of personal feelings), but simply because of his own airy, transcendental disposition. Julian's instincts had always been those of the mystic, almost totally the opposite of the Arian spirit in which he had been raised, where religion was primarily a matter of logical proofs and "having it all figured out."

Yet now—perhaps it was the wine speaking, watered as it may have been—the young Caesar acquiesced quite readily, alleging with a raised hand that the anti-Christian position was actually the more difficult side to defend. This elicited from the pagan portion of the assembly another round of shared glances and enigmatic smiles. Gregory was surprised that Basil, who had known Julian longer than he had, was still missing these alarming signals—but then Basil had always been pretty bad at picking up on body language or emotional cues. And now, sure enough, like the big black bull in a china cabinet that he was, Basil launched right into his opening statement, using a booming voice even a bit louder than usual—a circumstance that, as Gregory thought, might also be at least partially attributed to the evening's liberal use of good Greek wine.

Pulling at his bushy beard as he composed his thoughts, Basil launched immediately into a lengthy recapitulation of the argument from prophecy so memorably pioneered by Justin Martyr, that great patron of all who practice the art of Christian apologetics. God had chosen to reveal himself to the ancient race of the Jews, Basil avowed, gradually unveiling himself more and more clearly to their prophets as the Father of a coming deliverer, "through whom all the nations of the earth would be blessed." He employed numerous quotations from the Greek Septuagint, all of them indicating—or at least appearing to indicate—highly detailed prophecies of the life of Christ made centuries before the fact. These passages were, as even most heathen readers were willing to admit, highly suggestive facts calling, if not for faith, then at least for some other explanation. And when Basil finally concluded his opener, young Julian rose to his feet eagerly, ready to attempt just that.

Contemporary accounts tell us that Julian had a straight nose, elegant eyebrows, and (unusual for a Roman patrician in those days) a very long beard ending in a point. He also had big, broad shoulders that reminded people of his uncle, the Emperor Constantine.

Unlike Basil, his speaking voice was not impressive but it had an earnest quality in it, a nonverbal invitation to take life more seriously that was highly attractive, especially to young people. He responded to Basil's initial arguments just as the company expected he would: first, by debunking several of his prophecies in detail (claiming, for instance, that Jesus was not actually a physical descendant of Judah, as would seem to be necessary from the passages quoted), and then by magnifying the discontinuities between Jewish and Christian practices generally, in an effort to render untenable the whole conception of "Christianity as the fulfillment of Hebrew religion." Julian highlighted, for instance, the abandonment by Christians of practically all Judaism's most central distinctives: circumcision, the sacrificing of animals, the many dietary restrictions, and so forth. Had not Moses and Joshua pronounced the most dreadful warnings against those who should dare to alter God's everlasting law? And what of the Christian claim (and here Julian's line of argumentation began to reveal something of his Arian background) that the Hebrew God had created a being equal to himself in Christ—and thus a second God—when everyone knows that Judaism is the most adamantly monotheistic of all world religions?

Julian seemed to argue with great conviction here; and he did, as a matter of fact, have an excellent knowledge of Judaica at his command. Even so, his culminating counterattack was *anti*-Jewish in character. Is it not absurd to believe that the God who created the entire world had been content to waste his time shepherding so jealously a tiny, insignificant tribe in Palestine while simultaneously abandoning all other nations to the worship of false gods for century upon century? And if the God of the Hebrews is the only god, why was it that the Jews as a nation had accomplished so little in comparison to the Greeks, the Babylonians, even the ancient Egyptians from whom they separated themselves? Why had they been so often subjugated to barbarian races such as the Assyrians, the Philistines, or even the hated Persians? Concluding his rebuttal with this query, Julian again took his seat and received in response a round of applause quite a bit more enthusiastic than

Basil's had been; an unaccustomed gesture, as Gregory thought, from a group so traditionally equitable in its liberality.

When Basil rose again, however, he did so with a very distinct smile on his face. Had Julian stepped into some kind of trap the group hadn't yet noticed? Indeed he had, for somehow he had missed the elephant in the center of the *taberna*, so to speak. Had Caesar really been, asked Basil, so poor a student of recent history? Had he been so little impressed by his uncle's accomplishment? By the mercy of Christ, *Rome*—eternal Rome herself—was now Christian! The Messiah of those "insignificant" Hebrews, wearing the crown of David their king, had now become the King of Kings in truth, worshipped with humble obeisance by every local Roman satrap from Bithynia to Britannia! Christian missionaries, using the greatest highway system ever conceived by man, were now spreading their Gospel outside the imperial boundaries as well. Had Julian missed the recent conversion of savage Armenia—or that of the very Abyssinians he had just invoked? Even the current troubles with Persia had been caused, at least to some extent, by the massive, destabilizing conversions to Christianity taking place there! No, friends, no. Subject the Jews may have been for a season, just as the humble tortoise in Aesop's fable had been subject to the mockery of the hare for most of the course— but now, by God's grace, slow and steady had won the race!

And if, Basil continued, the insignificance of the Hebrew religion would have proved, as Julian would have it, the falseness of their revelations, does not their astounding new significance—*the conquerors of Rome!*—prove just the opposite? Genuinely puzzled, Basil let his question hang in the air, before stepping aside then wondering aloud (albeit respectfully) how his esteemed colleague could have "put his foot in it" with so elementary an error as this.

There was no applause at all this time but only silence. All eyes turned to Julian again, who sat impassive at first, stone-faced. Slowly, the pagans began to murmur among themselves; Gregory even saw—or thought he saw—some kind of curious hand signal being shared between them. Though everyone waited for it expectantly, the new governor of Gaul did not rise with a counter-reply. He simply sat seething in the firelight, his lower lip trembling, paralyzed completely by whatever interior battle was raging within. Finally, after what seemed an eternity, Julian merely indicated an unwillingness to continue; complaining, it seemed, to those immediately around him, that Basil's use of pagan wisdom (in the form of Aesop's fables) had constituted an unfair move somehow, an unmanly cheat that freed him from any necessity of mounting a reply.

Basil's expression changed from triumph to dismay. He watched in horror as his old friend rose to his feet and gathered up his things, apparently intent on leaving his own party early. Stepping across the circle to intervene, Basil wore an open, conciliatory expression and offered the outstretched hand of truce. He'd gotten carried away, perhaps, in the heat of the moment—too much wine, no doubt. Julian rounded on him harshly and produced, in the hearing of all, a bitter reversal of another fable: Aesop's old story about the ass that had once fooled the rest of the animals by wearing the skin of a lion. Perhaps, declared Caesar, Christian Rome might have to learn one day about a lion who had—while patiently biding his time for a season—worn the skin of an ass.

Basil stood thunderstruck and watched him go. Gregory's reaction was more vocal—and a little too unguarded for his own good, given the true state of affairs just revealed. Those, at any rate, who overheard it—pagan and Christian alike—remembered it for years to come: "What a monster the Roman Empire is nourishing within itself!"[142]

The Whole World Groaned

Athanasius's return from the West was, if anything, more glorious than from his first exile—but equally short lived.

Eusebius of Nicomedia himself had died while Athanasius was in Rome; yet he had, nevertheless,

> arrived at the summit of his hopes. He may really have believed Arian doctrine, but clearly his chief aim had ever been

his own aggrandizement, and the humiliation of those who had humbled him at Nicaea. He had succeeded. His enemies were in exile. His creatures stained the sees of Alexandria and Antioch. He was bishop of the imperial city, and the young emperor obeyed his counsels. If Epiphanius is right in calling him an old man even before Nicaea he must now have reached a great age. His work lived after him. He had trained a group of prelates who continued his intrigues, and who followed the court from place to place throughout the reign of Constantius. More than this, it may be said that the world suffers to this day from the evil wrought by this worldly bishop.[143]

Those Eusebian prelates, according to Athanasius himself, now went in a body to the emperor

and besought him, saying, "When we first made our request to you we were not believed; for we told you, when you sent for Athanasius, that by inviting him to come forward [i.e., to return from exile] you are expelling our heresy. For he has been opposed to it from the very first, and never ceases to anathematize it. He has already written letters against us into all parts of the world, and the majority of men have embraced communion with him; and even of those who seemed to be on our side, some have been gained over by him, and others are likely to be. And we are left alone, so that the fear is, lest the character of our heresy become known, and henceforth both we and you gain the name of heretics. . . . Therefore begin again to persecute, and support the heresy, for it accounts you its king."

Was it true, even after the triumphs of Eusebius, that "the majority of men" were still orthodox? Very much so, if by "the majority of men" one means the laity, not the clergy. Athanasius had witnessed this firsthand on his long journey back to Egypt from the West. Even in Syria and Palestine, where the leadership had been in Arian hands for nearly twenty-five years, he had been met from town to town by great outpourings of popular support and enthusiasm. Arianism, in other words, was still being imposed *from the top down*, not from religious motives but for the sake of political unity in the Roman Empire. [XCIII]

> "Subscribe, or withdraw from your churches, for the emperor has commanded you to be deposed!" . . . In this manner it was that the emperor forced so great a multitude of Bishops, partly by threats, and partly by promises, to declare, "We will no longer hold communion with Athanasius." For those who came for an interview, were not admitted to his presence, nor allowed any relaxation, not so much as to go out of their dwellings, until they had either subscribed, or refused and incurred banishment thereupon. And this he did because he saw that the heresy was hateful to all men. For this reason especially he compelled so many to add their names to the small number of the Arians . . . supposing that he will be able to alter the truth, as easily as he can influence the minds of men.[144]

When, in 350, his brother Constans was killed trying to put down a usurper of his own in the West, Constantius felt that he had, at last, a free hand. Yet Athanasius had become more than a troublesome subject by now; he was almost an imperial rival himself. "The circumstances of the times," as Newman writes,

---

[XCIII] "[The Orthodox party] relied on the greatest religious force of those times, the monks, as well as on the faith of the mass of devout believers . . ." Soloviev, *The Russian Church and the Papacy*, 30. "The people looked to the monks for the color of their theology. Arianism felt its weakness without them and ineffectually sought their suppression. The Nicene faith uniformly received the support of these communities, to which they remained devoted under all persecutions." Chester D. Hartranft, introduction to Sozomen, *Ecclesiastical History*.

had attached an adventitious importance to his fortunes; as if the cause of the *Homoüsion* were providentially committed to his custody, and in his safety or overthrow, the triumph or loss of the truth were actually involved. . . . Considering then Athanasius too great for a subject, Constantius, as if for the peace of his empire, desired his destruction at any rate. Whether he was unfortunate or culpable it mattered not; whether implicated in legal guilt, or forced by circumstances into his present position; still he was the fit victim of a sort of ecclesiastical ostracism, which, accordingly, he called upon the Church to inflict. He demanded it of the Church, for the very eminence of Athanasius rendered it unsafe, even for the emperor, to approach him in any other way.

It was vital to the emperor's cause that the *bishops* should punish Athanasius, rather than the secular power, because public opinion was still far too strong in his favor for Constantius to act alone:

The patriarch of Alexandria could not be deposed, except after a series of successes over less powerful Catholics, and with the forced acquiescence or countenance of the principal Christian communities. And thus the history of the [next] few years of the persecution, presents to us the curious spectacle of a party warfare raging everywhere, except in the neighborhood of the person who was the real object of it, and who was left for a time to continue the work of God at Alexandria, unmolested by the councils, conferences, and usurpations, which perplexed the other capitals of Christendom.[145]

Western leaders became the emperor's main targets at this stage, for he was embarrassed by the charge (perfectly true) that hatred for Athanasius was primarily an Eastern phenomenon and this primarily because Constantius already had the Eastern bishops in his pocket. His first notable catch in this

regard was Vincent of Capua, one of the two papal legates
who had signed for Sylvester at Nicaea. Vincent was tricked
into accepting the condemnation of Athanasius by a promise
that Arianism would be explicitly condemned along with him.
Unsurprisingly, the censure thus obtained was noised loudly
abroad, while the condemnation of Arianism remained "forth-
coming." After this, the emperor decided to stage a Western
council—a council in Italy, which no one might accuse of un-
due Eastern influence. He also planned, however, to attend
the proposed council himself, along with an entire legion of
troops. This council was held in the spring of 355—the Council of Milan—and more than 300 Western bishops turned up.
They were offered a creed that had only one real defect: it
omitted the word *homoousious*. In a building surrounded on
all sides by armed men, most of them signed it right away.[XCIV]
Next up on the docket: yet another condemnation of Athanasius was produced. When nearly half the assembly balked at it,
doubting the little patriarch's guilt, Constantius himself (who
had, up to this time, been content to listen in on the proceedings from an antechamber) rushed from behind a curtain with
his sword drawn and simply ordered the bishops to take his
word on the subject. The contrast with his father's conduct at
Nicaea could not have been more complete.

> When the bishops heard this they were utterly amazed, and
> stretching forth their hands to God, they used great boldness
> of speech against him teaching him that the kingdom was not
> his, but God's, who had given it to him, Whom also they bid
> him fear, lest He should suddenly take it away from him. And
> they threatened him with the day of judgment, and warned

[XCIV] "Those, who would rather have suffered death than have sanctioned
the impieties of Arius, hardly saw how to defend themselves in refusing
creeds, which were abstractedly true, though incomplete, and intolerable
only because the badges of a prevaricating party. Thus Arianism gained
its first footing in the West." Newman, *Arians of the Fourth Century,* 308.

him against infringing ecclesiastical order, and mingling Roman sovereignty with the constitution of the Church, and against introducing the Arian heresy into the Church of God. But he would not listen to them, nor permit them to speak further, but threatened them so much the more.[146]

Those who held firm in spite of this were dealt with summarily. Dionysius, the bishop of Milan, was deposed and replaced with a hard Arian, Auxentius. At least three other Western bishops were banished from the Roman Empire. One brave deacon, Hilarius, especially vocal in his denunciation of the irregular proceedings, was stripped, tied to a pillar, and flogged like his Lord before him.

> The deacon, while he was being scourged, praised the Lord, remembering his words, "I gave my back to the smiters [Isa. 50:6]"; but they while they scourged him laughed and mocked him, feeling no shame that they were insulting a Levite.[xcv] Indeed they acted but consistently in laughing while he continued to praise God; for it is the part of Christians to endure stripes, but to scourge Christians is the outrage of a Pilate or a Caiaphas.[147]

All in all, 147 Western clergymen were banished at Milan by order of Constantius; the rest of the 300, trembling and overawed, signed and went meekly back to their churches.

Finally, two unworthy bishops, Ursacius and Valens, urged the emperor to aim high—to go after the pope of Rome himself, Liberius (newly elected to replace Julius, who passed away not long after saying goodbye to Athanasius). Constantius saw the point right away. If the successor of Peter were to become Arian

---

[xcv] This comparison of Christian clergy to the priests of the Old Covenant is fairly widespread in Patristic literature and quite significant. The earliest example appears in Clement's *Epistle to the Corinthians*, a book written about the same time as the Gospel of John, by a coworker of the apostle Paul.

and start preaching Arianism, the battle would be practically over. Consequently, the emperor "strove with burning desire," according to the pagan historian Ammianus, "that the sentence [against Athanasius] should be confirmed by the higher authority of the bishop of the eternal city."[148]

The pope, accordingly, was asked politely to endorse the decrees of Milan. Liberius replied that he would rather die first and would defend the faith of Nicaea till the end. He was offered bribes of cash, which he flung into the streets. At last, Constantius ordered him seized immediately, by violence if necessary. Liberius was taken from Rome by soldiers and carried away to exile at Beroea in Thrace (modern Bulgaria). On the emperor's orders one of Liberius's deacons, Felix, was consecrated to replace him by Acacius, Arian bishop of Caesarea. "He preserved inviolate the doctrines set forth in the Nicene confession of faith, yet he held communion with those who had corrupted that faith. For this reason none of the citizens of Rome would enter the House of Prayer while he was in it."[149]

About the same time, the Eusebians called for the arrest of Hosius of Cordoba as well, now close to a hundred years old: "We have done everything," wrote Athanasius, in summarizing their appeal to the emperor.

> We have banished the bishop of the Romans; and before him a very great number of other bishops, and have filled every place with alarm. But these strong measures of yours, are as nothing to us, nor is our success at all more secure, so long as Hosius remains . . . He is the president of councils, and his letters are everywhere attended to. He it was who put forth the Nicene Confession, and proclaimed everywhere that the Arians were heretics. If therefore he is suffered to remain, the banishment of the rest is of no avail, for our heresy will be destroyed. Begin then to persecute him also and spare him not, ancient as he is. Our heresy knows not to honor even the hoary hairs of the aged.

The feeble old Spaniard was brought east, cajoled, bribed like Liberius, and finally threatened and terrorized. "Cease these proceedings, I beseech you," was his reply,

and remember that you are a mortal man . . . God has put into your hands the kingdom; to us he has entrusted the affairs of His Church; and as he who would steal the empire from you would resist the ordinance of God, so likewise fear on your part lest by taking upon yourself the government of the Church, you become guilty of a great offense. It is written, "Render unto Caesar the things that are Caesar's, and unto God the things that are God's" [Matt. 22:21].

Instead of so rendering, Constantius determined—not to banish Hosius as he had the pope—but to hold him a whole year at an imperial fortress in frigid Sirmium. "Godless, unholy, without natural affection," concluded Athanasius,

he feared not God, he regarded not his father's affection for Hosius, he reverenced not his great age . . . but all these things this modern Ahab, this second Belshazzar of our times, disregarded for the sake of impiety. He used such violence towards the old man, and confined him so tightly, that at last, broken by suffering, he was brought, though hardly, to hold communion with Valens, Ursacius, and their fellows, though he would not subscribe against Athanasius. Yet even thus he forgot not his duty, for at the approach of death, as it were by his last testament, he bore witness to the force which had been used towards him, and anathematized the Arian heresy, and gave strict charge that no one should receive it.

About this same time, Athanasius heard with dismay a report (though there was—and still is—some doubt of its accuracy) that Liberius had stumbled as well, signing "from fear of death"[150] an ambiguous confession of faith and thereby obtaining his own release.[XCVI]

Having reached such a summit at last, the emperor, only then, turned his sights directly upon Athanasius once more. Early in

---

[XCVI] In reporting that Liberius simply lapsed due to fear, Athanasius must surely have been either acting on incomplete information or perhaps deceived by Arian disinformation (we do know that Euxodius, the Arian bishop of Antioch, did circulate forged letters to this effect). At any rate, only he and one other orthodox writer (Hilary of Poitiers) relate the story in that way. Socrates, Theodoret, Rufinus, and Sulpicius Severus all tell us that the Romans rose up against Felix and drove him out, just as the Alexandrians had driven out the Arian Gregory, obliging Constantius to release the pope for fear of a general Western uprising. Even the Arian historian Philostorgius concurs with this account. Equally telling is the way in which Liberius was received at Rome upon his return: not spurned as a coward or turncoat, but restored immediately to the papacy by the very people who had just rejected Felix (entirely orthodox!) merely for *holding communion with Arians*. The emperor, likewise, would surely have crowed loudly about any victory over the pope—that, after all, was the whole point of his having been persecuted—and yet there is no record of any such pronouncement, nor did Liberius himself make any recantation or public confession of having fallen. It is possible (but not certain) that the pope *was* driven to sign the Creed of Sirmium during his exile; but this document had been deliberately designed to bear either an orthodox or an Arian interpretation and is thus no proof of actual heresy on his part. "Yet even this only shows," according to Athanasius himself, "the hatred of Liberius against the heresy . . . so long as he was suffered to exercise a free choice. For that which men are forced by torture to do contrary to their first judgment, ought not to be considered the willing deed of those who are in fear, but rather of their tormentors." (One added point: though it has often been brought up in that context, the case of Liberius adds nothing at all to the debate over papal infallibility. "Even if Liberius signed the document," as apologist Leslie Rumble writes, "and even if that document were heretical, and even if Liberius personally held and believed heretical doctrine, no argument even then could be drawn from the case against the Catholic doctrine of papal infallibility. For the Catholic Church has never defined that the Popes are always infallible in all that they personally believe. The Catholic Church declares that the Pope is infallible when he gives an official definition of doctrine concerning faith or morals, it being required that he acts freely, that he declares himself to be acting in his capacity as head of the whole Church, and that he intends his definition to be binding upon all the faithful throughout the world. Not one of these last requirements was verified in the case of Liberius, and whatever view one takes of the case historically, it is invalid as a test of infallibility."

February 356, Constantius sent a brutal and trusted general, Syrianus, to extract the patriarch from his bishopric at Alexandria, dead or alive. Athanasius later wrote down the story in his own words:

> The Arians [of the city] mixed with the soldiers in order to exasperate them against me and, as they were unacquainted with my person, to point me out to them . . . It was now night [at the Church of St. Thomas], and some of the people were keeping a vigil preparatory to a communion on the morrow, when the General Syrianus suddenly came upon us with more than 5,000 soldiers, having arms and drawn swords, bows, spears, and clubs, as I have related above. With these he surrounded the Church, stationing his soldiers near at hand, in order that no one might be able to leave the Church and pass by them. Now I considered that it would be unreasonable in me to desert the people during such a disturbance, and not to endanger myself in their behalf; therefore I sat down upon my throne, and desired the deacon to read a psalm, and the people to answer, "For his mercy endures forever" [Ps. 136], and then all to withdraw and depart home.
>
> But the general having now made a forcible entry, and the soldiers having surrounded the sanctuary for the purpose of apprehending us, the clergy and those of the laity, who were still there, cried out, and demanded that we too should withdraw. But I refused, declaring that I would not do so, until [the congregation] had retired one and all. Accordingly I stood up, and having bidden prayer, I then made my request of them, that all should depart before me, saying that it was better that my safety should be endangered, than that any of them should receive hurt. So when the greater part had gone forth, and the rest were following, the monks who were there with us and certain of the clergy came up and dragged us away.

At this dramatic point comes another of those curious Gospel parallels we have already noted: "And thus (Truth is my witness), while some of the soldiers stood about the sanctuary, and others were going round the church, we passed through [the midst of them], under the Lord's guidance, and with his protection withdrew without observation [cf. Luke 4:30]."[151]

Spirited away once more to the outskirts of the city, Athanasius saw the great darkened desert spreading southward into Africa again, beckoning him to begin his third exile. Once more, a tyrannical Caesar was behind him, seeking his life for the "good" of the empire; once more, camels had been prepared to help him vanish into the Thebaid. With his friends now banished, Hosius shamed, an antipope on the Chair of Peter, and eight out of ten Christian bishoprics occupied by deniers of the divinity of Christ, this was the period about which the scholar Jerome later spoke, when he wrote those famous words *Ingemuit totus or bis et Arianum se esse miratus est*—"The whole world groaned and was astonished to find itself Arian."

THE BRIAR PATCH

When Basil of Cappadocia joined Athanasius in the desert, some three years after the bachelor party at Athens, he was a different man altogether.[XCVII]

His brother Naucratius, dearest to him of all his siblings and the one most deeply committed to his faith, had drowned in a fishing accident. This ought, perhaps, to have been something a grown man gets over eventually—but it hadn't been. When he returned to see the boy buried, his sister Macrina (speaking rather too frankly in her grief) compared Basil's piety poorly to that of the deceased; she called him arrogant, "puffed up beyond measure" with the pride of his great learning, far more

---

[XCVII] While we don't know for sure that Basil met Athanasius personally during his sojourn among the ascetics (no recorded account of such a meeting has survived), their timetables for 357 certainly match well enough; and the letters they exchanged in the years to come do seem to indicate at least some previous acquaintance.

likely to quote Plato or Aristotle than our blessed savior. Under the circumstances, her words were like blows. Basil wept for a season—then renounced his recently obtained teaching chair at the university in Caesarea. He accepted baptism instead (after a long delay not unlike that of Constantine), and finally sold all his possessions just as Antony had and set out to find the locust eaters, the Children of Israel.

Athanasius, it is true, had been banished from his episcopal manse in the city to the harshness of the blistering desert, a home proper not for men but only for the scorpion and the adder. Yet like Br'er Rabbit in Chandler Harris's famous folktales, Athanasius had the last laugh, for he was "born and bred in the briar patch." During previous visits, as Payne describes, "the monks, wearing their sleeveless tunics, sheepskin cloaks and woolen cowls, would come running up to him in multitudes, offering him the loyalty he received less often in the great cities. They recognized him as one of themselves. Whenever he was in danger he had only flee to the desert to secure a hiding place."

This time, they welcomed him not only as an old friend but, as Athanasius learned upon his arrival, as the spiritual successor to their beloved founder, Antony of Coma, who had come to the end of his earthly journey not long before. Athanasius included the story as he heard it in the biography of Antony he composed during this exile:

> What the end of his life was like, it is fit that I should relate, and you hear eagerly. For it too is worthy of emulation. He was visiting, according to his wont, the monks in the outer mountain, and having learned from Providence concerning his own end, he said to the brethren, "This visit to you is my last, and I wonder if we shall see each other again in this life. It is time for me to set sail, for I am near a hundred and five years old." And when they heard that they wept, and embraced and kissed the old man. And he, as if he was setting out from a foreign city to his own, spoke joyfully, and exhorted them not to grow idle in their labors or cowardly

in their training, but to live as those who died daily, and (as I said before) to be earnest in keeping their souls from foul thoughts, and to emulate the saints . . . [but not] to have any communion with the Arians, for their impiety . . . is manifest to all. Neither if ye shall see the magistrates patronizing them, be troubled, for their phantasy shall have an end, and is mortal and only for a little while. Keep yourselves therefore rather clean from them, and hold that which has been handed down to you by the fathers, and especially the faith in our Lord Jesus Christ which ye have learned from Scripture, and of which ye have often been reminded by me. . . .

After a few months he grew sick, and calling those who were by—and there were two of them who had remained there with him fifteen years, exercising themselves and ministering to him on account of his old age—he said to them, "I indeed go the way of the fathers, as it is written, for I perceive that I am called by the Lord."

Of possessions, Antony had practically none, yet these few he distributed as a last will and testament. He gave a sheepskin to Athanasius, as well as a cloak that he would wear for the rest of his own life. He was no doubt wearing it when young Basil arrived, looking for role models.

Basil brought stories, too—he was, in fact, the bearer of bad news from the outside world. Alexandria had a new bishop, a figure familiar from Basil's own past in Cappadocia, an idle, wealthy Arian dilettante named George (he from whom Julian had borrowed pagan literature once upon a time); and of all their obnoxious tribe, George was perhaps the worst. Basil's friend Gregory Nazianzen called him "a man of low birth and lower mind," *nouveau riche*, as we might put it today, who "after sneaking into public life, and filling its lowest offices, such as that of contractor for swine's flesh, the soldiers' rations, and then having proved himself a scoundrel for the sake of greed in this public trust, and been stripped to the skin, contrived to escape, and after passing, as exiles do, from country to country and city to city, last of all, in an evil hour for the Christian community, like one of the plagues of Egypt, he reached Alexandria."[152]

It seemed almost as if Constantius, in seeking a replacement for the great Athanasius, had chosen the man least like him that he could find. George entered the city with great military pomp, supported by Syrianus the general, and then immediately commenced a persecution on behalf of Arianism more vicious even than that of the previous heretical interloper, that Gregory who had been killed by the mob. George even resorted to the use of a technique pioneered by Macedonius, the Nicomedian's replacement at Constantinople, in which those who refused to attend his communion services were "forcibly constrained . . . to be partakers of the holy mysteries, their mouths being forced open with a piece of wood, and then the consecrated elements thrust into them."[153]

Meanwhile, Basil's old companion Julian had ascended to undreamed-of heights of his own—a sudden rise in which his Christian friends, alas, perceived little but ominous danger. As governor of Gaul, Julian had set to work on what his old classmates would have considered the unlikeliest new course of study imaginable: military science and tactics. After starting from absolute scratch (he learned how to march by drilling with the foot soldiers), Julian soon excelled beyond all expectation, proving his mettle by stunning victories in the field against the Alamanni and the Franks, opening the Upper Rhine once again for shipping.

Constantius was flummoxed; indeed, he had even withheld reinforcements at a crucial juncture for fear that Julian would succeed and become more popular than himself—which was, of course, exactly what did happen. The only sense that Basil could make in any of this was that Julian, the gentle academic with the guitar, had now set his eyes set on Constantius's throne. What was his motivation? Revenge must have factored in surely, revenge against the man who "left me an orphan as a child . . . my father's murderer."[154] Yet Basil feared that even more was afoot, for though Julian had attended Epiphany services at Vienne as recently as the previous January, all of his friends found the façade of his Christianity less and less convincing. Could it be that he aspired to be more than merely Constantius's replacement— that Julian dreamed of becoming as great as Constantine himself . . . but in reverse? Truly, one's heart withered within at such a conception.

There was, however, at least a touch of good news for Basil to relate: the Arian movement showed signs of fissuring, was presenting a less united front than before. By making so many new creeds, apparently, and by making them sound as orthodox as possible, the Arians had actually succeeded in fooling (or confusing, at any rate) a good portion of their own congregants and in strengthening their own conservative wing! Those who had been willing to Arianize with the Eusebians as a way to conciliate the emperor, but who were in their hearts still mostly orthodox, were now becoming the actual majority and were finding themselves more and more drawn to the traditional view, less and less angry at Athanasius. In reaction to this, the more thoroughgoing Arians among them (such as the cold and relentless Antiochene layman, Aetius[XCVIII]) became even harder and more uncompromising in their Arianism—driving the emerging majority, in turn, even more decisively backward toward orthodoxy. Though their patron, Eusebius Pamphilus, died not long after Constantine, this large Semi-Arian middle still kept striving for peace; and peace, nowadays, was beginning to mean

---

[XCVIII] "Aetius . . . used to argue relentlessly that the principles of both monotheism and of divine impassibility could only be consistently maintained if one frankly asserted that the Son is not merely distinct from the Father but actually belongs to the created order; that all derived being is substantially dissimilar from the underived First Cause; in short, that the Son's essence is unlike (*anomoios*) the Father's. This position, quickly labelled Anomoean or 'dissimilarian,' was opposed not merely to the Nicene formula . . . but also to the predominant formula of the great majority of Greek bishops that the Son's essence is 'like' the Father's (*homoiousios*) as a perfect image resembles its archetype." Chadwick, *The Early Church*, 141.

peace with Christianity's past as well: with its traditional and Trinitarian past. And this provided an opening the little patriarch of Alexandria felt he could exploit.

So Athanasius immediately set about writing, during this period, a series of books and letters aimed directly at these wavering Semi-Arians with a view toward winning them over: among others, the *Apology to Constantius*, the *Apology for His Flight*, his *Letter to the Monks*, *History of the Arians*, even the *Life of Antony*. Many of the minor clergy's capitulations, he believed, really had been caused by confusion, by sincere bewilderment over the matters in question, not dissimilar to that which Constantine had felt during his periods of discouragement. Arianism had experienced great success at first because (as Newman puts it) it is, by nature, easier to find objections than to solve them. So in these books, Athanasius set about trying to clear up the mere misunderstandings and to start going beyond simple insistence on theological continuity into the more difficult work of actually expressing (if not explaining) the mysteries of the Holy Trinity.

He established, first of all, that the Arian position is really, at heart, no more than a clever sleight of hand. It assumes, at first, that Christ really is a son in the usual sense, by insisting that no son is as old as his own father. It then turns right around, however, and uses this premise to arrive at the conclusion that Christ is no true son at all, except by way of analogy, but rather, a mere creature of God, with little more than an honorary title to show from his adopted Father. Athanasius exposes these fallacies brilliantly in the desert books; indeed, his theological writing continues to be, as it was in the days of *De Incarnatione*, surprisingly sophisticated for a man with practically no formal education, who probably grew up in a cave. A monk at heart, he was an apologist in day-to-day practice. In this he reminds one, perhaps, of the great English apologist G.K. Chesterton, who admired the peasant ideal most of all, advocated a return to the land as a solution to the economic problem, but who never could actually bring himself to give up the excitement of life as a Fleet Street journalist. Probably Athanasius had allowed Antony to be simple for him, while he, himself, had been forced by circumstances to become complex. At any rate, he attacks the Arian weaknesses with great acumen as well as with zest . . . and was, apparently, actually *read* by his opponents.

> The generation of the Son from the Father is otherwise than that which accords with the nature of men; and he is not only like, but is in fact inseparable from the substance of the Father. He and the Father are indeed one, as he did say Himself;[155] and the Word is ever in the Father and the Father in the Word, as is the way of radiance in relation to light. The term itself indicates this; and the Council [of Nicaea], so understanding the matter, did well, therefore, when it wrote *homoousious*, so that it might defeat the perverseness of the heretics, while proclaiming that the Word is other than created things. . . .
>
> God creates, while creating is also attributed to men; and God, indeed, is Being, while men too are said to be, having received even this gift from God. And yet, does God create as men do? Or is his being like that of man? No indeed. Rather, we take these terms in one way in regard to God, and understand them a different way for men. Indeed, God creates by calling into existence that which did not exist, requiring nothing in order to do it; but men [must] work with some existing material . . . obtaining [even] the ability of making from that God who fashioned all things through his own proper Word. . . . Just as the way in which men create is not the same way in which God creates, so also man's generation is in one way, while the Son is from the Father in another way. For the offspring of men are as a portion of their fathers, since the very nature of bodies is not to be a simple thing, but unsettled and composed of parts. . . . God, however, being without parts, is Father of the Son without division and without being acted upon. . . .
>
> Being simple in nature, he is the Father of only one Son. On this account is that Son only-begotten, and alone is he

in the bosom of the Father; and alone is He acknowledged by the Father as being from him, when he says, "This is my beloved Son, in whom I am well-pleased."[156]

Yet what of David, the Arians sometimes inquired, "a man after God's own heart" (1 Sam. 13:14)? Or of Moses, who, like Christ, "interceded for the people" (Num. 21:7)? "Behold, it was through Moses," writes Athanasius, summarizing this argument, "that he led the people out of Egypt, and through him he gave them the law; and Moses, nevertheless, was but a man; therefore it is possible for like to be brought into existence through like." He then proceeds to tear it to pieces:

> When they say such a thing as that, they ought to veil their faces the better to hide their shame. Moses was not sent to be a creator, nor to call into existence things which were not, nor to fashion men like himself, but only to be the minister of words to the people and to Pharao, the King. This is quite a different matter; for to minister is the work of servants, of created beings; while to fashion and to create belongs to God alone, to His own Word and Wisdom. When it comes to the matter of creation, therefore, we shall find none but God's Word; for all things were made in Wisdom [Ps. 104:24], and without the Word, nothing was made [John 1:3].[157]

Ultimately, however, Athanasius does come back around to the argument from continuity, from Antony's list. Even Constantine, a military man steeped in history and reverence for longstanding tradition, had known to back the "original Church as he found her"—and had stuck to this position (however imperfectly) to the end of his life, no matter how expedient it became to do otherwise. Similarly, Athanasius spells out the difference between what the Nicene Council had done and the approach taken by the many lawless and arrogant synods held since that time:

[The Fathers of the Ecumenical Council of Nicaea], without prefixing consulate, month, and day, wrote concerning [the proper date on which to celebrate] Easter: "The following has been decided." And it was at that time decided that all should comply. But concerning matters of faith, they did not write "It has been decided," but "Thus the Catholic Church believes." And thereupon they confessed how they believed. This they did in order to show that their judgment was not of more recent origin, but was in fact of apostolic times; and that what they wrote was no discovery of their own, but is simply that which was taught by the apostles.[158]

Let us [as well, continue to] note that the very tradition, teaching, and faith of the Catholic Church from the beginning, which the Lord gave, was preached by the apostles, and was preserved by the Fathers. On this the Church was founded; and if anyone departs from this, he neither is nor any longer ought to be called a Christian: there is a Trinity, holy and perfect, acknowledged as God, in Father, Son, and Holy Spirit . . . and thus there is preached in the Church one God, "who is over all, and through all, and in all" [Eph. 4:6]. He is *over all* as Father, as beginning, as source; and *through all*, through the Word; and *in all*, in the Holy Spirit.[159]

How much, if any, direct tutoring in these matters Basil received from Athanasius we do not know. He lingered in the desert only about six months, while Athanasius's very active third exile lasted over six years. Basil was, nevertheless, destined to take up this great work himself and to become, in the decades ahead, Arianism's most deadly opponent. Inspired by what he had seen in the desert, Basil returned to Caesarea in the spring of 358, fired with enthusiasm for a new project. While there, he recruited his old friend Gregory Nazianzen, and yet another Gregory (one of his remaining siblings, later to be known as Gregory of Nyssa), and the three of them returned to their native district of Pontus, intending to found a new commune on the family's ancestral property on the river Ibora. It would, like

Antony's unintentional community, be based on prayer and fast-ing, and on works of mercy toward the homeless and hungry; but it would also be modeled after that same community *under Athanasius*—a "think tank," so to speak, in the great defensive war against state-sponsored heresy.

Athanasius himself returned to civilization because of Julian. The distant conflict with Persia had reached a turning point. King Sapor demanded, in exchange for peace, the cessation to Persia of large swaths of Roman territory along his borders. Constantius, hoping to kill two birds with one stone, ordered Julian, with his recently victorious Gauls, to march the length of the empire, and to engage Sapor's forces directly (though there were many nearer and fresher legions available close at hand). Julian's troops promptly rebelled, hauled him from his residence in Paris, and proclaimed him Augustus (instead of Constantius) on the spot. Though Julian, hoping to avoid a civil war, was conciliatory at first, Constantius was infuriated at the news and demanded him to surrender even his current title of deputy-emperor, and his position as governor of Gaul. The army took this as a signal to march on Constantius instead of Sapor—and, indeed, many Western Christians backed Julian's cause at this point, seeing him as a champion against their longtime persecu-tor in the East (and lacking, unfortunately, Basil and Gregory's "inside information" on the matter in question). Sapor now called his army back to Persia, hoping perhaps to sit back and watch at his leisure while the two Roman emperors destroyed each other. And Constantius, indeed, mustered the largest army he could create and marched westward to smash this new pre-tender to his throne, with the odds heavily in his favor.

The matter was settled, however, by fate—and rather anticli-mactically, one must confess. Constantius simply got sick during the long march and died, at Mopsuestia in Cilicia, on November 3, 361. He had himself baptized beforehand by an Arian bishop and then, surprising everyone, declared Julian his rightful suc-cessor. His troops turned back toward the capital, where they buried his body in the same crypt with that of his father. When word of the death of Constantius reached Alexandria, the pro-Christian party revolted once again and dislodged George of Cappadocia from his stolen bishopric. Emperor Julian, meanwhile, announced a general amnesty for all banished clerics and also his intent to cease any further religious persecutions in the empire whatsoever. Athanasius was thus free to return, which he did, accompanied once more by great rejoicings, on February 21, 362. He was about sixty-five years of age.

The Great Apostate

All his Christians had been Arians.

His mother Basilina, his guardian Eusebius, George, his benefactor growing up, his brother Gallus—all of them were Christological heretics. Gallus, in fact, fearing that his sibling was spending too much time studying pagan mysticism, once sent a Christian apologist to steady Julian's faith—Aetius, captain of the far-left wing of the movement, whose Arianism was so absolute that the orthodox called him "the Atheist"! Even Basil and Gregory, destined to become, in the centuries ahead, two of the most immortal heroes of orthodoxy, entered Julian's life at a period when they themselves were hardly to be considered good examples. It takes a callous observer indeed not to find at least some pity for the man now remembered to history as "Julian the Apostate"—but apostate is just what he became, an out-and-out pagan priest offering sacrifice to Zeus and Hermes, and now emperor of Rome, with a burning passion to undo the work of Constantine entirely.

By Julian's own account he "walked along the road" of the Christians "until his twentieth year" (350 or 351), but now "with the help of the gods" had been following a different path "for twelve years." By this timetable, we can determine that he had already ceased to consider himself a Christian some four years or more before joining Basil and Gregory at Athens—"Let that darkness be forgotten," as he would later write. The process had begun, however, much earlier than that; Socrates tells us that a pagan magician named Maximus set his sights on the future emperor while Julian was still in his teens, and from Maximus the young prince had "received, in addition to the principles of philosophy, his own religious sentiments, and a desire to possess the empire."[160] Desperately, in reaction to the dry, logic-chopping sophistry of his Arian upbringing, Julian was craving not more syllogistic proofs, but a *direct experience* of the divine, the supernatural—a psychological fact about their target with which his seducers were all too aware. Theodoret tells us (in a story he learned from Gregory Nazianzen) that Julian was taken, at one point, into a mysterious cavern, with promises of initiation into the arcane science of theosophy. His conductor (probably Maximus) "introduced him within the shrine, and called upon the demons of deceit."

"As Julian advanced farther and farther," explains Giuseppe Ricciotti,

he encountered terrors increasingly numerous and alarming—strange sounds, revolting exhalations, fiery apparitions, and other such prodigies. Since he was taking his first steps in the occult sciences, the strangeness of the apparitions terrified him. He made the sign of the cross. The demons were subdued and all the visions disappeared. Julian regained courage and began to advance. Then the dread objects started to reappear. The sign of the cross was repeated and they again disappeared. Julian wavered.[161]

"On the magician becoming acquainted with the cause of their flight," continues Theodoret,

he blamed him; but Julian confessed his terror, and said that he wondered at the power of the cross, for that the demons could not endure to see its sign and ran away. "Think not anything of the sort, good sir"; said the magician, "they were not afraid as you make out, but they went away because they abominated what you did." So he tricked the wretched man, initiated him in the mysteries, and filled him with their abominations.[162]

Probably the whole experience was nothing but an elaborate "spook house" tricked up by fraudsters; history records many such hoaxes perpetrated on behalf of various pagan cults, all the way back to the scheme exposed by the prophet Daniel in the Septuagint version of the book bearing his name (Dan. 14:1–21). Still, Julian was deceived—and fascinated.

By the time he reached Athens, Julian was actively (but surreptitiously) courting all kindred spirits, anyone unhappy for whatever reason with his uncle's great revolution of 313. "In their hearts there still lived," as Ricciotti writes, "a vague hope, and undefined suspicion, that the last word had not yet been spoken. The glorious patrimony of the Greeks could not suffer gradual eclipse that would end in darkness." His teacher, Libanius, became an active co-conspirator, who later felt free (during Julian's reign) to reveal that the group had met often in secret, sharing their eager expectation that the young prince would soon be able to overthrow the oppression of the "Galileans"[XCIX] and

---

[XCIX] Ironically, the pagans really were being oppressed by this point—not by Constantine or the Council of Nicaea, but by Constantius, on behalf of Arianism, the first emperor to actually persecute paganism. "'The accursed tolerance shall cease,' he declared in one of his edicts. He prohibited all heathen sacrifices under penalty of death and in 353, after his victory over the pagan usurper Magnentius, ordered all the pagan temples to be closed, dismantled, or converted to other purposes. These severe measures did not have the desired effect; they only gave dying paganism a new lease on life. By a strange inconsistency Constantius permitted those arch-enemies of Christianity, the pagan rhetoricians, sophists, and Neo-Platonist philosophers to teach in all the higher institutions of learning throughout the Empire. These men exhausted all their ingenuity to arrest the progress of the Christian religion. How much harm they did, appears from numerous examples mentioned in the writings of the Fathers, and especially from the apostasy of Julian, the successor of Constantius, who was seduced by men of this stamp." Laux, *Church History*, 95.

reconsecrate the empire to her traditional gods. Libanius spoke tenderly, as well, of the longings Julian privately shared: "What affected his heart most were the temples in ruins, the feasts not celebrated, the priests in exile, and the treasures of the temples distributed among the insolent."[163] And now, with the departure of Constantius, this dream had at last begun to come true.

Julian marched triumphantly into Constantinople. Unlike Constantine or his sons, he was crowned in the traditional Roman manner—the same ceremony by which Nero had been made emperor three centuries before. In the words of Ammianus, he now "laid bare the secrets of his heart and with plain and final decrees ordered the temples to be opened, victims to be brought to the altars [animal sacrifice], and the worship of the gods to be restored . . . he attacked the memory of Constantine as an innovator and disturber of the ancient laws and customs handed down from antiquity."[164] Assuming the duties of *Pontifex Maximus*, he ordered the erection of many new temples in Constantinople, since the more recent portions of the city had been constructed (on Constantine's orders) entirely without them. He even ordered several Christian churches to be demolished in order to obtain materials for this work, since those materials had originally been procured from the ruins of Byzantium's (already abandoned by that time) pagan shrines. Sporadic anti-Christian violence was reported as well—churches wrecked, cemeteries vandalized—and only halfheartedly put down by police.

Even so, Julian did stand by his orders to release all Christian clergy. In an elaborate show of contrast with his predecessor, he took no active steps to put down rival faiths; in fact, he even "summoned to his palace the Christian bishops, who were at odds with each other, and the people, who also were divided into factions, and politely advised them to set aside their differences, and each without fear or opposition to observe his own beliefs." Broadminded as this may sound to the modern reader, Julian's actual intent was a bit less progressive; as revealed by Ammianus (a personal friend, by the way, of the emperor's), Julian had granted this freedom "in order that he might have no fear thereafter of a united populace, because such a freedom [always] increased their dissentions."[165] In short, a Church splintered into a mere mass of rival sects could be counted upon to "go quietly." Julian also forbade the universities to hire any more Christians as teachers of grammar or philosophy, and he required Christian military officers to resign their commissions. "I declare by the gods that I do not want the Galileans[C] to be put to death, or unjustly beaten, or to suffer anything else; but I still emphatically maintain that those who reverence the gods must be preferred to them. For through the folly of the Galileans nearly everything has been upset, whereas through the good pleasure of the gods we are all preserved."[166] Oddly enough, however, Basil seems to have received from Julian, about this time, an offer to join his government. He politely refused (though Gregory Nazianzen's brother Caesarius received the same invitation and took it).

There were other signs besides this that Julian's emotions, even after his triumph, remained in their usual turmoil. As often happens with people who have succumbed finally to a long temptation, the emperor now began to show signs of regret, of nostalgia, of being tempted in the opposite direction, so to speak. On the whole, for instance, he was deeply disappointed by the actual state of the pagan cults he now found himself shepherding. Their priests were a sorry lot, idle and careless, many alcoholic; and the few remaining active worshippers were mostly cranks, who had redoubled their zeal for paganism primarily out of distaste for Christianity (or of some particular Christian). Julian, in his ingenuous idealism, had expected huge throngs of pagans—long gagged and stifled under the Christian emperors—to rush forward now in his support with great enthusiasm. Instead, he found apathy and indifference.

Once, he traveled all the way to Antioch to help celebrate a venerable old local festival in honor of Apollo. Afterward, the emperor wrote this extremely discouraged letter of protest to

---

[C] For the rest of his life, Julian used this term for Christians in order to avoid saying the word Christ.

the city fathers:

> I hurried thither . . . thinking that, if anywhere, I should there be delighted with your wealth and public spirit. And I pictured to myself, like a man seeing visions in a dream, what kind of procession it would be, and the beasts for sacrifice, the libations, the choruses in honor of the god, the incense, and the youths of your city there about the precinct, their souls adorned with the greatest reverence for the god, and their bodies decked with white and splendid garments. But when I entered into the precinct, I found there neither incense, nor cake, nor sacrificial victim. For a moment I was amazed, and I presumed that I was still outside the precinct and that you were waiting for the signal from me, doing me this honor as the high priest. But when I asked what sacrifice the city was going to offer to celebrate the annual festival of the god, the priest replied: "I have brought with me from my own house a goose as an offering to the god, but for the present the city has made no preparations."[167]

Clearly, some program of reform was needed. What kind of reforms? One can't help noticing that they all had a distinctly *Galilean* flavor: "Let each one of us," Julian wrote, in a letter addressed to priests, "abound in acts of piety, always trying to think piously of the gods, and by looking on their temples and statues with due honor and veneration, worship them as if we saw them present." His pagan clergy were encouraged, henceforth, to avoid writers such as Ovid, Epicurus, and Pyrrho, and to "leave to the common people the licentiousness of the theatre." Also, "Priests must keep themselves pure not only from unclean and shameful acts, but also from speaking or hearing words of such a character. Accordingly we must banish all offensive jests and scurrilous intercourse."

Other than in a few late, Neo-Platonic movements clearly influenced by contact with Christianity, no paganism had ever made such demands before—nor had any troubled itself with enjoining acts of forgiveness or charity. Julian, on the other hand, was soon writing thusly:

> I would say, even though it is a paradox, that it would be an act of piety to share our food and clothing with our enemies. . . . It is my opinion that when the poor came to be overlooked and neglected by the priests, the impious Galileans noticed it and devoted themselves to this kind of philanthropy. . . . For just as those who deceive children throw a cake to them two or three times and lure them on, and then, when they are far from their homes put them on board a ship and sell them . . . in the same manner the Galileans also, beginning with what they call their "love feast" or "hospitality," or "waiting on tables" (for the name is as diverse as their way of carrying it out) have led very many into atheism.[168]

The new emperor, in other words, quickly began asking pagans to behave like Christians. Not surprisingly, most of them shrugged—then mocked.

Yet when Christians noticed, and commented upon these things—several writers pointed out that his religious and philosophical writings often contained (perhaps unconscious?) paraphrases of New Testament phraseology applied to pagan use—Julian became furious and doubled down on his apostasy. He went elbow-deep, as it were—often literally. Ammianus writes that "he drenched the altars with the blood of too great a number of victims, at time sacrificing a hundred bulls at once . . . he was called a slaughterer rather than a priest by many . . . and though he took offense at this, he controlled his feelings and continued to celebrate the festivals."[169] Yet even despite such a spectacle as this, the ordinary people stayed home. "In the temples, after he had spent a long time with his tunic tucked up and sweating like a slave at quartering his victims, he would suddenly realize that almost all the spectators had quietly walked away."[170]

Finally, Julian had himself officially "unbaptized" by pagan

priests and underwent, according to Gregory Nazianzen, a ritual bath in bull's blood to "purify" his hands "from the unbloody
sacrifice through which we become partakers in the sufferings
and divinity of Christ."[CI] Sometimes, when his feelings raged
too hotly, he forgot his own program of tolerance—burning
a chapel, for instance, wherein a pastor had criticized him; or
undergoing fits during which he threatened (idly, thank God) to
renew the Great Persecution of Galerius. At last, when he grew
tired of hearing his arguments refuted by appeals to the Christian Scripture, Julian conceived a monstrous plan to discredit
the Bible and Christianity once and for all. He recalled from his
own reading that "the Galilean" (as he now called Jesus exclusively) once prophesied Herod's temple at Jerusalem would fall,
leaving not one stone on top of another (Mark 13:1–2). He had
heard, likewise, that the loss of that temple, beginning with the
veil that was rent at the time of the Crucifixion and culminating
in its destruction by Julian's predecessor Titus in A.D. 70, had
been a great sign of judgment upon the city's rejection of Christ;
and that any attempt to rebuild it apart from Christ's will would
only bring about calamity.

Here then, was a chance to put the Galilean to the test! Here
would be a public challenge to Christ's authority, a double-dog
dare to match his own power with that of imperial Rome, now
purged of his corrupting influence. And once the new temple
was complete—standing in the sunlight every day for all to

[CI] Gregory is, of course, referring to the Lord's Supper here, of which
Julian would often have partaken as a Christian. Clement of Rome wrote
of "the sacrifices of the episcopate" as early as A.D. 95, and Irenaeus, a
few decades later, tells us explicitly that "Sacrifice as such has not been
reprobated. There were sacrifices then, sacrifices among the [Hebrew]
people; and there are sacrifices now, sacrifices in the Church." The
eucharistic sacrifices young Julian participated in were *unbloody* only in
their outward appearance, for the early Church believed that the true
Body and Blood of Christ, offered "once, for all" at the Last Supper, were
made accessible to later generations by this means.

see—the people would realize at last the futility of the whole thing . . . and the Christian fad would pass. People would settle down once again to their old duties of making Rome great as she had been under Antoninus Pius, under Marcus Aurelius. The old gods had been good enough for these great men; they could be good enough again.

So, late in 361, Julian sent letters to the startled Hebrews, encouraging them to begin training new Levites to resume their own bloody sacrifices once more, and promising, "I will use all my zeal to make the temple of the most high God rise again."[171] (Rather than expressing his own views here, the emperor used the Jews' own favored terminology; he himself regarded God as real enough—the guiding spirit of the Hebrews, just as all nations have their own guiding spirit—but their insistence upon him as the only true God Julian viewed as a primitive nativist delusion.) He allotted enormous, immoderate sums for the project (for which he was roundly criticized by his friend Ammianus) and sent a trusted official, Alypius, to Jerusalem to begin drawing up plans for construction. In this way, the new oblation being offered every day on the altars of Christendom would be minimized and the Galilean himself shown up, once and for all, as a charlatan. Arian and Orthodox alike would be cast down in their pomposity, their foolish hairsplitting disputes rendered forever ridiculous and forgotten.

The word was given. Alypius began clearing the site of debris around Christmas of that year, and removing previous ruins.

9

Anastasia

"He has delivered us from the dominion of darkness and transferred us to the kingdom of his beloved Son, in whom we have redemption, the forgiveness of sins. He is the image of the invisible God, the first-born of all creation; for in him all things were created, in heaven and on earth, visible and invisible, whether thrones or dominions or principalities or authorities—all things were created through him and for him. He is before all things, and in him all things hold together. He is the head of the body, the church; he is the beginning, the first-born from the dead, that in everything he might be pre-eminent" (Col. 1:13–18).

One by one, the old voices were being silenced. Hosius and Pope Liberias were gone. Athanasius was back in Alexandria again but he was slowing down, growing old, already one of the last surviving delegates who had been present at Nicaea. One of the few remaining others, Marcellus of Ancyra, seems to have grown so tired of defending himself against the charge of being a modalist that he actually gave in and became one in truth, thus denying the Trinity in his own perverse way. "This was a period when, throughout the world, the orthodox bishops who remained in charge of churches could be counted on one's fingers, and probably on the fingers of one hand . . . Had doctrine been determined by popularity, today we should all be deniers of Christ and opponents of the Spirit."[172]

Nevertheless, the torch had been passed. Hilary of Poitiers, aided by the enthusiastic new crop of Western monks Athanasius had inspired during his second exile, was finding so much success in his efforts to reclaim Semi-Arians that the real Arians agitated unceasingly for his arrest. Hilarion, another disciple of Antony's, had angered the emperor by carrying the way of the deserts to Palestine, where Julian was building his new Temple.

And above all, the Three Cappadocians—Basil, Gregory Nazianzen, and Gregory of Nyssa (now taking Julian's place in the broken fellowship)—were soon called out of their seclusion to active service as well, just as Athanasius had been after Nicaea, rising to leadership roles in various churches of the East. This was the next generation of heroes, called, as the apostle Paul called his successor Timothy, to "follow the pattern of the sound words which you have heard from me, in the faith and love which are in Christ Jesus" and to "guard the truth that has been entrusted to you by the Holy Spirit who dwells within us" [2 Tim. 1:13–14].

How, ultimately, *did* the Church end up explaining the Trinity? How were the paradoxes of *On the Incarnation* finally resolved, those puzzles that kept Constantine awake nights? The answer, in one very important sense, is that they never were . . . and never will be, in all likelihood; not at least until that day when, as the apostle Paul writes, "the perfect comes, [and] the imperfect will pass away. . . . For now we see in a mirror dimly, but then face to face. Now I know in part; then I shall understand fully, even as I have been fully understood" [1 Cor. 13:9b, 12]. The effort against Arianism had, after all, never been an attempt to create a theology more convincing, more logical than theirs; indeed, the orthodox champions had not been trying to *create* a theology at all. Just as at the Nicene Council, their campaign was almost entirely negative—the ruling out of false explanations, without offering speculative "answers" of their own.

It had been the advantage of the Arian side throughout the crisis that they were able to say just exactly what they meant—and the orthodox couldn't. Where Arianism paraded a proud surface plausibility, the orthodox were forced to admit that their everlasting stubbornness really *was* forcing them to sound irrational, illogical—but that theirs was the truth somehow anyway. They were taunted for using a word not found in the pages of the Bible, but it was, ironically, precisely their anxiety to do full justice to the words of Scripture, which had painted them into this corner. With the Hebrews the Church must affirm one God only: "Hear O Israel! The Lord your God, the Lord is One!" (Deut. 6:4). Yet with the apostles, it must affirm the full divinity of the Man Jesus, worshipped as "My Lord and my God!" (John 20:28). Unwilling to mitigate or to explain away either of those bedrock Truths, the Nicene party were stuck with a cure worse than the disease, an answer that seemed to raise more questions than it solved. Consistent fidelity to all of the revealed truths of Scripture had led the orthodox to an abysm of mystery.^CII

A funny thing happened to this "Party of No," however, as they kept turning down one faulty analogy after another. Even though they were still mostly saying what God *isn't*, rather than what God *is*, they slowly began to notice that all of their accumulated "no's" were beginning to sketch out . . . a shape, if you will, an outline. A Thing that was, apparently, by its very nature invisible to reason was starting to suggest at least something of its true form *by the void it was creating*—rather like H.G. Wells's elusive Invisible Man, who was detected finally by his footsteps in the snow, by the cavity his body created as he moved amongst the falling flakes. No, the human mind cannot imagine a single God who is actually a communion of Three; and we really are forced to admit, as Newman once did frankly, "that my abstract idea of three is simply incompatible with my idea of one."[173] Yet should we be surprised, really, to find that a truly cosmic God like ours might, in his innermost life and essence, turn out to have aspects that are perhaps permanently impenetrable to our finite minds?

"I reckon that the comprehension of God's essence is beyond not just men alone but beyond every rational creature," wrote

---

^CII A mystery, in the Christian sense, is a Truth that, by its very nature, surpasses the powers of human reason and that can thus be expressed by the finite mind only in terms of imperfect analogies. The apostle Paul acknowledged this principle in his New Testament writings, where he speaks of "the mystery of faith [1 Tim. 3:9]" resting "not in plausible words of wisdom . . . but in the power of God [1 Cor. 4:4–5b]." "O the depth of the riches and wisdom and knowledge of God! How unsearchable are his judgments and how inscrutable his ways! [Rom. 11:33]."

Basil. "When I say rational, however, I mean created. For the Father is known by the Son alone, and by the Holy Spirit. 'No one,' the scriptures say, 'knows the Father except the Son' [Matt. 11:27], and 'the Spirit probes all things, even the depths of God' [1 Cor. 2:10] . . . It follows, then, that the essence of God is not perceivable by any except the Only-Begotten and the Holy Spirit."[174] Does this mean that God is *wholly* unknowable to us or that the very concept of God is irrational, to be accepted by humans as a mere leap in the dark? No, it only means that we can never hope—should never have expected—to fully understand a mind which is as vast, in comparison to ours, as the visible cosmos is to our own little neighborhood. "There is no one name sufficiently broad," Basil continues, "to take in the whole nature of God. There are names, however, many and varied, obscure and of little importance in view of the whole, but each of its own special significance, which, when assembled together, convey to us a sufficient understanding of God's nature. Among these names which are ascribed to him, some signify what qualities are inherent in God, whereas others indicate what qualities are not found in him. From the two categories, from the denial of what is absent and from the confession of what is present, we find expressed for us a certain character, as it were, of God."[175]

It isn't so much, then, that the Trinity is "taught in Scripture"—it's that Scripture teaches so many other things that, if held to with the tenacity of faith, make the Trinity absolutely necessary. "How often have I said to you," as Sherlock Holmes put it in another context, "that when you have eliminated the impossible, whatever remains, *however improbable*, must be the truth?" This was the position in which the Nicene champions now found themselves; it was *impossible* that the Christian Church could always have been wrong about its single most central doctrine, the divinity of Christ; merely *improbable* that Three might be One in some hitherto unimagined form of celestial geometry.

A fit analogy, perhaps, is the way in which scientists were driven to the discovery of that most astounding of natural objects, the "black hole." As early as 1783, mathematician (and Anglican clergyman) John Michell predicted—using the ordinary, established laws of motion and gravitation—that we might one day find a star whose gravitational pull was so strong that even its own light would not be able to escape, rendering it invisible. Later calculations, using Einstein's improved physical theories, projected characteristics even more unfathomable: a gravitational field so powerful that it would deform both space and time, leaving a center that could never be reached because time stands still before any traveler can arrive there, and a perimeter that could never be escaped because space itself would have *bent backwards*—so effectively that there are simply no longer any paths leading *away* from the black hole. Even backwards travel into one's own past was (and is) a valid interpretation of the data. No wonder, then, that "Black Hole Arians," if you will, looked for a more rational explanation.

Eddington, for instance, argued that some yet unknown mechanism would prevent the formation of such an object and even Einstein himself doubted that this application of his principles was anything more than a theoretical curiosity. And who could blame them? By their very nature, the proposed black holes would be not only contingently but *essentially* impossible to observe. No information of any kind can escape from them to the outside world; they have no detectable features, emit no signals, have swallowed their own past existence and are, from one point of view, frozen forever in a present with no future. This is a collection of descriptors that might understandably be called, as a hard-bitten old Hyde Park atheist once said when presented with a definition of what it means to be a pure Spirit, "The best definition of nothing I ever heard of." And yet it was forces we already understood—forces that were, indeed, fundamental to our most basic understanding of scientific law—that seemed to be driving us there, without any regard at all for our ordinary ideas of logic or reality. Grant the reasoning that leads to the black hole and you find a place where logic no longer reigns, "a point where time and space as we understand it no longer exists." Grant the mystery, however, and you get your math back. Deny the mystery, you deny the chain of laws that led to it.

And the strangest fact about the whole story? Black holes are *real*—confirmed, over the course of the twentieth century, to be astrophysical objects as factual as the Earth we stand on. How was their existence proved? It was done, to put it shortly, by indirect methods—not by viewing the things themselves, but by observing the deformation of space-time that they cause as they affect surrounding objects such as companion stars. In much this same way, the inconceivable Triune nature of the One God was not directly observed by these Nicene Fathers, but was deduced, rather, from the time-honored traditions of the early Church, by way of Antony, Athanasius, and others. "Concerning God," as a later council would put it, "we cannot grasp what he is, but only what he is not, and how other beings stand in relation to him."[176] No one ever "proposed" the doctrine of the Trinity—not Constantine, not Hosius, not Athanasius; no one "invented" it, the way Arius invented his "Xerox copy" hypothesis. In a way, the great doctrine invented itself. We were driven to it in spite of ourselves, because of the other things we already believed.[CIII]

"Truths turn into dogmas," wrote Chesterton, "the instant that they are disputed. Thus every man who utters a doubt defines a religion. And [opposition] does not really destroy the beliefs, rather it creates them; gives them their limits and their plain and defiant shape."[177] In this sense, it was the pressure of Arianism that caused

---

[CIII] "The systematic doctrine of the Trinity," according to Newman, "may be considered as the shadow, projected for the contemplation of the intellect, of the Object of scripturally-informed piety: a representation, economical; necessarily imperfect, as being exhibited in a foreign medium, and therefore involving apparent inconsistencies or mysteries; given to the Church by tradition contemporaneously with those apostolic writings, which are addressed more directly to the heart; kept in the background in the infancy of Christianity, when faith and obedience were vigorous, and brought forward at a time when, reason being disproportionately developed, and aiming at sovereignty in the province of religion, its presence became necessary to expel an usurping idol from the house of God." Newman, *Arians of the Fourth Century,* 145.

men like Basil and the Gregories (of Nyssa and Nazianzus) to begin unearthing the deeper significance of the Nicene formularies. In one sense, the effort was superfluous; for the most part, they were arguing theology with men for whom theology had been merely a pretext, a smokescreen to justify a political counterrevolution. To quote Chesterton once again, the Universal Church does "sometimes go on flogging a dead horse and killing a heresy long after it has killed itself. But even that is, properly understood, a fault on the side of chivalry. The [apologist] really takes the heresy more seriously than it is seen ultimately to deserve . . . [often] has more respect for the heresy than the heretics have."[178]

Nevertheless, there were at least a few, mostly in the Semi-Arian camp, who were worth wrestling with; and for their sakes this new generation of apologists did take up the challenge. "What was in the beginning?" Basil asks.

> "The Word," he says [John 1:1] . . . Why the Word? So that we might know that he proceeded from the mind. Why the Word? Because he was begotten without passion (change) . . . Why the Word? Because he is the image of the Father who begets him, showing forth the Father fully, in no way separated from him, and subsisting perfectly in himself, just as our word entirely befits our thought."[179]

Gregory Nazianen adds, "Common to the Father and the Son and the Holy Spirit is their having no coming into being, and their divinity. Common to the Son and Holy Spirit is their coming from the Father. Proper to the Father alone is unbegotteness; to the Son alone, His begotteness; to the Spirit alone, His being sent forth."[180] For the Persons of the Trinity, according to Gregory of Nyssa, "are separated from one another neither in time, nor place, nor will, nor practice, nor operation, nor passivity, nor any of the like things such as are perceived with men, but only in that the Father is Father and not Son, and the Son is Son and not Father, and likewise the Holy Spirit is neither Father nor Son."[181]

However sophisticated their writings later became, it is still the spirit of Antony that animates the writings of the Three Cappadocians, just as it did with their role model Athanasius: "[John 15:26 speaks] of 'the Holy Spirit, who proceeds from the Father,'" writes Gregory Nazianzen, "who, since he proceeds from there, is not a creature; who, since he is not begotten, is not a Son; and who, since he is between the unbegotten and the begotten, is God. . . . What, then is procession? Tell me first what is the unbegotteness of the Father, and then I will physiologize for you on the generation of the Son and the procession of the Spirit; and we will both be frenzy-stricken for prying into God's mysteries."[182] Misunderstandings they are ready to address, puzzles they are willing to ponder, but never are they willing to question "the list"—which must be received, like the gospel itself, "as a little child."

In his treatise on *The Holy Spirit*, Basil expresses this clearly:

Of the dogmas and kerygmas[CIV] preserved in the Church, some we possess from written teaching and others we receive from the tradition of the Apostles, handed on to us in a mystery. In respect to piety both are of the same force. No one will contradict any of these, no one, at any rate, who is even moderately versed in matters ecclesiastical. Indeed, were we to try to reject unwritten customs as having no great authority, we would unwittingly injure the Gospel in its vitals.[183]

Gregory of Nyssa, in arguing with Eunomius, one of the most "logical" of the Arians, indicates the bottom line with even more firmness:

Let him first show, then, that the Church has believed in vain that the only-begotten Son truly exists, not made through adoption by a Father falsely so-called, but existing as such

---

CIV Kerygmas are the original "factoids," so to speak, about the saving work of Christ as contained in the preaching of the apostles.

according to nature. . . . And let no one interrupt me and say that what we confess should be confirmed by constructive reasoning. It suffices for the proof of our statement that we have a tradition coming down to us from the Fathers, an inheritance, as it were, by succession from the apostles, through the saints who came after them.[184]

This principle of a "chain of custody" for God's revelation is, in one sense, the underlying reality of the whole crusade, both from the beginning and moving forward. "[T]he doctrines in question have," as Newman put it,

> never been learned merely from Scripture. Surely the Sacred Volume was never intended, and is not adapted, to teach us our creed; however certain it is that we can prove our creed from it when once it has been taught us. . . . From the very first the rule has been, as a matter of fact, that the Church should teach the truth, and then should appeal to Scripture in vindication of its own teaching. And from the first, it has been the error of heretics to neglect the information thus provided for them, and to attempt of themselves a work to which they are unequal, the eliciting of a systematic doctrine from the scattered notices of the truth which Scripture contains. . . . The insufficiency of the mere private study of Holy Scripture for arriving at the exact and entire truth which Scripture really contains is shown by the fact, that creeds and teachers have ever been divinely provided, and by the discordance of opinions that exists wherever those aids are thrown aside.[185]

No one could see the future at this point; neither Athanasius himself nor any of his successors knew how long the war would continue. Perhaps their struggle would, on the merely human level, accomplish nothing but the permanent return of paganism—and a new persecution to rival that of Galerius. Even so, the Faith *must* be passed down intact, the Christian way unaltered. This, after all, is how the churches had gained the approval of their founders from the beginning: "I commend you," as Paul wrote to the Corinthians, "because you remember me in everything and maintain the traditions even as I have delivered them to you" (1 Cor. 11:2). As they had from the start, the chips must fall where they may, any consequences left in the hands of God.

Downfall

The meteoric rise of Julian the Apostate quickly reached its zenith. He had been sole emperor of Rome for less than a year when he began making plans for a final showdown with Sapor of Persia—an expedition, in fact, into Persia itself with the ultimate goal of annexing it to his empire, of imposing his own Greek idolatry on a nation that had been almost completely monotheistic since before the time of the Magi. Having allowed his deceivers—led by Maximus and Libanius—to twist his mind into believing that he was nothing less than the reincarnation of Alexander the Great, virtually no plan seemed too grandiose any longer. Destiny had chosen him to bring peace and order to a chaotic world and he now set about the exhaustive preparations for this campaign with an energy and determination highly reminiscent of his departed uncle Constantine.

In the meantime, he had undergone some second thoughts about the blanket amnesty he granted for clergy to return—for Athanasius, clearly, was a special case. "One who had been banished by so many imperial decrees," Julian wrote to the people of Alexandria,

> issued by many emperors ought to have waited for at least one imperial edict, and then on the strength of that returned to his own country, and not displayed rashness and folly, and insulted the laws as though they did not exist. . . . Yet I learn that the most audacious Athanasius, elated by his accustomed insolence, has again seized what is called among them the episcopal throne. . . . By all the gods, I would see and hear nothing more gladly done by you than that Athanasius, the infamous wretch

who dared to baptize Greek women of noble birth during my reign, should be sent out of Egypt. Let him be driven forth.[186]

Julian had always been changeable, of course, but why this sudden reversal of policy? The fact is the new emperor wasn't so very different from his immediate predecessor after all. Once the crown had settled firmly upon his head, Julian began to feel the same fear Constantius had felt: that Athanasius and all he represented—nothing less than a Church absolutely independent of secular control!—might have to be bowed to one day. In a manner of speaking, Galerius's sudden edict of toleration, way back in 311, might be seen as a *glasnost* that had now gotten out of hand, with Julian's pagan revival a late, hard-line coup to restore the *status quo antebellum*. After all, had not every emperor since then—including Constantine himself—struggled to stay on top of this powerful horse he had hoped to bridle? Constantius turned more or less consciously backward to pagan thought forms, pagan ways of governing, yet he had tried to do so without the embarrassment of having to explicitly unsay what his own father had said.

"Rather than sacrifice its actual paganism," as Soloviev writes, "the Byzantine Empire attempted in self-justification to pervert the purity of the Christian idea"[187]—via Arianism, of course, the changeling in Christianity's cradle. Julian, in turn, simply abandoned the hypocritical fiction. Having done so, however, he now realized what the others had realized—that Athanasius was their common archenemy in these efforts, as he had been since the beginning. It was now apparent to everyone that, humanly speaking and in the eyes of the people, *this was the little man who had saved Christianity* . . . thus far, at any rate. Julian, therefore, reneged—in his apoplexy calling Athanasius "the head of a wicked and impious school," "unfit to be a leader," "a contemptible little fellow," and "hardly a man at all, only a little manikin." Athanasius, for his part, took the insults—and the new banishment—in his stride. As he boarded a boat on the Nile, headed southward once again into his briar patch, he called out to his disconsolate flock with an encouraging word of prophecy: "Be of good cheer. It is but a little cloud, and it will soon pass."[188]

Ironically, it was during this very same period that Julian pushed hardest when it came to reshaping Rome's reluctant pagan cults into something more like what he thought Christianity ought to have been. He began sending out what can only be called "encyclical letters" explaining his plan to reorganize the various pagan priesthoods of the empire into a regular episcopal hierarchy—"a real pagan church," as Ricciotti calls it, "with himself as supreme pastor." Local priests were henceforth to have an archpriest ruling over their diocese, then something like an archbishop to govern a whole district of such archpriests, with Julian himself as *Pontifex Maximus* presiding over all. Many of these new posts he granted to apostate Arians (such as Pegasius, formerly the Christian bishop of Ilium), scores of whom were all too willing to abandon altogether the Christ they had already devoted the last forty years to demoting.

Julian took an interest in every detail of life in this new church-to-be. He composed prayer books to be used by both priests and laity; and he worked up a catechetical lecture series on "Hellenic Dogma" that seems to have been patterned after that of the great second-century Christian apologist Clement of Alexandria. He also planned homes for single mothers, founded ministries to prisoners and to the poor, and established a chaplaincy for the military; in short, "he dared to take under consideration matters about which the pagan pontiffs before him had not cared in the least. In fact, if they had been confronted by projects of this nature, they would probably have looked upon them as the wild dreams of a fevered brain. . . . In his enthusiasm for paganism he unconsciously proffers contraband wares, representing as consequent to the worship of the gods a genuine product of Christianity."[189] Many of the pagans, in their turn, now called Julian a few choice names of their own: "nanny goat," "scold," "Greekish pedant," "talkative mole," and "an ape dressed in purple."[190]

Setbacks and discouragements only drove him harder to bring his face-off with the Galilean to a head. Midway through 362, he moved his entire court to Syria in order to lay the groundwork for his great Persian war. "After establishing himself at Antioch, Julian withdrew into complete retirement. Knowing that he was despised by the Christians and ridiculed by the pagans, he surrounded himself with a small company of intimate friends or, better, of 'initiates,' since they formed a small secret society."[191] The emperor pored over maps and charts, conducted countless interviews with spies and Persian expatriates familiar with the territory ahead. Yet even as these preparations were entering their final stages, Julian still found time to obsess over his private issues. All winter long he spent sleepless nights toiling over the composition of an elaborate polemic intended "to refute," as Libanius writes, "those books which make the man from Palestine a God and Son of God."[CV]

Eventually published as *Against the Galileans*, it contains (in addition to the arguments we pictured him using during our college debate scene) an example of Julian's own Great Apostasy theory. Based on no external evidence at all, it postulates an early, primitive Christianity founded by a purely human Jesus, overthrown to begin with, by that crafty rascal Paul—the first to entice otherwise educated Greeks into the folly of the Christian system—and then by the Gospel writer John, first to bestow the attributes of divinity upon the unremarkable Galilean. The apostasy, in other words, began more or less immediately after the Crucifixion and the "true message" scarcely outlived the Man himself.

Finally, as the war against Persia was about to begin, events in Jerusalem reached their climax. Master builder Alypius had been coping with various setbacks all throughout the early stages of construction. Multiple independent sources report the fact that a series of destructive earthquakes took place all along the Palestinian coast in late 362; one of them caused a portion of the uncompleted temple to collapse, killing a number of workmen. Some of the other workers revealed their misgivings about the project by fleeing into

---

[CV] Notice that Julian inadvertently provides us here with yet another hostile witness to the fact that the early Christians and their Scripture taught the Divinity of Christ.

a nearby Christian church during one of these temblors. Julian, however, merely redoubled the effort. At last, as the project was ready to begin again in earnest, there came an occurrence that, if it were not being reported by a pagan and a personal adviser of the emperor's, we should scarcely credit at all without feeling ourselves the victims of superstitious pro-Christian propaganda.

Nevertheless, Ammianus—Julian's friend and one of the last great Roman historians of antiquity—records the event as sober history: "But though Alypius pushed the work forward energetically, and though he was assisted by the governor of the province, frightful balls of flame kept bursting forth near the foundations of the temple and made it impossible for the workmen to approach the place, and some were even burned to death. And since the elements persistently drove them back, Julian gave up the attempt." After receiving the report, the emperor turned on the Jews bitterly, whom he had, obviously, been using merely for his own purposes. He actually blamed them for the disaster, their temple having been the site, apparently, of far too much talk against the gods through the centuries. "He abandoned them to their fate after disparaging their religion and culture."[192]

A kind of madness came over the emperor now, a determination to fling himself against the rock of Persia at any cost, almost as a final test of his mission in life. He foolishly spurned an offer from Sapor, in fact, to simply call the whole thing off. The Persian ruler had already seen what Julian could do, having followed reports of his exploits in the West; clearly, the young emperor was, unlike the pompous and windy Constantius, a man of action, who had already proved his mettle by taking the throne of the Caesars by force. So the king sent ambassadors to Antioch to suggest a negotiated settlement. Julian's reply shocked not only the Persians, but also his own advisers, who looked on this as a highly fortuitous chance to get out of a highly doubtful situation. Julian simply told the envoys that their services would no longer be needed—he would soon carry his reply to Sapor in person.

The expedition set out from Antioch on March 5, 363—
65,000 men, no longer carrying Constantine's *Chi Rho* on
their shields but once again the old pagan laurels. Half of them
were sent eastward to Carrhae as a feint, giving the impression that Julian's chosen route to Ctesiphon, the Persian capital,
was down the River Tigris. The other half marched down
the western bank of the Euphrates, accompanied by hundreds
of supply ships and a fleet of fifty pontoon boats to ferry the
army across when the proper time came. Near the end of April
the Romans captured the entrance canal leading to the gates
of the city. Despite the fact that the Persians broke the dikes
that had reclaimed this area, turning the plains around the city
into a swampy quagmire, Julian's forces reached the ramparts
of Ctesiphon by mid-May and defeated their Persian defenders. Nothing remained but to take the capital itself—yet the
city walls proved so formidable that a long, costly siege now
seemed inevitable.

Quick initial success gave way to disaster. The main Persian
army had not been placed at Ctesiphon; it was still at large,
strong and powerful, led by Sapor himself, and said to be approaching from the East. The Romans, meanwhile, having
reached the city and surrounded it, now lacked any real stra-
tegic objective. Julian was certain that reinforcements would
soon arrive from Armenia, but his generals helped him to see
that it was folly to merely camp out at Ctesiphon waiting for
the defenders to arrive. So the Romans set off for the Persian
interior, to wander aimlessly in hostile territory with no clear
means of retreat. Soon, their supply lines had been cut and Julian's legions went hungry. Pursued by Sapor, harassed by defending militias at every city where they hoped to scavenge
provisions, they were stopped repeatedly for one small battle
after another—none of them decisive, but each wearing down
Julian's forces by attrition. It was during one of these desperate
but rather futile skirmishes that the end finally came.

On June 26, 363, after turning back a Persian raid at the Battle of Samarra, the emperor called for a pursuit. "Careless of his

own safety," Ammianus writes, "Julian cried out that the enemy had fled in disorder. His guards, the *candidati*, shouted to him to get out of the way of the mass of fugitives, when suddenly a cavalryman's spear—no one knows whence—grazed the skin of his arm, pierced his ribs, and lodged deep in his liver. As he tried to pull it out with his right hand, he felt the sinews of his fingers cut through on both sides by the sharp steel. He fell from his horse, and all those about him rushed to his side. He was then taken to camp and given medical treatment."[193]

Philostorgius claims that on the battlefield Julian flung a handful of his own blood at the sky and cast a reproach upon the one who had hitherto been his favorite god, the Unconquered Sun: "Helios, thou hast ruined me." Libanius initially floated a theory that one of the emperor's own Christian troops had seen a chance to assassinate him; but when Ammianus and other pagan historians refused to corroborate the idea, he changed his story and began blaming a foreigner. Theodoret and Sozomen maintain (though the account is often doubted) that Julian's last words were, "You have won, O Galilean."[194] And though this verdict is undoubtedly true regarding the pointless contest between them Julian felt he had arranged, the victorious Galilean himself—inveterate friend of sinners, who prayed, "Father, forgive them for they know not what they do" on one memorable occasion—probably wept.

ATHANASIUS CONTRA MUNDUM

Though it took another seventeen years to play itself out, the remaining story of Arianism in Europe and the empire is largely a postscript. Julian had shown the world where the Arian spirit actually led—it was simply the spirit of subservience to secular authority, of rendering to Caesar the things that are God's. He had also spooked the poor peace party badly, sobering them up, making them realize that their quest for "common ground" had been a sucker bet all along, and that their experiment in "peace at the expense of orthodoxy" had, in practice, meant continuously less and less orthodoxy and no peace at all.[CVI] "Many Semi-Arians, disgusted by the excesses of the extreme Arian party and frightened by the appearance of an apostate on the throne, returned to the unity of the Church."[195]

Julian's troops chose his successor on the battlefield, a mild and sensible Christian general named Jovian. Sapor was notified of the change and immediately renewed his overtures for a truce. The Romans definitely got the worst of the peace that followed—five provinces in Mesopotamia returned to Persian sovereignty—but at least the defeated army was allowed to march back to Antioch intact. Once in Syria again, Jovian met personally with Athanasius, whose stay in the Thebaid had, as he himself predicted, been brief this time. Treated with deference and respect by the new emperor, Athanasius was informed that the policies of Constantine were now to be pursued once again and that no measures of revenge or repression against the pagans were being contemplated. Sadly, Jovian's reign was even shorter than Julian's two and a half years. Six months in, he was felled by nothing more than an unhappy accident, poisoned in his sleep one night by fumes from a malfunctioning stove. His brother Valens took his place (along with another largely irrelevant Western Caesar, Valentinian), and Valens, like Constantius before him, was inclined to see a golden throne as the proper place for "Christian" emperors, not so much the low stool. He rescinded Jovian's Church measures and once again began sponsoring Arian "solutions" to the problems of Church and state.

"After this the Arians, becoming bolder, grievously harassed

[CVI] The Semi-Arians had sought peace by "throwing a veil over heterogeneous doctrines" and by drawing up ever more artificial documents aimed at disguising fundamental disagreements instead of resolving them. "To attempt comprehensions of opinion, amiable as the motive frequently is, is to mistake arrangements of words, which have no existence except on paper, for habits which are realities; and ingenious generalizations of discordant sentiments for that practical agreement which alone can lead to co-operation." Newman, *Arians of the Fourth Century,* 147.

the orthodox party, frequently beating them, reviling them, causing them to be imprisoned, and fined; in short they practiced distressing and intolerable annoyances against them. The sufferers were induced to appeal to the emperor for protection against their adversaries if haply they might obtain some relief from this oppression. But whatever hope of redress they might have cherished from this quarter, was altogether frustrated, inasmuch as they thus merely spread their grievances before him who was the very author of them."[196] Athanasius thought it best to disappear again—no less than his fifth (and final) exile—but Valens feared a popular uprising in his case and gave, within a few weeks, a personal order that the little patriarch be reinstated at his see in Alexandria. Perhaps he felt that Athanasius, having grown old and feeble, was mainly a symbolic figure now at any rate—and equally powerful for such purposes whether living in the desert or the city. In any event, the bishop was back in his home church by February 365.

No, the man Valens really dreaded now—and the opponent he might actually be able to do something about—was Basil, bishop of Caesarea. With real abandon, Basil had taken on the mantle of his mentor and had flung himself into the work of reestablishing the orthodox Faith in the East. "The dogmas of the fathers are despised," he wrote, upon his initial arrival, "and apostolical traditions are set at naught; the discoveries of innovators hold sway in the Churches. Men have learned to be speculatists instead of theologians. The wisdom of the world has the place of honor, having dispossessed the glorying in the Cross. The pastors are driven away, grievous wolves are brought in instead, and plunder the flock of Christ. Houses of prayer are destitute of preachers; the deserts are full of mourners: the aged sorrow, comparing what is with what was; more pitiable the young, as not knowing what they are deprived of." In another letter, addressed to the bishops of Italy and Gaul, Basil says, "Unbelievers laugh at what they see, and the weak are unsettled . . . [even] those of the laity who are sound in faith avoid the places of worship, as schools of impiety, and raise their hands in solitude with groans and tears to the Lord in heaven."[197]

Basil's activity was tremendous. Not only did he preach orthodoxy, vividly and compellingly, to large crowds every morning, he also liquidated the remaining lands he inherited from his family and exhausted the funds for the relief of the poor, a constituency that his predecessor—an Arian—had entirely neglected. His most important achievement in this regard was the enormous "urban commune" he created just outside the city limits of Caesarea, a combination hospital and poor farm known during Basil's own lifetime as "the New Town" but after his death as the Basileiad. It was during this period that he composed many of his best theological works: the *Hexahemeron*, or *Account of the Six Days of Creation*, and *Against Eunomius the Arian*. He also composed a discourse addressed *To Our Young Men, How They Can Derive Benefit from the Study of Pagan Literature*, in which he encourages Christians to interact with non-Christian wisdom but to do so cautiously, like a bee "which only takes the honey out of the flower and leaves the poison." Basil also turned many unworthy ministers out of their positions during this period—a thorough housecleaning, at least in the regions under his administration. Despite this determination, however, Basil actually won over most of his opponents by his amiable temperament. He was so ready, in fact, to grant everything that could legitimately be granted to their position, so willing to confess the missteps of the orthodox party, and so quick to see the best in everyone, that he was actually accused of Semi-Arianism himself during this period by the more embittered of his coreligionists.

Fooled by this, as these diehards had been, the emperor briefly thought that Basil might be bought. He sent Modestus, the Praetorian prefect, to offer him bribes or an important position in the new government. Newman recounts the story well:

He summoned Basil into his presence, in his turn, and set before him the arguments which had been already found successful with others—that it was foolish to resist the times, and to trouble the Church about inconsiderable questions; and he promised him the prince's favor for him and his friends, if he complied. Failing by soft language, he adopted a higher tone; but he found his match. Gregory [Nazianzen] has preserved the dialogue which passed between them.

"What is the meaning of this, you Basil (said the Prefect, a bitter Arian, not deigning to style him bishop), that you stand out against so great a prince, and are self-willed when others yield?"

BASIL: What would you? And what is my extravagance? I have not yet learned it.

MODESTUS: Your not worshipping after the emperor's manner, when the rest of your party have given way and been overcome.

BASIL: I have a Sovereign whose will is otherwise, nor can I bring myself to worship any creature—I am a creature of God, and commanded to be a god.

MODESTUS: For whom do you take me?

BASIL: For a thing of naught, while such are your commands.

MODESTUS: Is it, then, a mere nothing for one like you to have rank like myself; and to have my fellowship?

BASIL: You are prefect, and in a noble place: I own it. Yet God's majesty is greater; and it is much for me to have your fellowship, for we are both God's creatures. But it is as great a thing to be fellow to any other of my flock, for Christianity lies not in distinction of persons, but in faith.

The prefect was angered at this, and rose from his chair, and abruptly asked Basil if he did not fear his power.

BASIL: Fear what consequences? What sufferings?

MODESTUS: One of those many pains which a prefect can inflict.

BASIL: Let me know them.

MODESTUS: Confiscation, exile, tortures, death.

BASIL: Think of some other threat. These have no influence upon me. He runs no risk of confiscation, who has nothing to lose, except these mean garments and a few books. Nor does he care for exile, who is not circumscribed by place, who does not make a home of the spot he dwells in, but everywhere a home whithersoever he be cast, or rather everywhere God's home, whose pilgrim he is and wanderer. Nor can tortures harm a frame so frail as to break under the first blow. You could but strike once, and death would be gain. It would but send me the sooner to Him for whom I live and labor, for whom I am dead rather than alive, to whom I have long been journeying.

MODESTUS: No one yet ever spoke to Modestus with such freedom.

BASIL: Peradventure Modestus never yet fell in with a bishop; or surely in a like trial you would have heard like language. O prefect, in other things we are gentle, and more humble than all men living, for such is the commandment; so as not to raise our brow, I say not against "so great a prince," but even against one of least account. But when God's honor is at stake, we think of nothing else, looking simply to him. Fire and the sword, beasts of prey, irons to rend the flesh, are an indulgence rather than a terror to a Christian. Therefore insult, threaten, do your worst, make the most of your power. Let the emperor be informed of my purpose. Me you gain not, you persuade not, to an impious creed, by menaces even more frightful.'

Modestus parted with him with the respect which firmness necessarily inspires in those who witness it; and, going to the emperor, repeated the failure of his attempt.[198]

Like Athanasius (with whom he exchanged many letters during this period), Basil had now become too popular with the laity to be directly attacked. As an alternative, Valens tried to limit his power through administrative tricks; he divided Cappadocia, for instance, into two smaller provinces, and installed a new bishop—an Arian, of course—over "New Cappadocia." Basil responded, we must confess, with a similar craftiness: he created two new dioceses in his own territories, new cathedral churches at the previously obscure little villages of Nyssa and Sasima, and pressured his compadres, the two Gregories, into being made bishops there. Neither man was at all happy to accept; both were much more contemplative by nature than Basil, much less ready for a fight, and the move created painful estrangements between the great heroes that lasted for years, rather like the unhappy falling out between Paul and Barnabas recorded in the book of Acts. Gregory of Nazianzus grudgingly took the post at Sasima—but abandoned it after just a few weeks; Gregory of Nyssa proved so incompetent as an administrator that he was actually charged with embezzlement (though the charge was false on the face of it—an embezzler who sleeps on the ground and lives off a couple of potatoes a day!).

Athanasius, meanwhile, somehow enjoyed seven final years of peace. In addition to his long correspondence with Basil, he wrote continuously in defense of the original Christian faith as it had been imparted to him as a youth in the desert. His repeated refrain?—"Let what was confessed by the Fathers of Nicaea prevail."[199] The sickly dwarf, the redheaded stepchild not expected to survive infancy, had outlived four Roman emperors, overcome five lonely exiles, outwitted a hundred hostile and heretical prelates, before earning, here at last, his well-deserved rest. Finally, as Theodoret tells it, "Athanasius the victorious, after all his struggles, each rewarded with a crown, received release from his labors and passed away to the life which knows no toil."

The date was May 2, 373; the little patriarch was seventy-five. "Then Peter, a right excellent man, received the see. His blessed predecessor had first selected him . . . and all the people strove to show their delight by their acclamations. He had shared the heavy labors of Athanasius; at home and abroad he had been ever at his side, and with him had undergone manifold perils. Wherefore the bishops of the neighborhood hastened to meet; and those who dwelt in schools of ascetic discipline left them and joined the company, and all joined in begging that Peter might be chosen to succeed to the patriarchal chair of Athanasius."[200]

"By one of those inexplicable ironies that meet us everywhere in human history," the *Catholic Encyclopedia* adds, "this man [Athanasius], who had endured exile so often, and risked life itself in defense of what he believed to be the first and most essential truth of the Catholic creed, died not by violence or in hiding, but peacefully in his own bed, surrounded by his clergy and mourned by the faithful of the see he had served so well."[201]

Basil—his spiritual understudy, if you will—still lived, but only a few years longer. He and the Emperor Valens both died around the end of 378, within a few months of each other—Valens by violence, in a new war against the Goths of the North; and Basil simply by ill health at the premature age of fifty, his career on earth shortened, perhaps, by the rigors of his fasting. These austerities ought not, however, to be regretted for the sake of Basil's lost productive years; they were essential to his entire mission, not external to it. Though the thing was worth doing in itself, of course, it had now become more than that, this lifestyle of the deserts; it had become, in the minds of the people, *the way of the Athanasians*—and inextricably bound up with the orthodox Faith itself. The Arians, significantly, almost never attempted it themselves; like the docetists and other gnostics of old, they sniffed at such gauche displays and maintained that "knowledge of the correct doctrine" was redemption enough. Antony's boys, on the other hand, lived this way precisely in order to avoid emulating the comfortable intellectualism of Arius. They chose to "put on Christ" by imitating his lifestyle

literally—homeless, hun   mpted in the wilderness—and
they did it as a more or l   scious strategy for avoiding the
trap of sophistry. If we ma   egret anything in his passing, we
may be sorry that Basil did not live to see his labors rewarded. At
the time of his departure, "his health was breaking, the Goths
were at the door of the empire, Antioch was in schism. . . .
He was surrounded by jealousies and dissensions at home; he
was accused of heterodoxy abroad; he was insulted and roughly
treated by great men; and he labored, apparently without fruit,
in the endeavor to restore unity to Christendom and stability to
its churches." His career had been, in one sense, one long, slow-
motion act of self-sacrifice so that all of us might have the truth;
it seems only fitting, then, that his last words were those of the
suffering savior whose honor he had spent his life defending:
"Father, into your hands I commend my spirit."

Yet if Basil had lived just a little longer he would have seen the
sunrise. Just three weeks after his death, Theodosius succeeded
Valens as emperor of the East, and not long after that, called for
the Second Ecumenical Council of the Christian Church, that of
Constantinople, which met in 381. The events leading up to this
decision were remarkable. Though Theodosius had received,
rather like Basil, a Christian upbringing by orthodox parents,
he seems to have devoted the greater part of his energies, earlier
in life, to a distinguished military career, taking little serious
thought of religious matters. But early in 379, while returning
from a victory over the marauding barbarians in the West, he
stopped for a respite at Thessalonica in Greece:

> There he was taken dangerously ill, and expressed a desire
> to receive Christian baptism. Now he had been instructed in
> Christian principles by his ancestors, and professed the *homo-
> ousian* faith. Becoming increasingly anxious to be baptized
> therefore, as his malady grew worse, he sent for the bishop of
> Thessalonica, and first asked him what doctrinal views he held?
> The bishop having replied, "that the opinion of Arius had not
> yet invaded the provinces of Illyricum, nor had the novelty

to which that heretic had given birth begun to prey upon the churches in those countries; but they continued to preserve unshaken that faith which from the beginning was delivered by the apostles, and had been confirmed in the Nicene Synod," the emperor was most gladly baptized by the bishop Ascholius; and having recovered from his disease not many days after, he came to Constantinople on the twenty-fourth of November, in the fifth consulate of Gratian, and the first of his own."[202]

Strikingly revealed to his mind, now, as the purely political thing it really was, spawned and nourished "inside the beltway," so to speak, of the new capital on the Bosphorus and still largely confined there, Theodosius conceived a newfound hatred for Arianism that lasted the rest of his life; and he returned to Constantinople as its unwavering enemy. Though he did not and could not overturn it at once simply by imperial fiat, he felt the common people at his back—and he joined Basil's old cause by encouraging, wherever he could, the ongoing exodus of Semi-Arians back into the Holy Land of orthodoxy, and by frowning on the ecclesiastical chicanery that had so long prevailed under his predecessors Constantius, Julian, and Valens. While still in Greece, in fact, he sent a rescript eastward ahead of him, making known "his intention of leading all his subjects to the reception of that faith which Peter, the chief of the apostles, had, from the beginning, preached to the Romans, and which was professed by Damasus, [the current] bishop of Rome, and by Peter, bishop of Alexandria. He enacted that the title of 'Catholic Church' should be exclusively confined to those who rendered equal homage to the three Persons of the Trinity."[203]

Theodosius saw signs of spring almost immediately upon his return to the capital. He heard reports that Basil's lieutenant Gregory Nazianzen had, since the death of Valens, been persuaded to come to Constantinople and take up a post as unofficial shepherd to that city's persecuted underground church of *homoousians*. Though this new congregation had begun as little more than a "home cell" meeting in a private residence, its growth was now becoming explosive. "It subsequently became," as Socrates records, "one of the most conspicuous [churches] in the city, and is so now, not only for the beauty and number of its structures, but also for the advantages accruing to it from the visible manifestations of God. For the power of God was there manifested, and was helpful both in waking visions and in dreams, often for the relief of many diseases and for those afflicted by some sudden transmutation in their affairs."

Just as he had when Antony called the Ghetto Church out of deadly nominalism, our Lord was confirming this new work of Antony's spiritual grandson by miraculous signs and wonders. "The name of *Anastasia* [which means, in Greek, *Resurrection*] was given to this church, because, as I believe, the Nicene doctrines which were fallen into disuse in Constantinople, and, so to speak, buried by reason of the power of the heterodox, arose from the dead and were again quickened through the discourses of Gregory." Some accounts, however, credited the name with a profound double meaning: "I have [also] heard some affirm with assurance that one day, when the people were met together for worship in this edifice, a pregnant woman fell from the highest gallery, and was found dead on the spot; but that, at the prayer of the whole congregation, she was restored to life, and she and the infant were saved. On account of the occurrence of this divine marvel, the place, as some assert, obtained its name."[204]

Theodosius saw, as well, how hotly the opposition raged against the *Anastasia*. Gregory had survived a stoning attempt, had been brought up before the civil authorities on charges of inciting a riot, and was attacked and injured in his own chapel while baptizing Easter converts "in the name of the Father, and of the Son, and of the Holy Spirit"—a formula which was beginning to fall out of favor in many churches, as savoring too much of the hated Trinity doctrine. Yet, as they usually do, these things had the opposite effect of that intended by their authors: Gregory's flock grew steadily larger, steadily more galvanized by his message. Not only faithful orthodox believers now, but throngs of former Semi-Arians, and even many actual heretics were drawn to the *Anastasia* (which had to be continually enlarged to meet the demand), where they heard some of the greatest Christian teaching ever given from a pulpit.

Theodosius had seen enough:

> When the emperor found the church in this state, he began to consider by what means he could make peace, effect a union, and enlarge the churches. Immediately, therefore, he intimated his desire to Demophilus, who presided over the Arian party [as bishop of Constantinople]; and enquired whether he was willing to assent to the Nicene Creed, and thus reunite the people, and establish peace. Upon Demophilus's declining to accede to this proposal, the emperor said to him, "Since you reject peace and harmony, I order you to quit the churches." When Demophilus heard this, weighing with himself the difficulty of contending against superior power . . . therefore went outside the city gates, and there in future held his assemblies. . . . Thus the Arians, after having been in possession of the churches for forty years, were in consequence of their opposition to the peace proposed by the emperor Theodosius, driven out of the city, in Gratian's fifth consulate, and the first of Theodosius Augustus, on the twenty-sixth of November. The adherents of the *homoousian* faith in this manner regained possession of the churches.[205]

Wasn't this, however, just another act of imperial interference in a purely ecclesiastical matter? Theodosius saw it otherwise. The Arian phenomenon had been, as everyone knew, the creation of Caesar from the start, made and nurtured entirely through imperial interference—and since Theodosius *was* Caesar, he felt fully within his rights to kill the thing that Caesar had created.[CVII]

[CVII] "Despite [all of its] victories, the prevalence of Arianism was more apparent than real. When the imperial favor and the play of interests which permitted the Arian leaders to obtain the most conspicuous episcopal sees for themselves would come to an end, the swollen sails of the movement would immediately collapse. The great majority of Christians remained orthodox." Ricciotti, *Julian the Apostate,* 33.

As regards the original Catholic Church however—well, that kingdom is not of this world and thus subject to a different Sovereign entirely. There even the Roman emperor is layman and vassal. In that spirit, Theodosius now returned to Constantine's low stool. Also like Constantine, Theodosius, in choosing to sponsor the health of the original Christian Church, wasn't so much taking the initiative as simply responding to the temper of the times. Arianism within the empire was already on its way out. It had run its course, produced a bumper crop of bad fruit for almost everyone who wasn't actually on its payroll, and Theodosius could feel the change in the air. When he received, from the faithful of the Constantinople diocese, a request for his permission to install a new bishop to fill the vacancy created by the desertion of Demophilus, he gave the people a chance to make the change themselves—and also to do more. He called upon their representatives, as Constantine had—all the bishops of the world (including the often excluded Western bishops)—to meet at the imperial city in council, in order to bring the Arian era to a close, a bookend to the great Nicaea of fifty-plus years before.

"In the month of June [381] . . . the bishops of every sect arrived from all places: the Emperor, therefore, sent for Nectarius [one of the orthodox leaders at Constantinople] and consulted with him on the best means of freeing the Christian religion from dissensions, and reducing the church to a state of unity. 'The subjects of controversy,' said he, 'ought to be fairly discussed, that by the detection and removal of the sources of discord, a universal agreement may be effected.'" While admiring the emperor's sense of fairness in calling for an open debate, Nectarius realized that dialectical tournaments had always been Arianism's bread and butter, ever since the days of the heresiarch himself. "Convinced that disputations, far from healing divisions usually create heresies of a more inveterate character," Nectarius, "knowing well that the ancients have nowhere attributed a beginning of existence to the Son of God, conceiving him to be co-eternal with the Father," passed along the following advice:

Let the emperor demand of the heads of each sect, whether they would pay any deference to the ancients who flourished before schism distracted the church; or whether they would repudiate them, as alienated from the Christian faith? If they reject their authority, then let them also anathematize them: and should they presume to take such a step, they would themselves be instantly thrust out by the people, and so the truth will be manifestly victorious. But if, on the other hand, they are not willing to set aside the fathers, it will then be our business to produce their books, by which our views will be fully attested.

Once the council was convened, Theodosius

carried [this plan] into execution with consummate prudence. For without discovering his object, he simply asked the chiefs of the heretics whether they had any respect for and would accept the teachings of those teachers who lived previous to the dissension in the Church? As they did not repudiate them, but replied that they highly revered them as their masters; the emperor enquired of them again whether they would defer to them as accredited witnesses of Christian doctrine?

And here, official Arianism within the Roman Empire foundered on the rocks, and came to a miserable, Pharisee-like finale:

At this question, the leaders of the several parties, with their logical champions—for many had come prepared for sophistical debate—found themselves extremely embarrassed. For a division was caused among them as some acquiesced in the reasonableness of the emperor's proposition while others shrunk from it, conscious that it was by no means favorable to their interests: so that all being variously affected towards the writings of the ancients, they could no longer agree among themselves, dissenting not only from other sects, but those of the same sect differing from one another.

Accordant malice therefore, like the tongue of the giants of old, was confounded, and their tower of mischief overturned. The emperor perceiving by their confusion that their sole confidence was in subtle arguments, and that they feared to appeal to the expositions of the fathers, had recourse to another method: he commanded every sect to set forth in writing their own peculiar tenets. Accordingly those who were accounted the most skillful among them, drew up a statement of their respective creeds, couched in terms the most circumspect they could devise; a day was appointed, and the bishops selected for this purpose presented themselves at the palace.

Nectarius and Agelius appeared as the defenders of the *homoousian* faith; Demophilus supported the [Semi-]Arian dogma; Euno-mius himself undertook the cause of the Eunomians [hard-core Arianism]; and Eleusius, bishop of Cyzicus, represented the opin-ions of those who were denominated Macedonians [an ominous new sect ready to grant the divinity of Christ but deniers of the Personhood of the Holy Spirit]. The emperor gave them all a courteous reception; and receiving from each their written avow-al of faith, he shut himself up alone, and prayed very earnestly that God would assist him in his endeavors to ascertain the truth.

Then perusing with great care the statement which each had submitted to him, he condemned all the rest, inasmuch as they introduced a separation of the Trinity, and approved of that only which contained the doctrine of the *homoousion*. . . . But the bishops of the other sects, on account of their disagreement among themselves, were despised and cen-sured even by their own followers: so that overwhelmed with perplexity and vexation they departed, addressing consola-tory letters to their adherents, whom they exhorted not to be troubled because many had deserted them and gone over to the *homoousian* party; for they said, "Many are called, but few chosen" [Matt. 20:16]—an expression which they never used when on account of force and terror the majority of the people was on their side.[206]

The Ecumenical Council of Constantinople (first of at least three more to be conducted there in the decades ahead) concluded its business on July 30, 381, when Emperor Theodosius issued an imperial decree declaring that the Christian churches of the empire should be restored to those bishops who confessed the equal divinity of the Father, the Son, and the Holy Spirit. As historian Philip Hughes writes, that council was merely "an epilogue to a drama just concluded. It does little more than register a *fait accompli*, and its essential importance is its demonstration to the world that the Christians of the 'East,' after more than fifty years of continuous disturbance and of oppression on the part of their rulers, remain Catholics, are not Arians . . . that the Arians were no more than a heretical faction—had never been anything more, despite their power—and were now finally discredited."[207] Theodosius also, at the behest of the ordinary Christians of the city, announced that Gregory of Nazianzus—outlaw pastor of the church called *Anastasia*—should now be enthroned as bishop of Constantinople. Theodosius himself accompanied the humbled Cappadocian to the church of Hagia Sophia, at the head of an enormous, joyful procession, and opened the door to the basilica personally.

Gregory of Nyssa was present as well, beaming with pride, no doubt; he seems to have served as the emperor's personal adviser in Church matters from this point on, "the supreme authority in all matters of theological orthodoxy."[CVIII] One vivid

---

[CVIII] Gregory of Nyssa seems also to have composed the additional amplifying phrases that were added to the original Nicene Creed at the Council of Constantinople; Greek scholars believe they can detect his literary style there. This is the version (more correctly called the Niceno-Constantinopolitan Creed) recited in churches today: "I believe in one God, the Father almighty, maker of heaven and earth, of all things visible and invisible. I believe in one Lord Jesus Christ, the Only Begotten Son of God, born of the Father before all ages. God from God, Light from Light, true God from true God, begotten, not made, consubstantial with the Father; through him all things were made. For us men and for our salvation he came down from heaven, and by the Holy Spirit was incarnate of the Vir-

detail preserved in the old records is quite unusual for its time: the new Constantinopolitan patriarch was met, it seems, on the steps outside, by a huge standing ovation of applause from the massive crowd. He, himself, must have thought of Basil,

> triumphing in his death, though failing throughout his life . . . all the objects either realized, or in the way to be realized, which he had so vainly attempted, and so sadly waited for. . . . Constantinople was now restored to Catholic unity; the emperor, by a new edict, gave back all the churches to Catholic use; Arians and other heretics were forbidden to hold public assemblies; and the name of Catholic was restricted to adherents of the orthodox and Catholic Faith.[208]

St. Antony of the Desert; St. Alexander of Alexandria; St. Athanasius, Doctor of the Church; St. Basil the Great; St. Gregory the Divine. Together, they make an unbroken chain leading backward through the chaos, bridging the gulf between pre-Constantinian Christianity and our own times, our guarantee that the Faith they preserved is, in fact, the "Faith once delivered to the saints." And Athanasius—the stone (or perhaps just a little chip off the Block) that the builders rejected—was the linchpin. It was he who, "after the Apostles, has been a principal instrument, by which the sacred truths of Christianity have been con-

gin Mary, and became man. For our sake he was crucified under Pontius Pilate, he suffered death and was buried, and rose again on the third day in accordance with the scriptures. He ascended into heaven and is seated at the right hand of the Father. He will come again in glory to judge the living and the dead and his kingdom will have no end. I believe in the Holy Spirit, the Lord, the giver of life, who proceeds from the Father and the Son, who with the Father and the Son is adored and glorified, who has spoken through the prophets. I believe in one, holy, catholic and apostolic Church. I confess one Baptism for the forgiveness of sins and I look forward to the resurrection of the dead and the life of the world to come. Amen."

veyed and secured to the world."[209] Even the hostile deist historian Thomas Carlyle conceded the importance of his victory: "If Arianism had not been conquered, Christianity would in time have dwindled into a legend."[210] Though he had the meek and humble folk behind him throughout—"the common people" who had, in their day, "heard Christ gladly" (Mark 12:37)—the Church is not wrong to remember his triumph as *Athanasius contra mundum*—Athanasius against the world!

ADESTE FIDELES

The damp basaltic cave was dark as a tomb, cold as the grave, and the grim, squinting scholar poring over his work there had to stop repeatedly to warm his fingertips against the single smoky candle. Up before dawn, his digestion had troubled him during the night as it almost always did—good for the progress of his work, no doubt, but hard on his disposition. He was, as another writer once said of a similar character, "hard and sharp as flint . . . secret, and self-contained, and solitary as an oyster. The cold within him froze his old features, nipped his pointed nose, shriveled his cheek, stiffened his gait; made his eyes red, his thin lips blue; and spoke out shrewdly in his grating voice. A frosty rime was on his head, and on his eyebrows, and his wiry chin."

The abstruse, ancient language he had come here to learn was still a struggle as well, especially in complex prophetic passages like this one from Habakkuk. He'd have to have the rabbis in again, he supposed—another half day lost to their inane small talk in exchange for one or two worthwhile insights. Confound it all, he thought, as he fumbled the pen worthlessly in his numbed hands, while the still uncountable foreign characters crawled across the pages of his expensive borrowed codices like so many insects. Confound this entire, interminable project! Perhaps he should just go back to bed and try to sleep some more . . .

But then came the noises from outside which would, of course, make that effort impossible—the all-too-familiar sounds of shuffling feet, of low muffled speech, and finally, of Psalm singing, from two dozen or so ill-trained voices. Pilgrims again!—with more of their everlasting interruptions! At this hour? Could they not give a man a single day's peace? Yet it was, in one sense, his own fault, he supposed—the inevitable downside of living in this particular cave, one of the sites on the tour. After all, he had come here as a pilgrim himself to begin with, as had so many others since Helena opened the traffic during the reign of Constantine; and he had helped popularize the practice by his own writings. Even so! How serious were these people anyway? Were their intentions in any way spiritual—or were they simply religious holidaymakers, collecting travel stories to tell back home? "Men rush here from all quarters of the world," he had written not long before, "the city is filled with people of every race, and so great is the throng of men and women that here you will have to tolerate in its full dimensions an evil from which you desired to flee when you found it partially developed elsewhere."[211] Merchants made the most of these travelers, of course, and his old master Gregory had thought these pilgrimages did more harm than good. Right now, the scholar was very much inclined to agree. In fact, the whole thing, he decided, was nothing more than a humbug.[CIX] And rising suddenly, he started up the steps to tell them so.

Our irascible scholar here, as some may have guessed already, is Eusebius Sophronius Hieronymus, better known as St. Jerome: the first great Bible translator. A native of Dalmatia in what is today Croatia, he was converted to Christianity as an adult, then spent time in Alexandria learning the Faith from former disciples

---

[CIX] Christians began making devotional pilgrimages to the Holy Land very early indeed; Eusebius the historian records the visit of a bishop of Cappadocia as early as 217, "in consequence of a vow and the celebrity of the place." Etheria of Spain, probably a relative of Theodosius, has left us a vivid account of her own trip to the shrines of Jerusalem during the year 385, where "you see nothing but gold and gems and silk. . . . The church vessels too, of every kind, gold and jewelled, are brought out on [holy days]." Just as in our own day, these trips created a lucrative tourism industry that brought with it very serious questions about their spiritual value; Gregory and Jerome did, in fact, come to believe that the abuses outweighed the benefits.

of Antony, before relocating to Constantinople so as to witness firsthand the miracles surrounding the great revival at the *Anastasia*. As a young man, he became the protégé of Gregory Nazianzen, sat next to Gregory of Nyssa at the Council of Constantinople and discussed the proceedings with him, and conceived, finally, his life's work—a great new translation of Holy Scripture directly from the original tongues into Latin.[CX] It was for this reason that he had moved to the Holy Land, to devote himself to Scripture in the land where it had been written, to familiarize himself with the actual settings in which the events recorded there had taken place, and to receive help with his Old Testament from native Hebrew speakers at a time when the knowledge of Hebrew had been effectively lost to Christendom.

But Jerome was, for all his undoubted virtues, a difficult personality. His bitterly satirical letters, the history of his career, his terrible row, later in life, with his best friend, Rufinus—all these reveal the very deep character defects that Paul Johnson would summarize as "a notoriously bad temper," and "a donnish love of savage controversy." It is true that Jerome was as hard on himself as he was on others; and his Latin Bible, once completed, was, in a sense, the ultimate fruit of Antony's efforts—the scriptures saved from Ghetto-era indifference across nearly a century of violent upheaval. Nevertheless, the man who stepped out of the cave to grouse about noisy pilgrims was a man who redeemed his claim to sanctity only through constant use of the Spirit's gift of repentance—another opportunity for which awaited him even now at the top of the stairs.

[CX] Jerome's Bible became known as "the Vulgate"—meaning "common," in the sense of the common people or "vulgar" as opposed to "for the elite." Latin had been and still was the language used by practically all Western Christians who could read or write and remained so for another five hundred years at least. The Vulgate is very valuable to Bible scholars even today because the oldest surviving copy is older than practically all existing manuscripts in the original tongues. Equally important: Jerome translated it by comparing six editions of the Bible that were already very old in his day—none of which exists any longer. The first printed Bible—the Gutenberg Bible—is an edition of Jerome's Latin Vulgate.

Jerome emerged from his cavern to see the very first glimmerings of dawn in the east. A dry, light snow was falling—something of a novelty there in Palestine, but certainly not unheard of—and it was dusting the shoulders of a group of foreigners carrying torches. The group was larger than he expected, perhaps half a hundred men and women, assembled, as it would appear, from all across the empire and beyond: Armenians, Persians, Indians, Ethiopians, and many others. It was the *words* of their hymn, however, that finally began to awaken the scribe to the true meaning of their visit.

Of the Father's love begotten,
Ere the worlds began to be,
He is Alpha and Omega,
He the source, the ending he,
Of the things that are, that have been,
And that future years shall see,
Evermore and evermore!

He is found in human fashion,
Death and sorrow here to know,
That the race of Adam's children
Doomed by law to endless woe,
May not henceforth die and perish
In the dreadful gulf below,
Evermore and evermore!

O that birth forever blessed,
When the virgin, full of grace,
By the Holy Ghost conceiving,
Bare the savior of our race;
And the babe, the world's Redeemer,
First revealed his sacred face,
Evermore and evermore![CXI]

[CXI] This song, written about 380 by the Christian poet Prudentius, is the earliest known Christmas carol.

At the back of the group, Jerome saw a shepherd's crook sticking into the sky, like the banner of a legion heading into war. The bishop was present then, though Jerome could not see his face or vestments, overseeing this procession—and that was something that only happened on special days! The scholar's eyes widened, his expression changing immediately into one of confused astonishment. He saw a ten-year-old boy standing near the front of the group. Jerome stepped forward and took him by the shoulder.

"What's today?" the old man called into the lad's young ear.

"Eh?" returned the boy, with all his might of wonder.

"What's this all about? What day is it?"

"Today!" replied the boy. "Why, Christmas Day."

Christmas Day! December the twenty-fifth! So lost in Habakkuk had he been, that Jerome had quite lost track of the days—the weeks, even. And Christmas, after all, was a recent arrival here in Palestine in the Year of Our Lord 390. Though the feast had been celebrated on this day at Rome some fifty years earlier, it was Gregory Nazianzen who made himself *exarchos* (initiator) of it in the East, while still pastoring the little chapel of the *Anastasia*. Yet it would be more accurate to call Gregory the sponsor of it rather than true initiator, for the real drive behind this sudden explosion had come from below— from the ordinary, orthodox Christians of the empire. Far from being the creation of any emperor or Church council (neither of which can be shown to have had anything to do with setting the date of Christmas or ordering its celebration), Christmas had become, over the course of the past half century, not only a popular Christian festival but a fiery, "vulgar" protest against the Arian denials.[CXII] Arius, Eusebius, Eunomius, and their ilk

[CXII] Despite the common assertion that the date of Christmas was set where it is in order to co-opt a pagan festival for Christ, there is a surprising amount of early evidence that December 25 really is the anniversary of the Nativity—or was believed to be so, at least, by the early Christians. Hippolytus of Rome, for instance, in a passage written more than one hundred years before the accession of Constantine, says straight up that "the first advent of our Lord in the flesh, when he was born in Bethlehem,

had forced us to think—long and hard, over a whole, long human lifetime—about things we already believed but had not,
as yet, properly staggered over. The Church had, with a shock
of wonder, been driven to unpack her Christmas presents, so
to speak, the gifts that had been sitting in her own house since
the beginning, though she had not yet the eyes to see: the Trinity, the depths of the Incarnation, the Virgin Mother who bore
her own Creator into our world, the unbreakable coinherence
between the infallible Scripture written by the apostles and the
infallible Traditions of interpretation they passed on.

And now the proud scholar Jerome experienced a shock of his

was December 25th, [a] Wednesday." Likewise, the *Depositio Martyrum*, a
very old calendar of early martyrs, shows written under December 25:
"Birth of Christ in Bethlehem of Judaea." Pope Julius (who hosted Athanasius at Rome in the 350s) was asked to assign a date for the feast for the
churches of Armenia; and he chooses, in another set of records, December
25 based on "census documents brought by Titus to Rome." (Both Tertullian and Justin Martyr refer, in their second-century apologetic writings, to these now-lost census records in the Roman archives). As for the
feast of Christmas itself, it was certainly being celebrated in Rome by 354,
but had not yet reached Constantinople in 379 when Gregory Nazianzen
began sponsoring it there: "Hence, almost universally has it been concluded that the new date reached the East from Rome by way of the Bosphorus during the great anti-Arian revival, and by means of the orthodox
champions." It is true that the minor pagan feast of *Sol Invictus* was also set
on December 25; but this cult was the creation of the Emperor Aurelian
in the year 274 and there is no mention of its winter festival until eighty
years after that; meaning, of course, that the pagan holiday in question is
far more likely to have been invented as a pagan alternative to Christmas
rather than the other way around. For his part, John Chrysostom, writing in the early fifth century, seems to have believed that the correspondence between the two dates was simply another interesting (or perhaps
providential) coincidence: "But Our Lord, too, is born in the month of
December . . . the eight before the calends of January [25 December] . . .
But they call it the 'Birthday of the Unconquered.' Who indeed is so unconquered as Our Lord . . . ? Or, if they say that it is the birthday of the
Sun, He is the Sun of Justice." Chrysostom also believed that the rapid
spread of Christmas in response to the Arian denials had been a miracle
that proved the genuineness of the December date.

own, humbling and devastating. He had taken it all for granted. Like the presumptuous and complacent children of Israel, he had "grown comfortable in Zion" . . . literally. Turning away from the still-caroling pilgrims back toward his own cave, he dropped to his knees and wept—for this was *the very cave*, once used as a shelter for livestock, which had hosted the first Christmas here in Bethlehem of Judaea, some 350 years ago. Jerome had chosen it as the place to do his work, so that his translation of the Word of God might come into the world at the same spot where the Word of God himself had come into it. ^{CXIII} And he had—God help him!—forgotten momentarily, lost the wonder of it, the reality behind all the theology, the Word made flesh and dwelling among us.

Sometimes, because of this very danger—that of losing the fact of God in the tangled thickets of our theology of God—people since Jerome's time have called out for a "simple religion" free of complicated dogmas such as the Trinity. Yet it was the work of the *homoousians* that had saved the true significance of the cave—and brought out its fullness. "If there is one question," Chesterton wrote,

> which the enlightened and liberal have the habit of deriding and holding up as a dreadful example of barren dogma and senseless sectarian strife, it is this Athanasian question of the co-eternity of the divine Son. On the other hand, if there is one thing that the same liberals always offer us as a piece of pure and simple Christianity, untroubled by doctrinal disputes, it is the single sentence, "God is Love." Yet the two statements are almost identical; at least one is very nearly nonsense without the other. The barren dogma is only the logical way of stating the beautiful sentiment. For if there be a being without beginning,

---

CXIII The pilgrim Etheria, writing once again in 385, records that "vigils are kept in Bethlehem, in the church wherein is the cave where the Lord was born . . . reciting hymns and antiphons." The chamber that Jerome used is separated from the Grotto of the Nativity only by a thin wall, and it is still visited by pilgrims today.

existing before all things, what was he loving when there was nothing to be loved? If through that unthinkable eternity he is lonely, what is the meaning of saying he is love?

The only justification of such a mystery is the mystical conception that in his own nature there was something analogous to self-expression; something of what begets and beholds what it has begotten. Without some such idea, it is really illogical to complicate the ultimate essence of deity with an idea like love. If the moderns really want a simple religion of love, they must look for it in the Athanasian Creed.[CXIV] The truth is that the trumpet of true Christianity, the challenge of the charities and simplicities of Bethlehem or Christmas Day never rang out more arrestingly and unmistakably than in the defiance of Athanasius to the cold compromise of the Arians. It was emphatically he who really was fighting for a God of Love against a God of colorless and remote cosmic control; the God of the stoics and the agnostics. It was emphatically he who was fighting for the Holy Child against the grey deity of the Pharisees and the Sadducees. He was fighting for that very balance of beautiful interdependence and intimacy, in the very Trinity of the divine nature, that draws our hearts to the Trinity of the Holy Family. His dogma, if the phrase be not misunderstood, turns even God into a Holy Family.[212]

Jerome's tears turned into laughter—laughter at his own folly and at the sheer, cosmic scale of the joke: the Christian theologian who spent Christmas Eve inside the original Nativity scene . . . grumbling about his digestion. The pilgrims must have taken him for a madman. Even so, they were happy when he joined them in one more rousing Christmas carol—a song used even in our own day, but often without some of its greatest verses. It may be, in fact, the greatest of all Christmas carols, calling all of

---

[CXIV] The Athanasian Creed is a fifth- or sixth-century compendium of his Trinitarian theology, not an actual work of Athanasius himself (though for a long time many believed it to be so). It seems to have been composed in Latin, perhaps by Vincent of Lerins.

us—all of humanity—to Jerome's cave, both literally and figuratively, so that we may experience our own shock of wonder:

> *O come all ye faithful, joyful and triumphant,*
> *O come ye, o come ye to Bethlehem.*
> *Come and behold him, born the king of angels.*
> *O come let us adore him, O come let us adore him,*
> *O come let us adore him, Christ the Lord.*

> *God of God, light of light,*
> *Lo! He abhors not the Virgin's womb.*
> *Very God, begotten not created;*
> *O come let us adore him, O come let us adore him,*
> *O come let us adore him, Christ the Lord.*

> *Yea, Lord, we greet Thee, born this happy morning,*
> *Jesus, to thee be all glory given.*
> *Word of the Father, now in flesh appearing;*
> *O come let us adore him, O come let us adore him,*
> *O come let us adore him, Christ, the Lord.*

> *There shall we see him, his eternal Father's*
> *Everlasting brightness now veiled under flesh.*
> *God shall we find there, a babe in infant clothing;*
> *O come let us adore him, O come let us adore him,*
> *O come let us adore him, Christ the Lord.*

> *Child, for us sinners, poor and in the manger,*
> *We would embrace thee, with love and awe.*
> *Who would not love thee, loving us so dearly?*
> *O come let us adore him, O come let us adore him,*
> *O come let us adore him, Christ the Lord.*[CXV]

[CXV] Though our earliest written copies of *Adeste Fideles* date from much later, there are good reasons to believe that the original words were passed down from the age of the Arian controversies.

Afterword

Believe it or not, A.J. Tomlinson is actually the hero of my book—along with Athanasius, of course. But I'll come back around to that theme a little later . . .

For now, let's simply pause to draw a few basic conclusions from the material we've covered. Surely we can agree, to begin with, that some of the more absurd versions of the Great Apostasy theory bear, on the plainest face of things, very little resemblance to reality. Dan Brown's Constantine, for instance, imposes his own will at Nicaea, persecutes the large, enlightened minority there who held out for a plain, Gandhi-like Jesus, then bans Arius and burns all of his books, wiping out any evidence for Christianity's original message of feminism and goddess worship. In reality, Constantine rehabilitated Arius completely within two years, allowed him to republish his books, and flirted with the heresiarch's movement himself, right up to receiving baptism at the hands of his patron, Eusebius! Popular radio host Glenn Beck recently credited the emperor with inventing the Apostle's Creed at Nicaea (not the Nicene), then blamed him for suppressing the Dead Sea Scrolls because they didn't square with it. In reality, the Dead Sea Scrolls were lost 200 years before Constantine was born, and none of them have anything to do with Christianity, being of exclusively Jewish origin.

Other groups explain the absence of any early documents favorable to their cause—those that might prove the existence of a fourth-century Mormonism or Seventh-day Adventism or some such—with the same expedient Beck employed: that Constantine or one of his successors ordered them burned. Yet the existence of fourth-century Arianism (against which the Nicene Faith really did make war) is as plain in the records as Caesar's conquest of Gaul; and its teachings have survived without any ambiguity at all, not only in orthodox defenses against them, but also in large excerpts from the actual Arian writings—even Julian's venomous screed *Against the Galileans* is largely preserved. The voices of Arius and Eunomius, in other words, can still be "heard" today; but when we listen for the sounds that might prove the existence of some primitive, original Swedenborgianism or Anabaptistry—only crickets.

More sober versions of the tale than these, however, would also seem to call for further review. Every single plank, in fact, of the Great Apostasy platform seems shakier than when we started, as I think you must also agree. Not only was Constantine *not* the first emperor to legalize Christianity (that was Galerius), nor the man who made it the official religion of Rome (that was Theodosius, forty years after Constantine's death)—Constantine wasn't even the first Christian emperor! Neither was the Nicene the first Christian creed (the Apostle's Creed, Tertullian's Old Roman Creed, even Eusebius's Creed of Palestine are all much older—none of which were "substituted for the word of God" any more than any other supplemental précis or doctrinal statement ever is). And the "pure early Church" that pre-dated Constantine was just as prone to nominalism as the Church that came after (as is proved by the mass defections of the Great Persecution era) and just as likely to fall off into errors (such as modalism). It was also just as likely to require correcting by Christianity's "clerical class" (meaning the bishops and presbyters), a hierarchy that did not arise during the age of Constantine but can, rather, be shown to have been in place at least since the time of Ignatius—a personal disciple of the apostle Peter.

We might add, as well, that the New Testament these officers preached from contained the same books Pope Pius I preached from during his reign (A.D. 142–157, the era of the Muratorian Fragment); Constantine neither created it nor suppressed it (apostasy theorists, recall, can't quite agree which it was), and it was "locked away" in Greek because that's the way the apostles and evangelists had written it—locked away, that is, until Jerome translated it for the common man into Latin (Jerome, a staunch supporter of Nicaea, who would have died rather than see its rulings overthrown).

More important than these details, however, is the fact that the whole broad picture of the era is wrong. Yes, the formerly pagan empire became Christian, but the process was largely complete before Constantine ever started. And paganism, for all intents and purposes, was already dead, as is proved by the apathetic reception Julian received for his pitiful, polytheistic church a few decades later. If it were true that the pagans only converted to Christianity to please Constantine, then they would have converted back to paganism to please Julian but, of course, they did not—though many insincere Arian leaders certainly did. Were there emperors who persecuted on behalf of a creed? Certainly there were, but Constantine wasn't one of them, though his son Constantius was—Constantius, who persecuted for the Creed of Antioch, the Creed of Rimini, the Creed of Sirmium, the Lengthy Creed, any creed but the one the free, original Church created at Nicaea while his father looked on quietly. Is there, then, any sign of a Great Apostasy here at all? Yes, in a sense, there is . . . the apostasy foreseen by Alexander and Antony. It was Arianism—"the last heresy," "worse than serpent's poison," an "apostasy such as one may justly consider and denominate the forerunner of Antichrist"—but it was an apostasy that failed. The original Christian Church defeated it, survived it, and thrived after it was gone. The theory, remember, is, that "Christianity did not really rise . . . it was imposed from above." Chesterton summarizes the notion in his masterpiece *The Everlasting Man*:

> It is an example of the power of the executive, especially in despotic states. The Empire was really an Empire; that is, it was really ruled by the emperor. One of the Emperors happened to become a Christian. He might just as well have become a Mithraist or a Jew or a Fire-Worshipper; it was common in the decline of the Empire for eminent and educated people to adopt these eccentric eastern cults. But when he adopted it, it became the official religion of the Roman Empire; and when it became the official religion of the Roman Empire, it became as strong, as universal and as invincible as the Roman Empire. It has only remained in the world as a relic of that empire; or, as many have put it, it is "but the ghost of Caesar

still hovering over Rome" . . . [As for the Nicene Faith] it was only officialism that ever made it orthodoxy.

Thus the theory, at any rate. Chesterton continues:

Now the most extraordinary thing about this is that it is all quite true; it is true in every detail except that it happens to be attributed entirely to the wrong person. It is not true of the Church; but it is true of the heretics condemned by the Church. It is as if one were to write a most detailed analysis of the mistakes and misgovernment of the ministers of George the Third, merely with the small inaccuracy that the whole story was told about George Washington; or as if somebody made a list of the crimes of the Bolshevists with no variation except that they were all attributed to the czar.

There really was an attempt to create a new religion in the fourth century, entirely through imperial power, but it was not Constantine who made it—and the religion involved was certainly not that of Nicaea.

The whole great history of the Arian heresy might have been invented to explode this idea. . . . In so far as there ever was a merely official religion, it actually died because it was merely an official religion; and what destroyed it was the real religion. Arius advanced a version of Christianity which moved, more or less vaguely, in the direction of what we should call Unitarianism; though it was not the same, for it gave to Christ a curious intermediary position between the divine and human. The point is that it seemed to many more reasonable and less fanatical; and among these were many of the educated class in a sort of reaction against the first romance of conversion. Arians were a sort of moderates and a sort of modernists. And it was felt that after the first squabbles this was the final form of rationalized religion into which civilization might well settle down. It was accepted by Divus Caesar himself and became the official orthodoxy; the generals and military princes drawn from the new barbarian powers of the north, full of the future, supported it strongly. But the sequel is still more important. Exactly as a modern man might pass through Unitarianism to complete agnosticism, so the greatest of the Arian emperors ultimately shed the last and thinnest pretense of Christianity; he abandoned ever Arius and returned to Apollo. . . . If there really was something that began with Constantine, then it ended with Julian.[213]

In short, the story of Constantine and his Creed is just the opposite of the one told by so many conspiracy theorists. "[It] was the orthodox Athanasius who resisted Constantine when he thought the emperor wrong," according to Leithart, "while it was the soft Arian Eusebius of Caesarea who delivered orations in praise of Constantine and the harder Arian Eusebius of Nicomedia who was more likely to be hobnobbing at the imperial court." The Nicene party, on the other hand, was the party of the common herd, the *hoi polloi*, both the Christian laity and their democratically minded well-wishers. And their creed, laid out at the very start of the crisis before any tampering had even begun, expressed the faith of these common folk—which is why it succeeded. The Nicene Creed, in other words, was actually the great *roadblock* to the paganization of Christianity in the age of Constantine—and the Great Apostasy is exactly what its champions were struggling (and suffering) to prevent.

Every version of the Great Apostasy scenario implies the existence of an early, "original" body of New Age Christians, Scotch Covenanters, or what have you, brutally put down by agents of the later Roman orthodoxy. Yet only one modern church can show any evidence of such an occurrence—that of the Jehovah's Witnesses. Theodosius really did suppress Arianism, and Jehovah's Witnesses are today's modern Arians, the only group currently in existence that affirms Arius's strange mix of godlike honors afforded to the man Jesus and bitter denials of his actual divinity. It should be noted, however, that Jehovah's Witnesses are not actual successors of Arius, Eusebius, and the like; their nineteenth-century founders, Russell (a former Presbyterian) and Rutherford (a former Baptist), reasoned themselves into the same theological dead end independently, using the same "logical" thought processes, the same set of Bible-alone arguments. They seem to have had no awareness of fourth-century Arianism at all, though the cult they founded has since discovered its existence and now sends inquirers there for an ancient witness to their beliefs.

There is, however, one Great Apostasy religion—the greatest of them all, surely—that really can be legitimately traced back to fourth-century Arianism. That religion is Islam. You see, all of Muhammad's Christians had been Arians as well—or adherents, at least, of some later Christologically defective heresy descended from Arianism. While the prophet of Islam was still a dreamy young merchant in Mecca, frustrated and confused by the chaotic religious scene on the Arabian peninsula circa 610 (a mixed population of Jews, pagans, but practically no Nicene Christians), he, too, climbed a mountain to pray; he, too, was allegedly told to join no existing religion but to restore the old one instead, which had been sadly eclipsed by the powers that be. Surrounded only by hostile witnesses to what Christians within the empire believed, Muhammad seems to have heard their Trinity explained as "the Father, the Son, and the Virgin Mary," and heard Christ's virginal conception explained in a manner more like that of Pollux in the myth of Leda and the swan. The Romans, in other words, had turned Christ into another of their typical half-human demigods.

Muhammad reacted with disgust—an honorable reaction, given the lies he was told—and set out to remedy the situation. How did this disaster come about? What was it that fertilized the field for Islam in this way? Pope Julius's warning to Athanasius had been fulfilled in spades: the Roman army had carried Arianism, its favorite heresy, to the ends of the earth (including Arabia), and ensured that Arian ideas continued to survive long after being cast out of the empire. "The army [had gone solidly]

Arian," as Belloc wrote in his book *The Great Heresies*, "because it felt Arianism to be the distinctive thing which made it superior to the civilian masses, just as Arianism was a distinctive thing which made the intellectual feel superior to the popular masses."

As what Belloc called a "derivative" from Arianism, Islam

> began as a heresy, not as a new religion. It was not a pagan contrast with the Church; it was not an alien enemy. . . . It differed from most (not from all) heresies in this, that it did not arise within the bounds of the Christian Church. The chief heresiarch, Mohammed himself, was not, like most heresiarchs, a man of Catholic birth and doctrine to begin with. . . . He came of, and mixed with, the degraded idolaters of the Arabian wilderness, the conquest of which had never seemed worth the Romans' while. He took over very few of those old pagan ideas which might have been native to him from his descent. On the contrary, he preached and insisted upon a whole group of ideas which were peculiar to the Catholic Church and distinguished it from the paganism which it had conquered in the Greek and Roman civilization . . . But the central point where this new heresy struck home with a mortal blow against Catholic tradition was a full denial of the Incarnation. Mohammed did not merely take the first steps toward that denial, as the Arians and their followers had done; he advanced a clear affirmation, full and complete, against the whole doctrine of an incarnate God. He taught that our Lord was the greatest of all the prophets, but still only a prophet: a man like other men. . . .

> In other words, he, like so many other lesser heresiarchs, founded his heresy on simplification. Catholic doctrine was true (he seemed to say), but it had become encumbered with false accretions; it had become complicated by needless man-made additions, including the idea that its founder was divine, and the growth of a parasitical caste of priests who battened on a late, imagined, system of sacraments which they alone could administer. All those corrupt accretions must be swept

away. . . . Alone of all the great heresies Mohammedanism struck permanent roots, developing a life of its own, and became at last something like a new religion. So true is this that today very few men, even among those who are highly instructed in history, recall the truth that Mohammedanism was essentially in its origins *not* a new religion, but a *heresy* . . . which rapidly became a counter-religion; the implacable enemy of all the older Christian bodies.[214]

The Church councils that set themselves against Christological heresy—Nicaea, first, but then Constantinople, Ephesus, Chalcedon, and a second Constantinople—had not been well received in the Roman south and east, leaving these portions of the empire wide open to Islam. The new heresy was, in other words, merely encouraging them to go ahead and complete the long process they'd been toying with since the days of Arius himself; and this entirely logical encouragement—combined with the power of the new and ruthless Islamic armies—was quite sufficient to do the trick.

> No earlier attack had been so sudden, so violent or so permanently successful. Within a score of years from the first assault in 634 the Christian Levant had gone: Syria, the cradle of the Faith, and Egypt with Alexandria, the mighty Christian See. Within a lifetime, half the wealth and nearly half the territory of the Christian Roman Empire was in the hands of Mohammedan masters and officials, and the mass of the population was becoming affected more and more by this new thing. . . . The death of Arianism in the East was the swamping of the mass of the Christian Eastern Empire by Arabian conquerors.[215]

Arianism had paved the way, but Arianism quickly gave way to its new and more wholehearted progeny. In that sense, Arianism is still with us. Islam is Great Apostasy religion taken to its logical conclusions—swamping all lesser, more timid versions of the idea, and so exasperated in its drive for simplicity that it does not, even today, scruple to subdue irrational, Trinitarian "polytheists" by force and violence.

Yet aren't there at least a few legitimate points in the various apostasy scenarios, in spite of these extreme examples? Isn't it true that pagan survivals do exist in the churches claiming continuity with the Nicene authorities? Rome became Christian in those days, to be sure, but isn't there at least a little evidence that Christianity also became Roman? The answer—in one sense and for some people groups—is *yes*; but another question, less often contemplated, needs to be asked at this point as well: was this a good thing or a bad thing? The Church's task, you see, was to help the Romans stop being pagans without making them stop being Romans. Just as modern missionaries have learned that it is not necessary to dress a Bantu tribesman in a three-piece suit before allowing him to come to church, so the early Christians realized that it was not necessary to make a Roman citizen renounce his own national identity either before or after coming to Christ (though there will undoubtedly be, in both cases, at least some wholly "indigestible" things that really will have to be simply left behind). It's actually one of the chief glories of Christianity that it does baptize and redeem and transform pagan things, ourselves included! There is not and never was any "Christian culture" with which to replace Roman culture (or English, or American, what have you); Christianity is a Faith, not a culture—though it is a highly transformative catalyst for the making of new cultural distinctives. What Christianity does do is to *save* Roman culture, not replace it. And this saved culture remains recognizably Roman, even recognizably pagan, in a manner of speaking.

Once again, G.K. Chesterton gets to the bottom of things: "It is often said by the critics of Christian origins that certain ritual feasts, processions or dances are really of pagan origin. They might as well say that our legs are of pagan origin. Nobody ever disputed that humanity was human before it was Christian; and no Church manufactured the legs with which men walked or danced, either in pilgrimage or in a ballet." The fact is that a good deal of what all of us do every day has pagan origins. The mathematics we use has pagan origins; our form of government has pagan origins; the very letters with which this sentence is written have pagan origins. Wedding rings have pagan origins, bridal gowns, lilies at funerals. In fact, many of the churches from which one hears antipaganism sermons are, architecturally speaking, Greek revival temples in the "neoclassical style"! We can't even speak the name of our savior, most of us, without using the language of Rome—for "Jesus" (as opposed to *Yeshua* in Aramaic or *Iésous* in Greek) is Latin and came into common usage for people like us only by way of Jerome's Vulgate Bible. So the claim that such and such an aspect of Christian practice might have roots in paganism isn't simply false. These things really are there. The mistake is about what these holdovers signify, about what is their meaning, their importance.

As we've seen in previous notes, some of these survivals have simply been interpreted (perhaps, once again, by hostile witnesses) in an unnecessarily jaundiced way—the origins of Christmas, for example, or the use of the word Easter. Others came in much later than the Athanasian era, by routes other than Roman; Christmas trees appear only in the tenth century, for instance, by way of Islam! Likewise, the fundamentalist who finds "Babylon mystery religion" in the Universal Church's teachings about the Eucharistic supper or honors paid to Mary is acting mainly through misunderstanding, rooted in historical ignorance. In discovering—and then railing against—a pre-Christian "virgin queen" or a pagan feast of bread and wine transformed, he stops too soon, and at an arbitrary point; for the blood atonement is there in paganism as well, along with Satan, the angels, and more than one virgin-born redeemer. The doctrine of hell is perhaps the best example of this: the Greeks believed in a place of eternal punishment (which they called Tartarus) while the Old Testament Hebrews were still debating whether the soul of man is immortal at all!

Other debunking writers have not been so arbitrary but have gone on to conclude that even the pared-down fundamentalist version of the story is nothing but a later transmogrification of heathen legends and superstition. Newman got to the truth, however:

> Now, the phenomenon, admitted on all hands, is this:—that a great portion of what is generally received as Christian truth, is in its rudiments or in its separate parts to be found in heathen philosophies and religions. For instance, the doctrine of a Trinity is found both in the East and in the West; so is the ceremony of washing; so is the rite of sacrifice. The doctrine of the divine Word is Platonic; the doctrine of the Incarnation is Indian; of a divine kingdom is Judaic; of angels and demons is Magian; the connection of sin with the body is gnostic; celibacy is known to Bonze and Talapoin; a sacerdotal order is Egyptian; the idea of a new birth is Chinese and Eleusinian; belief in sacramental virtue is Pythagorean; and honors to the dead are a polytheism. Such is the general nature of the fact before us; [and the critic] argues from it—"These things are in heathenism, therefore they are not Christian": we, on the contrary, prefer to say, "these things are in Christianity, therefore they are not heathen."

To say that the Church merely "Christianized" what it found in paganism is to miss the point badly. As St. Paul dramatically points out in his Epistle to the Romans, paganism already had a good deal of inchoate truth in it already. What the Church actually did was to gather up some of these inchoate truths, sift out what was patently unusable, and then point the pagans to the final fulfillment of their ancient longings as revealed in the faith of Christ. "We are not distressed," Newman continues, "to be told that the doctrine of the angelic host came from Babylon, while we know that they did sing at the Nativity; nor that the vision of a mediator is in Philo, if in very deed he died for us on Calvary. Nor are we afraid to allow, that, even after his coming, the Church has been a treasure-house, giving forth things old and new, casting the gold of fresh tributaries into her refiner's fire, or stamping upon her own, as time required it, a deeper impress of her master's image." This, after all, is simply Basil's analogy of the bee again, of taking the honey and leaving the poison. Yet isn't such a process inherently dangerous? Mightn't mistakes be made in this area, perverting the purity of the original system? No doubt about it—in fact, Ambrose, fifth-century bishop of Milan, was forced to suppress several superstitious Christmas devotions during his watch; while Jerome, on the other hand, wrote against Vigilantius, "who deprecated manifestations of popular devotion, such as vigils and memorials of the saints, as pagan infiltrations into the Church" (this was the same Jerome, mind you, who held out for the Nicene Faith, against those who believed the Trinity itself to be a pagan infiltration).

This is the point: Ambrose and Jerome were both shepherds of the very same Undivided Church. Ambrose suppressed when suppression was warranted—without throwing the baby out with the bathwater; and Jerome encouraged when other leaders were excessively timid or reactionary. After all, is it likely that the same Church that got the Trinity right, quickly got everything else wrong? Those who see the Christian Faith as an archeological dig, always scratching around in search of "the pure, New Testament church" that was lost in time, seem to doubt that that Church has this power—the power to distinguish between a corruption and a treasure. "They are ever hunting," as Newman goes on, "for a fabulous primitive simplicity . . . [while] we consider that a divine promise [that "the gates of hell shall not prevail," Matt 16:18] keeps the Church Catholic from doctrinal corruption; but on what promise, or on what encouragement, they are seeking for their visionary purity does not appear."

This image—of Christianity conquering the old world by absorbing it, like Israel carrying away the spoils of Egypt—actually brings us very close to the deepest truth about the age of Constantine. The goal of Christianity had never been to simply impose Judeo-Christian folkways and theology on the rest of ignorant and contemptible humanity. The goal was to reunite what had been sundered at the Tower of Babel, and bring all of

Adam's children together again into one family. In fact, that is very close to what the word "Church" means, etymologically speaking: *the Great Gathering.* As the apostle Paul writes in his epistle to the largely Gentile church at Ephesus:

> Remember that you were at that time [during the Old Testament era] separated from Christ, alienated from the commonwealth of Israel, and strangers to the covenants of promise, having no hope and without God in the world. But now in Christ Jesus you who once were far off have been brought near in the blood of Christ. For he is our peace, who has made us both one, and has broken down the dividing wall of hostility, by abolishing in his flesh the law of commandments and ordinances, that he might create in himself one new man in place of the two, so making peace, and might reconcile us both to God in one body through the cross, thereby bringing the hostility to an end. And he came and preached peace to you who were far off and peace to those who were near; for through him we both have access in one Spirit to the Father. So then you are no longer strangers and sojourners, but you are fellow citizens with the saints and members of the household of God, built upon the foundation of the apostles and prophets, Christ Jesus himself being the cornerstone, in whom the whole structure is joined together and grows into a holy temple in the Lord; in whom you also are built into it for a dwelling place of God in the Spirit (Eph. 2:12–22).

In many ways, Paul himself was the bridge: both Jew and Roman in the same man, with a respectful knowledge of the heathen poets as well as the Tanakh. Peter, on the other hand, struggled with this concept. All of his life he had associated everything good and decent and godly with Israel and her religion . . . and everything cruel and lawless and superstitious with the goyim and their pagan ways. Yes, he received Cornelius . . . but even after that he had required a special revelation from God (the sheet full of animals, descending from heaven in Acts 10) to grasp the true depths of the new thing that had happened to Israel. Peter, in other words, couldn't separate the Hebrew faith from the Hebrew culture; he simply equated the two. Paul was forced to "withstand him to his face" (Gal. 2:11) over it. Paul was mentally agile enough to unpack the deeper implications of a Gentile church, when hardly anyone else could—and he knew that the Proto-Christians were waiting for an answer.

With regards to Roman religion, then, as well as Jewish, our Lord came to fulfill—not to destroy. He came not only to be Isaiah's Suffering Servant, he came to be Osirus rising, to be Aesculapius the Great Physician, to be Prometheus's deliverer and Suetonius's King of the Romans. When unfriendly critics speak of the Nicene Fathers as "under influence of Hellenism" the very phrase itself Judaizes; it assumes that Christianity is a Jewish thing being exported to Greeks—and that the Greek element is alien to it, something to be tolerated at best. And yet the New Testament is written in Greek, because it is for Greeks (for all Gentiles, that is, most of whom were, at the time, Greek-speaking Romans). As Clement of Alexandria writes, from about A.D. 200: "The whole Christ, if we may be allowed the phrase, the total Christ, is not divided: for he is neither barbarian, nor Jew, nor Greek, nor man, nor woman, but the new Man, wholly transformed by the Spirit." Irenaeus, writing even earlier, puts it more beautifully still: "By the wood of the Cross the work of the Word of God was made manifest to all: his hands are stretched out to gather all men together. Two hands out-stretched, for there are two peoples scattered over the whole earth. One sole head in the midst, for there is but one God over all, among all, and in all." This is the glorious vision Basil had celebrated when recalling the conversion of Rome, and what Julian had been so blind to, through his bitterness and prejudice.

What then, if there was no Great Apostasy? What if it simply never happened—neither the complete abandonment version imagined by the Mormons and company or the "remnant theory" that sends us searching for our own favorite denomination hiding out amongst the Sabellians and Montanists of 1,700-plus years ago? "How" (as Francis Schaeffer once asked, in a slightly different context) "should we then live?" If that's the case, then the Christianity of the Universal Church—of the first millennium A.D.—*is* Christianity. An indefectible Church admits of any amount of reformation, but never a revolution. What distinguishes the two? Continuity—continuity, as opposed to innovation. If the one single Church founded by Christ, established by the apostles, preserved by Athanasius and the other Fathers, is still here, and still the same Church with which we have to deal today, then we must learn to apply, henceforth, Theodosius's test at Constantinople to our own beliefs: that test which asks us whether we will "pay any deference to the ancients who flourished before schism distracted the church" or whether we will "repudiate them, as alienated from the Christian faith?" Will we "defer to them as accredited witnesses of Christian doctrine" or go on "dissenting not only from other sects, but those of the same sect differing from one another"?

Apostasies do happen, without any doubt, great "fallings away," and they can be very great, indeed—without being the Great Apostasy. But no Christian teaching that breaks continuity with those of the Undivided Church in any serious way can pass Theodosius's test, and those who fail Theodosius's test must be content to take their place with Arius. This is not a matter, as some would have it, of siding with the Fathers when the Fathers differ from Scripture; it's a matter of siding with the Fathers when their interpretation of Scripture differs from our own. As John Wesley once recounted, when speaking of his experiences with the early Methodists:

> From five to seven (each morning) we read the Bible together; carefully comparing it that we might not lean to our own understandings with the writings of the earliest ages . . . The Rule of Faith is delivered to us in the oracles of God, and in the writings of the ancient Fathers of the Christian Church. May we be followers of them in all things, as they were of Christ.

Even Martin Luther, it is said, did not intend to form a new Church, but only to reform the old one. Whether this is true, or how his own movement lines up in regard to this test of continuity, is, once again, outside the scope of this book. But the impulse, at least, is another sound one, the instinct that approves *this* version of what the Protestant Reformation was meant to be, rather than any other.

And this, I think, brings us back around to A.J. Tomlinson. Twenty years after my original trip, I went back to Fields of the Wood, and what I found there is also worth telling. When I departed from those pleasant hills in the 1980s, challenged to the core by my visit, there had been no doubt at all of what Preacher Tomlinson was claiming. The initial Christian Church, "covered over with creeds and the doctrines of men," had been lost completely; the sixteenth-century Anabaptists were given some praise for pegging the Apostasy to Nicaea, but the Protestant Reformers had "fallen short"; and the ordinary Evangelical churches with which Fields of the Wood was surrounded were not even true churches—the best that could be hoped was that their members might be part of that "other fold" Jesus hopes to reach someday in John 10:16.

Yet by the time of this return trip everything had changed. The original markers that once spelled out Preacher Tomlinson's radical vision had been removed (though I still have photographs of them dating from my first visit) and they had all been replaced by new ones, featuring much less grandiose claims. The Church of God of Prophecy now appeared only to be one of the better examples of typical American Pentecostalism—insisting upon the validity and importance of tongues and other spiritual gifts for today, as all Pentecostal churches do, but otherwise eager, it seemed, to be thought of as just one more denominational option the visitor might very well wish to consider.

Another trip to that gift shop left very little doubt: the previously exclusive collection of quaintly old-fashioned material from COGOP's own publishing house had now been largely supplanted by books from Billy Graham and Charles Stanley. One might think that somebody like me would be happy to see the crazier, more cultish claims repudiated—but I couldn't help feeling differently, a little blue, in fact, sorry, in some strange way, for Preacher Tomlinson, and suspecting that there had simply arisen, since his day, "a generation that knew not the Lord."

By chance, I heard that the chief bishop of the entire church was present on the property that day, having his lunch in the on-site cafeteria. This thought, too, affected me strangely. It had been Fields of the Wood (at least in part) that had driven me to discover the writings of the Fathers in the first place, to experience the incredible story you have encountered in these pages, and which had forced me, over the course of the previous two decades, to some of the most dramatic choices of my Christian life. When I heard, therefore, that A.J. Tomlinson's lineal successor—they call him the "General Overseer," a title not dissimilar to that worn by Basil or Julius, by Athanasius himself—was eating a hot dog in that building over there and that I might simply step up, introduce myself to him, and ask him any question I liked . . . well, I felt a little irrational thrill of awe, almost as if I were being invited to an audience with the pope or an interview with the ecumenical patriarch of all the Russias.

The actual experience, however, was more than a little disappointing. The general overseer, though a very nice man (whose pronounced mountain accent reminded me of my own grandfather's), was not very impressive. He seemed more than a little uncomfortable, in fact, when I mentioned the missing markers and appeared eager to convince me that the Church of God of Prophecy has now renounced what it calls "exclusivity." He directed me to the COGOP Web site, which currently assures visitors that "The Church is working hard to correct the negative impression that this assumption has caused"—the "assumption" being, I suppose, that anything very interesting had happened at all here at Fields of the Wood. Oddest fact of the day: the general overseer had trouble remembering A.J. Tomlinson's name. He got it wrong, in fact, and I had to—gently—correct him.

This is the sense in which A.J. Tomlinson is my hero. Though I can't agree with either his premises or the conclusion he reached, at least he knew enough to keep searching for the true Church. He knew that a splintered body of bickering sects would surely go quietly in the coming century—and about this he was right. He "denounced denominationalism," according to the old COGOP tracts, "for being divisive and contrary to God's plan for his people (John 17:21–23, Eph 2:14–22, 4:1–16, 1 Cor 3:3–9, 12:12–31)," and he insisted, instead, on a visible church meant for everyone, arguing (as many of the Fathers did) from Matthew 18:15–17 and Matthew 5:14. Also very Patristic: Preacher Tomlinson argued from the Song of Solomon that the Church of God, "my dove, my perfect one, is only one, the darling of her mother, flawless to her that bore her" (Song of Sol. 6:9).

Unlike Arius then, Preacher Tomlinson wasn't really a heresiarch. His search was backward toward the Faith of the Fathers. He seems to have believed in the Real Presence of Christ in the Lord's Supper and in some kind of holy orders for ministers. He calls Fields of the Wood "a sacred place," and seems, obviously, to have had a rather Catholic instinct for the building of holy shrines, the marking of hallowed spots. In all of this he was reinventing the wheel, of course, no more aware of the fourth-century records than Judge Rutherford and his JWs—but there's just the point. Rutherford, in his pride, chose to reinvent that religion which had been perfectly content "to say what had never before been heard in the churches"; Preacher Tomlinson, contrariwise, almost managed to recreate the one that always said just the opposite.

To me, the man who had "prayed and prevailed" was still a figure to fire the imagination; but the current management, apparently, now preferred to look on their bearded prophet as just another guy with an opinion. Well, I liked Preacher Tomlinson better when he was still grabbing hold of God and refusing to let go. I hope you, my readers, will now do the same. Learn about the early Fathers. Their writings are, in a way, "the Christian Talmud"—not inspired Scripture themselves, but, like the central text of rabbinic Judaism, a sacred commentary on the

Bible hallowed by the usage of saints; and our main protection against shooting away, like Arius, into the void of our own "logical" interpretations. And this Faith of the Fathers, mind you, is *still preserved*—and with amazingly little ambiguity, all told. In a way, it's another elephant hiding in the center of the *taberna*. Surprising as it may seem, it is a cold statistical fact that something like seventeen-twentieths of the world's Christians are united around it still, at least in their official creeds and formularies: those of the Latin or Western Catholic communion, those of the Eastern or Greek Orthodox churches, and also the worldwide Anglican family of churches (including, in a sense, the proto-Evangelicalism of John Wesley in its initial form). Except for a few final vexing questions among these churches (almost all of which deal with issues of polity and governance, the least urgent matters, surely, for laypeople), these three great bodies are undivided still; still saying, on perhaps 98 points out of 100, just what Athanasius said, what Antony, and all of the earlier Fathers before them said. And this, if you don't mind my quoting Professor Tolkien's fictional wizard Gandalf, "is an encouraging thought"—a solid footing, perhaps, from which to begin your own journey away from Fields of the Wood.

For those of you who may, like me, be already affiliated with one of these great historic bodies—let me entreat you to *live* the Fathers. As in the days of the Ghetto Church, it is not enough to simply have one's name on the rolls of a church where the Patristic Faith is "still on the books." Orthodoxy alone would not have conquered Arianism; orthodoxy (right thinking) must always be linked to orthopraxis (right living). As the apostle Paul wrote, in his first letter to the Corinthians: "If I have prophetic powers, and understand all mysteries and all knowledge, and if I have all faith, so as to remove mountains, but have not love, I am nothing" (1 Cor. 13:2). In this regard, the traditional churches are as much in need of reform as any others—and more in need of it than many. What *all* of us need to listen for once again is the voice of Antony (and his chain of disciples, of course). He calls out to us, as he did in those days, not only for continuity with the *dogmas* of the patristic past, but with the *lifestyle* of the Athanasians as well. It is a lifestyle of miracles, of prayer, of self-mastery, of self-giving love, and it has the power, even today, to save the Church from nominalism—and by saving the Church, the whole world as well. The Faith on display in the early Fathers calls out to all of us, in other words—calls us back to that gospel which was not lost or destroyed during the age of Constantine but which must, nevertheless, be discovered anew by every generation.

Appendix

Christian Teaching Before Constantine

THE CONSTITUTION OF THE CHURCH

You shall not make a schism. Rather, you shall make peace among those that are contending. — *The Didache (The Teaching of the Twelve Apostles)*, c. A.D. 70.

The apostles received the Gospel for us from the Lord Jesus Christ; and Jesus Christ was sent from God. Christ, therefore, is from God, and the apostles are from Christ. Both of these orderly arrangements, then, are by God's will. Receiving their instructions and being full of confidence on account of the resurrection of our Lord Jesus Christ, and confirmed in faith by the Word of God, they went forth in the complete assurance of the Holy Spirit, preaching the good news that the Kingdom of God is coming. Through countryside and city they preached; and they appointed their earliest converts, testing them by the spirit, to be bishops and deacons of future believers. Nor was this a novelty: for bishops and deacons had been written about a long time earlier. Indeed, Scripture somewhere says: "I will set up their bishops in righteousness and their deacons in faith" [cf. 2 Sam. 7:13]. — Clement of Rome, *Epistle to the Corinthians*, c. A.D. 95.

Take care to do all things in harmony with God, with the bishop presiding in the place of God and with the presbyters in the place of the council of the apostles, and with the deacons, who are most dear to me, entrusted with the business of Jesus Christ, who was with the Father from the beginning and is at last made manifest. . . . Be subject to the bishop and to one another, as Jesus Christ was subject to the Father, and the apostles were subject to Christ and to the Father, so that there may be unity in both body and in spirit. — Ignatius of Antioch, *Epistle to the Magnesians*, c. A.D. 107.

As I said before, the Church, having received this preaching and this faith, although she is disseminated throughout the whole world, yet guarded it, as if she occupied but one house. She likewise believes these things just as if she had but one soul and one and the same heart; and harmoniously she proclaims them and teaches them and hands them down, as if she possessed but one mouth. For, while the languages of the world are diverse, nevertheless, the authority of the tradition is one and the same . . . nor will any of the rulers in the Churches, whatever his power of eloquence, teach otherwise, for no one is above the teacher. . . . It is necessary to obey those who are presbyters in the Church, those who, as we have shown, have succession from the apostles; those who have received, with the succession of the episcopate, the sure charism of truth according to the good pleasure of the Father. But the rest, who have no part in the primitive succession and assemble wheresoever they will, must be held in suspicion. . . . But since it would be too long to enumerate in a volume such as this the successions of all the Churches, we shall confound all those who . . . assemble other than where is proper, by pointing out here the succession of the bishops of the greatest and most ancient Church known to all, founded and organized at Rome by the two most glorious apostles Peter and Paul, that Church which has the tradition and faith which comes down to us after having been announced to men by the apostles. For with this Church, because of its superior origin, all Churches must agree, that is, all the faithful in the whole world; and it is in her that the faithful everywhere have maintained the Apostolic tradition. — Irenaeus of Lyons, *Against Heresies*, c. A.D. 180.

[The apostles] founded Churches in cities one after another, from which other Churches borrow the sprout of faith and the seeds of doctrine, and are daily borrowing them, so that they may become Churches. And it is in this way that they may regard themselves as apostolic; for they are the offspring of apostolic churches. Any group of things must be classified according to its origin. Therefore, although the Churches are so many and great, there is but one primitive Church of the apostles, from which all the others are derived. Thus, all are primitive, all are apostolic, because all are one. . . . From this, then, we draw up our demurrer: if the Lord Jesus Christ sent the apostles to preach, no others ought to be received except those appointed by Christ. For no one knows the Father except the Son, and him to whom the Son gives a revelation [cf. Matt. 11:27]. Nor does it seem that the Son has given revelation to any others than the apostles, whom he sent forth to preach what he had revealed to them. But what they preached, that is, what Christ revealed to them—and here again, I must enter a demurrer—can be proved in no other way except through the same Churches which the apostles founded, preaching in them themselves viva voce as they say, and afterwards by their epistles. If these things are so, then it follows that all doctrine which agrees with the apostolic Churches, those nurseries and original depositories of the faith, must be regarded as truth, and as undoubtedly constituting what the Churches received from the apostles. And, indeed, every doctrine must be prejudged as false, if it smells of anything contrary to the truth of the Churches and of the apostles of Christ and God. — Tertullian of Carthage, *Demurrer against the Heretics*, c. A.D. 200.

Even here in the Church the gradations of bishops, presbyters, and deacons happen to be imitations, in my opinion, of the angelic glory and of that arrangement which, the Scriptures say, awaits those who have followed in the footsteps of the apostles, and who have lived in perfect righteousness according to the Gospel. — Clement of Alexandria, *Stromateis*, c. A.D. 202.

From that time the ordination of bishops and the plan of the Church flows on through the changes of time and successions; for the Church is founded upon the bishops, and every act of the Church is controlled by these same rulers. Since this has indeed been established by divine law, I marvel at the rash boldness of certain persons who have desired to write to me as if they were writing letters in the name of the Church, "since the Church is established upon the bishop and upon the clergy and upon all who stand firm in the faith." — Cyprian of Carthage, *Letter to the Lapsed*, A.D. 250.

Christ breathed upon the apostles alone, saying to them: "Receive the Holy Spirit: if you forgive any man his sins, they shall be forgiven; and if you retain any man's sins, they shall be retained" [John 20:22–23]. Therefore, the power of forgiving sins was given to the apostles and to the Churches which these men, sent by Christ, established; and to the bishops who succeeded them by being ordained in their place. — Firmilian of Caesarea, *Letter to Cyprian*, c. A.D. 255.

THE RULE OF FAITH

You shall not abandon the commandments of the Lord; but you shall keep what you have received, adding nothing to it nor taking anything away. — *The Didache (The Teaching of the Twelve Apostles)*, c. A.D. 70.

You have studied the Holy Scriptures, which are true and are of the Holy Spirit. You well know that nothing unjust or fraudulent is written in them. — Clement of Rome, *Epistle to the Corinthians*, c. A.D. 95.

The true *gnosis* [knowledge] is the doctrine of the apostles, and the ancient organization of the Church throughout the whole world, and the manifestation of the body of Christ according to the successions of bishops, by which successions the bishops have handed down the Church which is found everywhere; and the very complete tradition of the Scriptures, which have come down to us by being guarded against falsification, and which are received without addition or deletion; and reading without falsification, and a legitimate and diligent exposition according to the Scriptures, without danger and without blasphemy; and the pre-eminent gift of love, which is more precious than knowledge, more glorious than prophecy, and more honored than all the other charismatic gifts. — Irenaeus of Lyons, *Against Heresies*, c. A.D. 180.

Moreover, if there be any [heresies] bold enough to plant themselves in the midst of the apostolic age, so that they might seem to be handed down by the apostles because they were from the time of the apostles, we can say to them: let them show the origins of their Churches, let them unroll the order of their bishops, running down in succession from the beginning, so that their first bishop shall have for author and predecessor some one of the apostles or of the apostolic men who continued steadfast with the apostles. For this is the way in which the apostolic Churches transmit their lists: like the Church of the Smyrnaeans, which records that Polycarp was placed there by John; like the Church of the Romans where Clement was ordained by Peter. In just this same way the other Churches display those whom they have as sprouts from the apostolic seed, having been established in the episcopate by the apostles. Let the heretics invent something like it. After their blasphemies, what could be unlawful for them? But even if they should contrive it, they will accomplish nothing; for their doctrine itself, when compared with that of the apostles, will show by its own diversity and contrariety that it has for its author neither an apostle or an apostolic man. The apostles would not have differed among themselves in teaching, nor would an apostolic man have taught contrary to the apostles, unless those who were taught by the apostles then preached otherwise. Therefore, they will be challenged to meet this test even by those Churches which are of much later date—for they are being established daily—and whose founder is not from the apostles or from among apostolic men; for those which agree in the same faith are reckoned apostolic on account of the blood ties in their doctrine. Then let all heresies prove how they regard themselves as apostolic, when they are challenged by our Churches to meet either test. — Tertullian of Carthage, *Demurrer against the Heretics*, c. A.D. 200.

Although there are many who believe that they themselves hold to the teachings of Christ, there are yet some among them who think differently from their predecessors. The teaching of the Church has indeed been handed down through an order of succession from the apostles, and remains in the Churches even to the present time. That alone is to be believed as the truth which is in no way at variance with ecclesiastical and apostolic tradition. — Origen, *The Fundamental Doctrines*, c. A.D. 225.

BAPTISM

Baptize as follows: after first explaining all these points, baptize in the name of the Father and of the Son and of the Holy Spirit, in running water. But if you have no running water, baptize in other water; and if you cannot in cold, then in warm. But if you have neither, pour water on the head three times in the name of the Father and of the Son and of the Holy Spirit. . . . Let none eat or drink of your Eucharist but those baptized in the name of the Lord; for concerning this also did the Lord say: "Do not give to dogs what is sacred." — *The Didache (The Teaching of the Twelve Apostles)*, c. A.D. 70.

What else does [God] say? "And there was a river flowing on the right, and beautiful trees grew beside it, and whoever shall eat of them shall live forever" [Ezek. 47:12]. In this way he says that we descend into the water full of sins and foulness, and we come up bearing fruit in our heart, having fear and hope in Jesus in the spirit. — *The Epistle of Barnabas*, c. A.D. 79.

"They had no need," [the Shepherd] said, "to come up through the water, so that they might be made alive; for they could not otherwise enter into the kingdom of God except by putting away the mortality of their former life. These also, then, who had fallen asleep, received the seal of the Son of God, and entered into the kingdom of God. For," he said, "before a man bears the name of the Son of God, he is dead. But when he receives the seal, he puts mortality aside and again receives life. The seal, therefore, is the water. They go down into the water dead, and come out of it alive." — Hermas, *The Shepherd*, c. A.D. 140.

Whoever is convinced and believes that what they are taught and told by us is the truth, and professes to be able to live accordingly, is instructed to pray and to beseech God in fasting for the remission of their former sins, while we pray and fast with them. Then they are led by us to a place where there is water; and there they are reborn in the same kind of rebirth in which we ourselves were reborn: in the name of God, the Lord and Father of all, and of our Savior, Jesus Christ, and of the Holy Spirit, they received the washing of water. For Christ said, "Unless you are reborn, you shall not enter into the kingdom of heaven." — Justin Martyr, *First Apology*, c. A.D. 155.

Moreover, those things which were created from the waters were blessed by God, so that this might also be a sign that men would at a future time receive repentance and remission of sins through water and the bath of regeneration—all who proceed to the truth and are born again and receive a blessing from God. — Theophilus of Antioch, *To Autolycus*, c. A.D. 180.

And again, giving the disciples the power of regenerating in God, he said to them: "Go and teach all nations, and baptize them in the name of the Father, and of the Son, and of the Holy Spirit." . . . The Lord promised to send us the Paraclete, who would make us ready for God. Just as dry wheat without moisture cannot become one dough or one loaf, so also we who are many cannot be made one in Christ Jesus, without the water from heaven. Just as dry earth cannot bring forth fruit unless it receive moisture, so also we, being at first a dry tree, can never bring forth fruit unto life, without the voluntary rain from above. Our bodies achieve unity through the washing which leads to incorruption; our souls, however, through the Spirit. Both, then, are necessary, for both lead us on to the life of God. — Irenaeus of Lyons, *Against Heresies*, c. A.D. 180.

When we are baptized, we are enlightened. Being enlightened, we are adopted as sons. Adopted as sons, we are made perfect. Made perfect, we are become immortal. "I say," he declares, "you are gods and sons all of the Most High" [Ps. 81:6]. This work is variously called grace, illumination, perfection, washing. It is a washing by which we are cleansed of sins; a gift of grace by which the punishments due our sins are remitted; an illumination by which we behold that holy light of salvation—that is, by which we see God clearly; and we call that perfection which leaves nothing lacking. — Clement of Alexandria, *The Instructor of Children*, c. A.D. 202.

Formerly there was Baptism, in an obscure way, in the cloud and in the sea; now however, in full view, there is regeneration in water and in the Holy Spirit. — Origen, *Homily on Numbers*, A.D. 244.

And I myself was bound fast, held by so many errors of my past life, from which I did not believe that I could extricate myself. I was disposed, therefore, to yield to my clinging vices; and, despairing of better ways, I indulged my sins as if they were actually part and parcel of myself. But afterwards, when the stain of my past life had been washed away by the water of re-birth, a light from above poured itself upon my chastened and now pure heart; afterwards through the Spirit which is breathed from heaven, a second birth made of me a new man. And then in a marvelous manner, doubts immediately clarified themselves, the closed opened, the darkness became illuminated, what before had seemed difficult offered a way of accomplishment, and what had been thought impossible was able to be done. Thus it had to be acknowledged that what was of the earth and was born of flesh and had lived submissive to sins, had now begun to be of God, as the Holy Spirit was animating it. — Cyprian of Carthage, *To Donatus*, A.D. 246/247.

The Lord's Supper

Assemble on the Lord's Day, and break bread and offer the Eucharist; but first make confession of your faults, so that your sacrifice may be a pure one. Anyone who has a difference with his fellow is not to take part with you until they have been reconciled, so as to avoid any profanation of your sacrifice. For this is the offering of which the Lord has said, "Everywhere and always bring me a sacrifice that is undefiled, for I am a great king, says the Lord, and my name is the wonder of nations" [Mal. 1:11]. — *The Didache (The Teaching of the Twelve Apostles)*, c. A.D. 70.

Take note of those who hold heterodox opinions on the grace of Jesus Christ which has come to us, and see how contrary their opinions are to the mind of God. For love they have no care, nor for the widow, nor for the orphan, nor for the distressed, nor for those in prison or freed from prison, nor for the hungry and thirsty. They abstain from the Eucharist and from prayer, because they do not confess that the Eucharist is the flesh of our savior Jesus Christ, flesh which suffered for our sins and which the Father, in his goodness, raised up again. They who deny the gift of God are perishing in their disputes. . . . Let that be considered a valid Eucharist which is celebrated by the bishop, or by one whom he appoints. Wherever the bishop appears, let the people be there; just as wherever Jesus Christ is, there is the Catholic Church. — Ignatius of Antioch, *Epistle to the Smyrnaens*, c. A.D. 107.

Then there is brought to the president of the brethren bread and a cup of water and of watered wine; and taking them, he gives praise and glory to the Father of all, through the name of the Son and of the Holy Spirit; and he himself gives thanks at some length in order that these things may be deemed worthy. When the prayers and thanksgivings are completed, all the people call out their assent, saying: "Amen!" *Amen* in the Hebrew language signifies *so be it*. After the president has given thanks, and all the people have shouted their assent, those whom we call deacons give to each one present to partake of the Eucharistic bread and wine and water; and to those who are absent they carry away a portion. We call this food Eucharist; and no one is permitted to partake of it, except one who believes our teaching to be true and who has been washed in the washing which is for the remission of sins and for regeneration, and is thereby living as Christ has enjoined. For not as common bread nor common drink do we receive these; but since Jesus Christ our savior was made incarnate by the word of God and had both flesh and blood for our salvation, so too, as we have been taught, the food which has been made into the Eucharistic prayer set down by him, and by the change of which our blood and flesh is nourished, is both the flesh and blood of that incarnated Jesus. — Justin Martyr, *First Apology*, c. A.D. 155.

[To Trypho the Jew] . . . the offering of fine wheat flour which was prescribed to be offered on behalf of those cleansed from leprosy was a type of the Bread of the Eucharist, the celebration of which our Lord Jesus Christ prescribed in memory of the passion he suffered on behalf of those men who are cleansed in their souls of every evil . . . [but] concerning the sacrifices which you at that time offered, God speaks through Malachias, one of the twelve [prophets] as follows: "I have no pleasure in you, says the Lord; and I will not accept your sacrifices from your hands; for from the rising of the sun until its setting, my name has been glorified among the gentiles; and in every place incense is offered to my name, and a clean offering: for great is my name among the gentiles, says the Lord; but you profane it" [Mal. 1:10–12]. It is of the sacrifices offered to him in every place by us, the gentiles, that is, of the bread of the Eucharist and likewise the Cup of the Eucharist, that he speaks at that time; and he says that we glorify his name, while you profane it. — Justin Martyr, *Dialogue with Trypho*, c. A.D. 155.

For as the bread from the earth, receiving the invocation from God, is no longer common bread but the Eucharist, consisting for two elements, earthly and heavenly, so also our bodies, when they received the Eucharist, are no longer corruptible but have the hope of resurrection into eternity. — Irenaeus of Lyons, *Against Heresies*, c. A.D. 180.

The sacrament of Eucharist . . . we take even before daybreak in congregations, but from the hand of none others except the presidents. — Tertullian, *The Crown*, c. A.D. 211.

The deacon shall then bring the offering to [the bishop] and he, imposing his hand on it, along with all the presbytery, shall give thanks, saying: "The Lord be with you." And all shall respond, "And with your spirit." "Hearts aloft!" "We keep them with the Lord." "Let us give thanks to the Lord." "It is right and just." And then he shall continue immediately: "We give thanks, O God, through your beloved Son Jesus Christ, whom in these last days you have sent to us as savior and redeemer and as the angel of your will; he that is your inseparable Word, through whom you made all things, and who is well-pleasing to you; whom you sent from heaven into the womb of a virgin, and who, dwelling within her, was made flesh and was manifested as your Son, born of the Holy Spirit and of the virgin; who, fulfilling your will and winning for himself a holy people, extended his hands when it was time for him to suffer, so that by his suffering he might set free those who believed in you; who also, when he was betrayed to his voluntary suffering, in order that he might destroy death and break the bonds of the devil and trample hell underfoot and enlighten the just and set a boundary and show forth his resurrection, took bread and gave thanks to you, saying: 'Take, eat: this is my body, which is broken for you.' Likewise with the cup, too, saying: 'This is my blood, which is poured out for you. Whenever you do this, you do it in my memory.' Remembering, therefore, his death and resurrection, we offer to you the bread and the cup, giving thanks to you, because of your having accounted us worthy to stand before you and minister to you. And we pray that you might send your Holy Spirit upon the offering of the holy Church. Gather as one in the fullness of the Holy Spirit your saints who participate; and confirm their faith in truth so that we may praise and glorify you through your Son Jesus Christ, through whom be glory and honor to you, to the Father and the Son with the Holy Spirit, in your holy Church, both now and through ages of ages. Amen." — Hippolytus of Rome, *The Apostolic Tradition*, c. A.D. 215.

You are accustomed to take part in the divine mysteries, so you know how, when you have received the Body of the Lord, you reverently exercise every care lest a particle of it fall, and lest anything of the consecrated gift perish. You account yourselves guilty, and rightly do you so believe, if any of it be lost through negligence. But if you observe such caution in keeping his Body, and properly so, how is it you think neglecting the word of God a lesser crime than neglecting his Body? — Origen, *Homilies on Exodus*, c. A.D. 244.

If Christ Jesus, our Lord, is himself the high priest of God the Father; and if he offered himself as a sacrifice to the Father; and if he commanded that it be done in commemoration of himself—then certainly the priest, who imitates that which Christ did, truly functions in the place of Christ. — Cyprian of Carthage, *Letter to a Certain Cecil*, c. A.D. 250.

Saints, Purgatory, Other Distinctives

For our God, Jesus Christ, was conceived by Mary in accord with God's plan: of the seed of David, it is true, but also of the Holy Spirit. — Ignatius of Antioch, *Epistle to the Ephesians*, c. A.D. 107.

[Christ] we worship as the Son of God; but the martyrs we love as disciples and imitators of the Lord; and rightly so, because of their unsurpassable devotion to their own king and teacher. . . . We took up [Polycarp's] bones, more precious than costly gems and finer than gold, and put them in a suitable place. The Lord will permit us, when we are able, to assemble there in joy and gladness; and to celebrate the birthday of his martyrdom . . . — *The Martyrdom of Polycarp*, c. A.D. 155.

Since it is written of him in the Memoirs of the apostles that he is the Son of God, and since we call him Son, we have understood that before all creatures he proceeded from the Father by his will and power . . . and that he became Man by the virgin so that the course which was taken by disobedience in the beginning through the agency of the serpent, might be also the very course by which it would be put down. For Eve, a virgin and undefiled, conceived the word of the serpent, and bore disobedience and death. But the Virgin Mary received faith and joy when the angel Gabriel announced to her the glad tidings that the Spirit of the Lord would come upon her and the power of the Most High would overshadow her, for which reason the Holy One being born of her is the Son of God. And she replied, "Be it done unto me according to thy word" [Luke 1:38]. — Justin Martyr, *Dialogue with Trypho*, c. A.D. 155.

The Virgin Mary . . . being obedient to his word, received from an angel the glad tidings that she would bear God. — Irenaeus of Lyons, *Against Heresies*, c. A.D. 180.

. . . Through a virgin, the Word of God was introduced to set up a structure of life. Thus, what had been laid waste in ruin by this sex, was by the same sex re-established in salvation. Eve had believed the serpent; Mary believed Gabriel. That which the one destroyed by believing, the other, by believing, set straight. — Tertullian of Carthage, *The Flesh of Christ*, c. A.D. 210.

We offer sacrifices for the dead on their birthday anniversaries . . . We take anxious care lest something of our Cup or Bread should fall upon the ground. At every forward step and movement, when coming in and going out, when putting on our clothes, when putting on our shoes, when bathing, when at table, when lighting the lamps, when reclining, when sitting, in all the ordinary occupations of our daily lives, we furrow our forehead with the sign [of the Cross]. — Tertullian, *The Crown*, c. A.D. 211.

The Church received from the apostles the tradition of giving baptism even to infants. For the apostles, to whom were committed the secrets of divine mysteries, knew that there is in everyone the innate stains of sin, which must be washed away through water and the Spirit. — Origen, *Commentaries on Romans*, c. A.D. 244.

Lawrence and Ignatius, though they fought betimes in worldly camps, were true and spiritual soldiers of God; and while they laid the devil on his back with their confession of Christ, they merited the palms and crowns of the Lord by their illustrious passion. We always offer sacrifices for them, as you will recall, as often as we celebrate the passions of the martyrs by commemorating their anniversary day. — Cyprian of Carthage, *Letter to the Clergy and People*, c. A.D. 250.

. . . Christ breathed upon the apostles alone, saying to them: "Receive the Holy Spirit: if you forgive any man his sins, they shall be forgiven; and if you retain any man's sins, they shall be retained" [John 20:22–23]. Therefore, the power of forgiving sins was given to the apostles and to the Churches which these men, sent by Christ, established; and to the bishops who succeeded them by being ordained in their place. — Firmillian of Caesarea, *Letter to Cyprian*, c. A.D. 268.

Because, however, all the various groups of heretics are confident that they are the Christians, and think that theirs is the Catholic Church, let it be known: that is the true Church, in which there is confession and penance, and which takes a salubrious care of the sins and wounds to which the weak flesh is subject. — Lactantius, *The Divine Institutions*, c. A.D. 305.

Notes

1 Francis de Sales, *The Mission of the Church*.

2 Henry M. Chadwick, *The Early Church* (Baltimore: Penguin Books, 1967), 25, 33.

3 Ibid.

4 Eusebius Pamphilus, *History of the Church,* translated by Rev. Anthony Bull in Abbot Giuseppe Ricciotti's *The Age of Martyrs* (Rockford, IL: TAN Books, 1999), 47.

5 Johannes Quasten, *Patristics,* Vol. 3 (Allen, TX: Christian Classics RCL, 1995), 146.

6 Rev. Charles Kingsley, *The Hermits* (New York: Macmillan & Co., 1913), 132.

7 Cf. 1 John 4:18.

8 Cf. Rom. 1:20.

9 Kingsley, *The Hermits,* 136.

10 Ricciotti, *Age of Martyrs,* 73.

11 G.K. Chesterton, *Collected Works of G.K. Chesterton, Vol. 1: The Everlasting Man* (San Francisco: Ignatius Press, 1991), 285.

12 Fulton J. Sheen, *The Electronic Christian* (New York: Macmillan Co., 1979), 16–17.

13 Quoted in Paul Johnson, *History of Christianity* (New York: Macmillan Co., 1976), 12.

14 Cf. Luke 7:9.

15 Irenaeus of Lyons, *Against Heresies,* IV:2:7–8.

16 Hilaire Belloc, *Europe and the Faith* (Rockford, Ill., TAN Books and Publishers, 1992), 33.

17 Eusebius Pamphilus, *History of the Church,* VIII:8–9.

18 Ibid., VIII:10.

19 Athanasius, *History of the Arians,* VIII:64.

20 Kingsley, *The Hermits,* 48.

21 Sozomen, *Ecclesiastical History,* II:12.

22 Athanasius, *Life of Antony, translated by* Kingsley in *The Hermits,* 46, 61, 73.

23 Kingsley, *The Hermits,* 49.

24 Ibid.

25 Kingsley, *The Hermits,* 77.

26 Ibid., 48.

27 Ibid., 59–60, 13.

28 Athanasius, *On the Incarnation of the Word,* chapter 56:1, 2.

29 Ibid., 4:4.

30 Ibid., 13:1–2, 5–6.

31 Ibid., 15:2.

32 Ibid., 4:3.

33 Ibid., 8:2, 3.

34 Ibid., 9:1, 2.

35 Ibid., 16:4.

36 Ibid., 18:4, 19:3.

37 Ibid., 17:1, 2, 5, 6.

38 John Henry Newman, *Arians of the Fourth Century* (Notre Dame, IN: University of Notre Dame Press, 2001), 146.

39 Dionysius, in ibid., 173.

40 Sozomen, *Ecclesiastical History,* II:15.

41 Socrates, *Ecclesiastical History,* I:5.

42 Ibid.

43 Sozomen, *Ecclesiastical History,* II:15.

44 Ibid.

45 Irenaeus, *Fragment 2,* quoted in Eusebius, V:20:7.

46 Sozomen, *Ecclesiastical History,* II:15.

47 Socrates, *Ecclesiastical History,* I:6.

48 Cf. 2 John 1:7.

49 *Epistle of Alexander,* quoted in Socrates, *Ecclesiastical History,* I:6.

50 Robert Payne, *The Holy Fire* (Crestwood, NY: St. Vladimir's Seminary Press, 1980), 77.

51 Eusebius, *Life of Constantine* II, 64–65, 69–72.

52 Socrates, *Ecclesiastical History,* I:7.

53 Sozomen, *Ecclesiastical History,* I:16.

54 Cf. James 3:17.

55 Newman, *Arians of the Fourth Century,* 242–44.

56 Socrates, *Ecclesiastical History,* I:6.

57 Theodoret, *Ecclesiastical History,* I:5.

58 Ignatius of Antioch, *Epistle to the Smyraeans,* 8.

59 Payne, *Holy Fire,* 75.

60 Sozomen, *Ecclesiastical History,* II:17.

61 Eusebius, quoted in Socrates, *Ecclesiastical History,* I:8.

62 Sozomen, *Ecclesiastical History,* I:17.

63 Ibid., II:18.

64 Theodoret, *Ecclesiastical History,* I:6.

65 Eusebius Pamphilus, *Life of Constantine,* III:10.

66 Theodoret, *Ecclesiastical History,* I:6.

67 Eusebius Pamphilus, *Life of Constantine*, III:12.

68 Theodoret, *Ecclesiastical History,* I:16.

69 Cf. Gal. 6:17.

70 Theodoret, *Ecclesiastical History,* I:10.

71 Eusebius Pamphilus, quoted in Socrates, *Ecclesiastical History,* I:8.

72 Newman, *Arians of the Fourth Century,* 237.

73 Arius's speech, preserved in Theodoret, *Ecclesiastical History,* I:4.

74 Thalia, translated by Newman in *Arians of the Fourth Century,* 216.

75 Eusebius of Nicomedia, quoted in Theodoret, *Ecclesiastical History,* I:5.

76 Athanasius, *De Decretis,* 2.

77 C.S. Lewis, *Mere Christianity* (New York: HarperCollins Books, 2001).

78 Eusebius of Nicomedia, quoted in Theodoret, *Ecclesiastical History,* I:5.

79 Newman's translation from *Arians of the Fourth Century,* 218.

80 Ibid.

81 Cf. Phil. 2:6.

82 Dorothy L. Sayers, *The Emperor Constantine* (Grand Rapids, MI: Wm. B. Eerdmans Publishing Co., 1976), 148.

83 Chadwick, *The Early Church,* 151.

84 Eustathius, in Theodoret, *Ecclesiastical History,* I:7.

85 Ibid.

86 Athanasius, quoted in ibid., I:7.

87 Newman, *Arians of the Fourth Century* 142.

88 Socrates, *Ecclesiastical History,* I:8.

89 Athanasius, *Ad Afros Epistola Synodica,* 6.

90 Peter J. Leithart, *Defending Constantine* (Downer's Grove, IL: InterVarsity Press, 2010), 152.

91 Sozomen, *Ecclesiastical History,* I:20.

92 Socrates, *Ecclesiastical History,* 1:9 (emphasis in the original).

93 Ibid., 1:8.

94 Eustathius preserved in Theodoret, *Ecclesiastical History,* I:8.

95 Newman, *Arians of the Fourth Century,* 255.

96 Sozomen, *Ecclesiastical History,* I:21

97 Leithart, *Defending Constantine,* 152.

98   Sozomen, *Ecclesiastical History*, I:25.

99   Ephraim the Syrian, *Hymns for the Feast of Epiphany*, 15.

100 Athanasius, quoted in Sozomen, *Ecclesiastical History*, II:17, translated by Philip Schaff in *Athanasius: Select Works and Letters*.

101 Henry Wace and William C. Percy, *A Dictionary of Christian Biography* (London: John Murray, 1911).

102 Leithart, *Defending Constantine*, 196, 207.

103 The story about the nail is recorded in Socrates, *Ecclesiastical History*, XVII.

104 Ibid., 1:25, 26.

105 Sozomen, *Ecclesiastical History*, II:19.

106 Socrates, *Ecclesiastical History*, I:23.

107 Chapman, *The Catholic Encyclopedia* (New York: Robert Appleton Co., 1907).

108 Socrates, *Ecclesiastical History*, I:23.

109 Sozomen, Ecclesiastical History, II:21, 22.

110 Athanasius, *Life of Antony*, quoted in Kingsley, *The Hermits*, 67.

111 Socrates, *Ecclesiastical History*, I:29.

112 Sozomen, *Ecclesiastical History*, I:13.

113 Athanasius, *Life of Antony*, quoted in Kingsley, *The Hermits*, 68.

114 Hilaire Belloc, *The Great Heresies* (Charlotte, NC: TAN Books, 1991), 28.

115 Sozomen, *Ecclesiastical History*, II:34.

116 Quasten, *Patristics*, Vol. 3, 319.

117 Socrates, *Ecclesiastical History*, I:40.

118 Payne, *Holy Fire*, 94.

119 Athanasius, *The Monk's History of Arian Impiety*, as quoted in William A. Jurgens, *Faith of the Early Fathers* (Collegeville, MN: Liturgical Press, 1979), 326.

120 Belloc, *The Great Heresies*, 23.

121 Vladimir Soloviev, *The Russian Church and the Papacy* (El Cajon, CA: Catholic Answers, 2001), 25.

122 Socrates, *Ecclesiastical History*, I:37.

123 Ibid., II:34.

124 Payne, *Holy Fire*, 94.

125 Sozomen, *Ecclesiastical History*, III:6.

126 Chadwick, *The Early Church*, 137.

127 G.K. Chesterton, *Collected Works of G.K. Chesterton, Vol. 21: The Resurrection of Rome*, 311.

128 Julius, in Jurgens, *Faith of the Early Fathers*, 346.

129 Chadwick, *The Early Church*, 138.

130 Chesterton, *The Resurrection of Rome*, 313.

131 Newman, *Arians of the Fourth Century*, 288.

132 Payne, *Holy Fire*, 95.

133 Athanasius, in Jurgens, *Faith of the Early Fathers*, 322.

134 Athanasius, translated by Newman in *Arians of the Fourth Century*, note 5.

135 Ibid., 290.

136 Julian, *To the Athenians*, quoted in Ricciotti, *Julian the Apostate* (Rockford, IL: TAN Books and Publishers, Inc., 1999), 7.

137 Gregory Nazianzen, *Oration 43*.

138 Julian, *To the Athenians*, quoted in Ricciotti, *Julian the Apostate*, 14.

139 Julian, *Hymn to Helios*, quoted in Ricciotti, *Julian the Apostate*, 43.

140 Libanius, *Orations*, ibid., 35.

141 Julian, *To the Athenians*, ibid., 10.

142 Ricciotti, *Julian the Apostate*, cites Ammianus 5:23–24.

143 P.J. Harrold, "The Alleged Fall of Pope Liberius," *American Catholic Quarterly Review*, vol. 8, 1883, 529–49.

144 Athanasius, *History of the Arians*, IV.

145 Newman, *Arians of the Fourth Century*, 309–10.

146 Athanasius, *History of the Arians*, IV:34.

147 Ibid., V:41.

148 Ammianus, quoted in *The Catholic Encyclopedia*, "Liberius."

149 Theodoret, *Ecclesiastical History*, II:14.

150 All quotes from Athanasius, *History of the Arians*, V:46.

151 Athanasius, *Apologia De Fuga*, 24.

152 Gregory Nazianzen, *Oratio*, XXI:16.

153 Socrates, *Ecclesiastical History*, II:38.

154 Julian, quoted in Ricciotti, *Julian the Apostate,*149.

155 Cf. John 10:30, 17:1.

156 Athanasius, *Letter Concerning the Decrees of the Council of Nicaea*, in Jurgens, *Faith of the Early Fathers*, 324.

157 Athanasius, *Discourses Against the Arians*, in ibid., 328.

158 Athanasius, *Letter Concerning the Councils of Rimini and Seleucia*, in ibid., 338.

159 Athanasius, *Four Letters to Serapion of Thmuis*, ibid., 336.

160 Socrates, *Ecclesiastical History*, III:1.

161 Ricciotti, *Julian the Apostate*, 41.

162 Theodoret, *Ecclesiastical History*, III:1.

163 Libanius, quoted in Ricciotti, *Julian the Apostate*, 47.

164 Ammianus, quoted in ibid., 179.

165 Ammianus, quoted in ibid., 225.

166 Julian, *To Artabius*, quoted in Ricciotti, *Julian the Apostate*, 202.

167 Julian, *Misopogon*, quoted in ibid., 189.

168 Ibid., 20.

169 Ammianus, quoted in ibid., 188.

170 Ibid., 189.

171 Julian, quoted in ibid., 224.

172 Jurgens, *Faith of the Early Fathers*, Vol. 2, 39.

173 John Henry Newman, *Apologia Pro Vita Sua*.

174 Jurgens, *Faith of the Early Fathers*, Vol. 2, 12..

175 Ibid.

176 Fourth Lateran Council, 1213.

177 G.K. Chesterton, *Collected Works of G.K. Chesterton, Vol. 1: Heretics*, afterword, 74.

178 G.K. Chesterton, *Collected Works of G.K. Chesterton, Vol. 3: The Catholic Church and Conversion*, 86.

179 Jurgens, *Faith of the Early Fathers*, Vol. 2, 23.

180 Ibid., 29.

181 Ibid., 51.

182 Ibid., 33.

183 Ibid., 18.

184 Ibid., 52.

185 Newman, *Arians of the Fourth Century*, 50–51.

186 Quoted at www.tertullian.org/fathers/index.htm#Julian_Letters.

187 Soloviev, *The Russian Church and the Papacy*, 25.

188 Pilkington's translation, quoted in Payne, *Holy Fire*, 108.

189 Ricciotti, *Julian the Apostate*, 22.

190 All quoted in ibid., 104.

191 Ibid., 213.

192 Ibid., 226.

193 Ammianus quoted in ibid., 252.

194 Theodoret, *Ecclesiastical History*, III:20.

195 Fr. John Laux, MA, *Church History*, 118.

196 Socrates, IV:15. Laux adds that Valens "persecuted both Catholics and Semi-Arians, with the result that scores of the latter returned to the Church."

197 Quoted by John Henry Newman in *Historical Sketches*, Vol. II, *The*

Church of the Fathers (London; Longmans, Green & Co., 1906).

198 Ibid., 14–17.

199 Athanasius, Letter 71, quoted in *The Catholic Encyclopedia*.

200 Theodoret, *Ecclesiastical History*, IV:17.

201 *The Catholic Encyclopedia*, "Athanasius."

202 Socrates, *Ecclesiastical History*, V:6.

203 Sozomen, *Ecclesiastical History*, VII:4.

204 Ibid., VII:3.

205 Socrates, *Ecclesiastical History*, V:7.

206 Ibid., V:10.

207 Philip Hughes, *The Church in Crisis: A History of the General Councils* (New York: Hanover House, 1961), 41, 47.

208 Newman, *The Church of the Fathers,* 130.

209 Newman, *Arians of the Fourth Century,* 264.

210 Quoted in Laux, *Church History,* 158.

211 Jerome, *Letter 58.*

212 G.K. Chesterton, *Collected Works of G.K. Chesterton, Vol. 2: The Everlasting Man,* 360.

213 Ibid., 362.

214 Belloc, *Great Heresies,* 42–44.

215 Ibid., 41.